THE THREE PILLARS OF RADICALIZATION

Additional Praise for *The Three Pillars of Radicalization:*
Needs, Narratives, and Networks

"This book is a welcome antidote to the common misconception that the brutally violent tactics of terrorist groups like ISIS and al Qaeda can only be understood as pathology. The authors offer a convincing argument that terrorist violence is the flip side of normative and even altruistic behavior: a tragic juxtaposition of the compelling individual need to seek personal significance joined with an ideological argument that prioritizes violence and a reference group to provide validation."

—Gary LaFree, Chair of the Department of Criminology and Criminal Justice and the Founding Director of the National Consortium for the Study of Terrorism and Responses to Terrorism (START), University of Maryland

"A fine work that uses case studies and profiles from across the world to reveal, through accumulated empirical evidence and statistical models, the drivers and pathways to radicalization. The authors soundly argue that the scourge of Islamic extremism is far from over, and that its ultimate defeat requires interventions to reconfigure the intimate links between social networks and ideological narratives into alternative routes to personal significance that transcend mere material opportunities."

—Scott Atran, Emeritus Director of Research in Anthropology, National Center for Scientific Research, France, Founding Fellow, Centre for the Resolution of Intractable Conflict, University of Oxford, and Research Professor of Psychology and Public Policy, University of Michigan

THE THREE PILLARS OF RADICALIZATION

Needs, Narratives, and Networks

Arie W. Kruglanski, Jocelyn J. Bélanger,
and Rohan Gunaratna

Oxford University Press is a department of the University of Oxford. It furthers
the University's objective of excellence in research, scholarship, and education
by publishing worldwide. Oxford is a registered trade mark of Oxford University
Press in the UK and certain other countries.

Published in the United States of America by Oxford University Press
198 Madison Avenue, New York, NY 10016, United States of America.

Library of Congress Cataloging-in-Publication Data
Names: Kruglanski, Arie W., author. | Bélanger, Jocelyn J., author. |
Gunaratna, Rohan, 1961– author.
Title: The three pillars of radicalization : needs, narratives, and networks /
Arie W. Kruglanski, Jocelyn J. Bélanger, Rohan Gunaratna.
Description: New York, NY : Oxford University Press, [2019]
Identifiers: LCCN 2018048100 | ISBN 9780190851125 (hardcover : alk. paper)
Subjects: LCSH: Radicalism. | Terrorism. | Religious fundamentalism.
Classification: LCC HN49.R33 K78 2019 | DDC 303.48/4—dc23
LC record available at https://lccn.loc.gov/2018048100

9 8 7 6 5 4 3

Printed by Sheridan Books, Inc., United States of America

CONTENTS

ABOUT THE AUTHORS

Arie W. Kruglanski is Distinguished University Professor of Psychology at the University of Maryland. He is the recipient of several awards including the National Institute of Mental Health Research Scientist Award, the Distinguished Scientific Contribution Award from the Society of Experimental Social Psychology and the Donald Campbell Award for Outstanding Contributions to Social Psychology from the Society for Personality and Social Psychology. He is Fellow of the American Psychological Association and the American Psychological Society, and presently serves as co-founder and senior investigator at the National Center for the Study of Terrorism and the Response to Terrorism. His research interests are in the domains of human judgment and decision making, the motivation-cognition interface, group and intergroup processes, the psychology of human goals, and the social psychological aspects of terrorism.

Jocelyn J. Bélanger is Assistant Professor of Psychology at New York University Abu Dhabi. His research seeks to understand why, and under which circumstances, individuals are willing to sacrifice their lives for a cause. Dr. Bélanger is the architect behind Montreal's Centre for the Prevention of Radicalization Leading to Violence. He also trains psychologists and social workers on the rehabilitation and reintegration of violent extremist offenders. Dr. Bélanger is the recipient of several awards such as the APA Dissertation Research Award and the Guy Bégin Award for the Best Research Paper in Social Psychology.

Rohan Gunaratna is Professor of Security Studies at the S. Rajaratnam School of International Studies, Nanyang Technology University, and Founder of International Center for Political Violence and Terrorism Research, Singapore. The author and editor of 20 books including *Inside al Qaeda: Global Network of Terror* (Columbia University Press), Gunaratna edited the *Insurgency and Terrorism Series* of the Imperial College Press, London.

A trainer for national security agencies, law enforcement authorities, and military counter-terrorism units, he has interviewed terrorists and insurgents in Afghanistan, Pakistan, Iraq, Yemen, Libya, Saudi Arabia, and other conflict zones. For advancing international intelligence cooperation, Gunaratna received the Major General Ralph H. Van Deman Award in June 2014.

1 A CLEAR AND PRESENT DANGER FOR THE 21ST CENTURY

This book represents a unique collaboration between colleagues with divergent backgrounds and field of expertise. One of the authors (R.G.) is founder of International Centre for Political Violence and Terrorism Research at the Nanyang Technological University in Singapore and a security expert with considerable hands-on experience with international terrorism in its varied manifestations. The other authors (A.K. and J.B.) are social psychologists (at the University of Maryland and New York University at Abu Dhabi, respectively) with expertise in human social behavior crossing the boundaries of motivation, cognition, and group dynamics, especially as these play out in phenomena of violent extremism. Bringing us all together is a keen sense that the wave of violent extremism that has been recently sweeping the globe represents a clear and present danger to the community of nations and poses a formidable challenge to societies world wide of arresting its pernicious advent. We also agreed that the social sciences, and psychology in particular, have a unique part to play in this endeavor. After all, radicalization happens when an individual decides to join a terror organization and construct an explosive device or don a suicide belt to kill unknown others who are personally innocent of all harm to the perpetrators or members of their group. What factors drive persons to risk life and limb and engage in untold acts of callous cruelty against other human beings? In subsequent chapters of this volume, we consider possible answers to these questions that we gleaned from a considerable body of empirical evidence and from other social science theories and analyses of violent extremism. But, first let us remind ourselves why the problem of violent extremism is currently so salient to most nations' daily policy agenda and what attempts have been made to combat it.

It is no exaggeration to state that the specter of world terrorism is among the defining characteristics of the 21st century's first two decades (Engel, 2016; MacAskill, 2014). The 2001 attacks on the World Trade Center and the Pentagon in the United States, as well as subsequent attacks in Bali, London, Madrid, Jakarta, Paris, Brussels, San Bernardino, and Orlando, among an increasing number of others, attracted major media attention to Islamist terrorism. Admittedly, the problem of terrorism is considerably broader, as hundreds of terrorist groups around the globe—as many as 442 according to a recent approximation (Bureau of Counterterrorism, 2014)—practice their lethal trade on a nearly daily basis. Nonetheless, likely because of its global aspirations, Islamist terrorism remains the main focus of public attention and continues to receive the lion's share of media coverage (Kearns, Betus, & Lemieux, 2017).

In response to the September 11, 2001 attacks on the United States, president George W. Bush declared a global war on terror. As of this writing, this war is in its 17th year with no end in sight; already, it has cost many billions of dollars and claimed hundreds of thousands of lives, the large majority of which are innocent civilians, mostly Muslims (see Chapter 10). Even though Al Qaeda core in the Pakistan–Afghanistan region has been badly wounded, its affiliates in other parts of the world—Syria, the Maghreb, and the Arabian Peninsula among others—have been undeterred. Moreover, the rise and fall of the Islamic State (IS) and its proclamation of the caliphate[1] on June 30, 2014 injected a new energy into Islamist extremism.

As of this writing in mid-2018, IS is largely defeated in Iraq and Syria, and the territory under its control, at one time the size of Great Britain, has largely been wrested from its control. As a consequence, Islamist terrorism seems to be seeking alternative outlets for expression, reflected in an uptick of attacks in the Western countries, attempts to capture territories in Southeast Asia (witnessed by the 2017 occupation of the town of Marawi in the southern Philippines), and so on. The competition between IS and Al Qaeda also seemed to enter a new phase with the emergence of Osama Bin Laden's son, the youthful Hamza bin Laden, as a dynamic force hoping to create enduring enthusiasm for the extremists' cause (Burke, 2017). Hardly anyone expects the

---

1. According to the Oxford Dictionary of Islam, a caliphate (2003) is an Islamic state under the leadership of a caliph, a person considered the successor to the Prophet Muhammad as the political-military ruler of the Muslim community. The caliph's functions classically are the enforcement of law, defense and expansion of the realm of Islam, distribution of funds (booty and alms), and general supervision of government.

struggle against Islamist extremism to end any time soon (Hodgson, 1996). The question now is: How should this fight against this particular brand of terrorism be conducted? What promises to constitute the optimal strategy of defeating this ominous phenomenon?

The fight against terrorism has a hard dimension and a soft dimension. Both are critically important for a successful counterterrorism effort, and both are quintessentially psychological. The hard approach, also referred to as kinetic, refers to the fight carried out by the military and the police. It involves defeating the extremists on the ground in Afghanistan, Syria, and Iraq; killing or apprehending their leaders; denying them territory and resources; and thwarting their plots. It is said that nothing succeeds like success and that nothing fails like failure. Indeed, the early successes of IS, its conquests of territory, and its ability to hold its ground despite pressures of the US-led coalition inspired thousands of foreign fighters to join its ranks (Tierney, 2016). Similarly, its failures and loss of territory appear to have dimmed its luster and dampened foreigners' enthusiasm about joining (Chulov, Grierson, & Swaine, 2017). From the psychological perspective, defeating extremists on the ground is important in reducing the attraction of their enterprise and lowering the motivation to identify with IS's cause.

The soft approach seeks to convince supporters of violent extremism through argumentation and social influence to abandon their aggression-justifying beliefs and/or relinquish their engagement in violence. It relies on psychologists, sociologists, educators, and clerics to open a dialogue with potential or committed extremists and persuade them that there is a better way to handle their personal and/or collective concerns. The soft approach has been applied preventively to discourage individuals from embracing extremism (cf. El-Said & Harrington, 2010) and reactively in specific deradicalization programs (i.e., programs that aim to reverse radicalization; Angell & Gunaratna, 2012; El-Said & Harrington, 2010). The latter enjoin detained militants to participate in educational, religious, and spiritual activities engineered to dissuade them from maintaining their commitment to the violence-justifying ideology and its implementation of violent action.

It is in this latter connection that we seek to understand the psychological factors involved in the kind of radicalization that progresses toward violent extremism. We assume that these factors are critical drivers of embarkation on violent extremism and also of its relinquishment in the appropriate circumstances. Our *significance quest theory* described in Chapter 3 suggests that radicalization involves the interplay of three determinants. We call them the 3Ns of violent extremism (Kruglanski et al., 2014; Webber & Kruglanski,

2016). The first N pertains to the individual's motivation—the *need* to feel that one is significant and that one matters. The second N pertains to the ideological *narrative* that enshrines violence as the means best suited for the attainment of significance. Finally, the third N pertains to the social *network*—the group or category of people whose acceptance and appreciation one seeks and whose validation of the ideological narrative is essential to its believability for the individual. Throughout the following chapters, our 3N framework serves as the lens for examining various aspects of radicalization and deradicalization and the interpretation of empirical data that bear on these phenomena.

Our book thus attempts an in-depth analysis of violent extremism contextualized in terms of the current world trends in this domain. To that end, in Chapter 2 we provide a brief history of the war against terror as it has unfolded since its declaration by the United States in 2001. In Chapter 3, we describe our 3N theory of radicalization and its implications. Chapter 4 shows how the present theoretical framework relates to major alternative models proposed by social scientists, and Chapter 5 reviews the empirical evidence that supports our theory. Chapter 6 reviews the profiles of diverse violent extremists and shows how, despite their seemingly unbridgeable differences, they all share in common the 3Ns of radicalization. Chapter 7 discusses the deradicalization process, and Chapter 8 considers the problem of recidivism, or reradicalization. Chapter 9 describes a way of assessing the risk of radicalization, and Chapter 10 is an epilogue that considers the impact that the recent waves of terrorism and radicalization have had on the world at large.

References

Angell, A., & Gunaratna, R. (2012). *Terrorist rehabilitation: The U.S. experience in Iraq.* Boca Raton, FL: Taylor and Francis.

Bureau of Counterterrorism. (2014). *Country reports on terrorism 2014.* Retrieved from http://go.usa.gov/3scv9

Burke, J. (2017, May 30). Hamza bien Laden—a potent weapon in the rivalry between al-Qaida and ISIS. *The Guardian.* Retrieved from https://www.theguardian.com/world/2017/may/30/hamza-bin-laden-a-potent-weapon-in-the-rivalry-between-al-qaida-and-isis

Caliphate. (2003). *The Oxford Dictionary of Islam* (John L. Esposito, Ed.). Oxford, England: Oxford University Press. http://www.oxfordreference.com/view/10.1093/acref/9780195125580.001.0001/acref-9780195125580-e-400?rskey=4B6QoP&result=401

Chulov, M., Grierson, J., Swaine, J. (2017, April 26). Isis faces exodus of foreign fighters as its "caliphate" crumbles. *The Guardian*. Retrieved from https://www.theguardian.com/world/2017/apr/26/isis-exodus-foreign-fighters-caliphate-crumbles

El-Said, H., & Harrington, R. (2010). *Globalisation, democratisation and radicalisation in the Arab world*. New York, NY: Palgrave Macmillan.

Engel, P. (2016, September 11). The terrorist threat is worse now than it was before 9/11. *Business Insider*. Retrieved from http://www.businessinsider.com/are-we-safer-now-than-on-911-2016-9

Hodgson, G. (1996, August 15). Terrorism will never go away. *Independent*. Retrieved from http://www.independent.co.uk/voices/terrorism-will-never-go-away-1309941.html

Kearns, E. M., Betus, A., & Lemieux, A. (2017). *Why do some terrorist attacks receive more media attention than others?* Unpublished manuscript. Retrieved from https://papers.ssrn.com/sol3/papers.cfm?abstract_id=2928138

Kruglanski, A. W., Gelfand, M. J., Bélanger, J. J., Sheveland, A., Hetiarachchi, M., & Gunaratna, R. (2014). The psychology of radicalization and deradicalization: How significance quest impacts violent extremism. *Political Psychology, 35*, 69–93.

MacAskill, E. (2014, November 18). Fivefold increase in terrorism fatalities since 9/11, says report. *The Guardian*. Retrieved from https://www.theguardian.com/uk-news/2014/nov/18/fivefold-increase-terrorism-fatalities-global-index

Tierney, D. (2016, April 28). Isis and the "Loser Effect": Could the Islamic State's recent failures signal its demise? *The Atlantic*. Retrieved from https://www.theatlantic.com/international/archive/2016/04/is-isis-losing/480336/

Webber, D., & Kruglanski, A. W. (2016). Psychological Factors in Radicalization: A "3 N" Approach. In G. LaFree & J. D. Freilich (Eds.), *The handbook of the criminology of terrorism* (pp. 33–46). West Sussex, England: Wiley.

2 THE RISE OF CONTEMPORARY VIOLENT ISLAMIST EXTREMISM

THE THREAT AND THE RESPONSE

Scientific research often evolves in response to significant problems in the world at large. So it has been the case with scientific research on violent extremism. Especially in the aftermath of the fateful attacks on September 11, 2001, in New York City and Washington, DC, social scientists' interest in this phenomenon and its determinants has multiplied by manifold, and there has been a significant upsurge in scientific publications on the topic.[1] Work featured in this volume on the psychological bases of radicalization is part and parcel of the scientific response to an acute social problem posed by extremism. But, what exactly is the problem, and where has it been trending? In this chapter, we provide a brief historical depiction of a major brand of contemporary violent extremism that commanded the world's attention like hardly any other, namely, violent Islamic extremism.

Generations of Threat

Islamist extremism developed over three generations of mujahidin, each more violent than its predecessor. The first generation were members of the Muslim Brotherhood. This group emerged in response to the failure of secular Muslim states and, throughout the 20th century, struggled in various ways to replace these states with

---

1. Google Scholar shows that from 1900 to 2000, around 120,000 books or articles were published on the topic of terrorism, and 12,500 books or articles were published on the topic of violent extremism. However, in the much shorter timespan from 2001 to 2018, there were 704,000 books or articles on terrorism and 34,700 on violent extremism.

Islamist ones. The Brotherhood ideology was fashioned by Hasan Al Banna (1906–1949) and Sayyid Qutb (1906–1956) in the Middle East and by Abdul Ala Maududi (1903–1979) in Asia. Most states reacted by unleashing their intelligence, police, and the military to suppress and repress the Brotherhood. The failure of the Brotherhood to succeed politically led to the creation of Islamist groups willing to use violence for political ends. As the mainstream Brotherhood found political accommodation within the secular regimes, the hardline Islamists and their supporters regarded the Brotherhood as compromised.

Much like the US invasion and occupation of Iraq in 2003, the Soviet invasion of Afghanistan in December 1979 created opportunities and conditions for disparate Islamist groups to grow in strength, size, and influence. Furthermore, they mastered the art of warfare during the Afghan campaign. Abdullah Azzam, a Palestinian-Jordanian, who rejected the Brotherhood, politically articulated and operationalized the concept of jihad.

In addition to Western assistance to mujahidin groups fighting in Afghanistan, the fallout from the revolution in Iran (1979) and the Iran–Iraq War (1980–1988) led Western governments, especially the United States, to assist Iraq and the Sunni groups worldwide. Furthermore, the Saudi campaign against the Shias empowered the Sunni groups throughout the 1980s, leading to the unintended consequence of Sunni fundamentalism with severe implications for international security (Baer, 2003; Gold, 2003).

In this context, the second mujahidin generation consisted of veterans of the anti-Soviet multinational Afghan campaign. As the launching pad to fight the Afghan jihad, Pakistan hosted both Muslim recruits and Islamist groups from around the world. Maktab Khadamāt al-Mujāhidīn al-'Arab (MAK), founded by Abdullah Azzam, was the principal transnational organization that disseminated propaganda, recruited followers, raised funds, offered training, and armed the mujahidin, as well as provided welfare to the mujahidin families. After the mujahidin's stunning victory over the Soviet army—the largest land army in the world—MAK evolved into Al Qaeda al Sulbah in 1988.

Al Qaeda was specifically created to support the Islamist struggle[2] worldwide. As the vanguard of the Islamist movement, wherever Muslims were oppressed by Western-oriented regimes, Al Qaeda was duty bound to play a

---

2. The goals were withdrawal of the United States and its Western allies from the Middle East, eradication of West-oriented regimes in Muslim majority countries and replacement with the rule of Sharia, and renewal of the Islamic Caliphate.

pivotal role by providing arms, weapons, finance, training, and fighters. The organization was able to achieve this preeminent status because it inherited the Western and Middle Eastern sponsored state-of-the-art guerrilla training and operational infrastructure. Furthermore, a merger with the Egyptian Islamic Jihad (EIJ) gave Al Qaeda the ability to attack civilian targets in urban environments. Thus, not only did Al Qaeda develop global jihadist orientation and truly lethal and sophisticated capabilities, but it imparted them to Islamist groups worldwide.

The mujahidin who fought the Soviets did not deliberately seek death—martyrdom operations or suicide terrorism was a later invention. Furthermore, these fighters did not believe in killing civilians, only combatants. When the Soviet military withdrew and the jihad against the Soviets ended, several tens of thousands of foreign mujahidin returned to their home countries. Their bulk returned to civilian life, but a minority either founded or joined Islamist groups in their home countries with the purpose of creating Islamist states. A few thousand mujahidin remained in Pakistan. They were members of Islamist groups such as the EIJ and the Islamic Group of Egypt that had formerly employed violence against their home governments. With time, the Pakistan- and Afghanistan-based mujahidin traveled to other lands with large Muslim populations. In Tajikistan, Kashmir, Bosnia, Chechnya, Dagestan, Somalia, Algeria, Mindanao, and Afghanistan, these mujahidin worked with local Muslim groups, enhancing their fighting capabilities.

After the collapse of the Soviet Union, the decline of communism, and the end of the Cold War, the international community neglected Afghanistan and Pakistan, previously frontline states in the fight against communism. Al Qaeda recruited from the abandoned mujahidin pool in those states and provided them with a home (Gunaratna, 2011) and, likely, a purpose in life—a mission that made them feel they really mattered.

The third generation of mujahidin are members of Al Qaeda and three dozen Asian, Middle African, and Caucasian Islamist groups trained in Afghanistan. In the post-9/11 environment, these groups engaged in insurgency and conducted terrorist attacks. Operationally active in their local and regional conflicts, Al Qaeda empowered some of these groups. By breaking away from the Al Qaeda orbit, IS surpassed it in developing a global reach. In comparison with Al Qaeda, IS was distinguished by its brutality. Although Al Qaeda and its associated groups have invested in significant chemical, biological, and radiological research, including in anthrax and ricin poison, IS has actually used chlorine and mustard gases against their targets, mostly in the Mosul area, and experimented with a range of agents (US Central Intelligence

Agency [CIA], 2003; Schmitt, 2016; K. Weston, Police International Counter Terrorism Unit, personal communication, October 18, 2003). The propensity of Islamist extremists to use unconventional agents with greater lethality has grown under IS influence.

The Current Global Landscape

The current global landscape of violent Islamist extremism has been shaped by three pivotal events: (a) the multinational Afghan mujahidin[3] campaign (1979–1989) and the defeat of the Soviet bloc in that campaign; (b) the terrorist attack by Al Qaeda on American landmarks in 2001 and the US-led coalition response; and (c) the emergence of IS in 2004 and the global response to the threat it poses. These events have coincided with the following three phases of Islamist extremism.

In Phase 1, the decade-long anti-Soviet multinational Afghan mujahidin campaign mobilized Muslims worldwide. The Soviet defeat strengthened the resolve of radical and violent Muslims to fight in territories where they perceived fellow Muslims to be suffering. In this context, in Afghanistan and beyond, Al Qaeda and their associates set up infrastructural bases to provide ideological indoctrination, training, weapons, and financing for like-minded groups and their current and future recruits.

In Phase 2, the September 11, 2001 assaults in New York City and Washington, DC, demonstrated that even a global superpower such as the United States can be attacked successfully. This, in turn, inspired a number of radical Muslim threat groups, instigating them to launch a worldwide fight against US targets and their allies. The fight was broadly framed as a perpetual battle against the Crusaders[4] and Jews who were targeting the Muslim religion and its faithful observants (Kean & Hamilton, 2004).

---

3. According to the *Oxford Dictionary of Islam,* mujahidin is the plural form of mujahid, "one who engages in jihad" ("Mujahidin," 2003). The term does not have a necessary connection with war. In literal terms, it means "one who struggles on behalf of Islam." In recent years, however, it has been adopted by those who consider themselves engaged in armed defense of Muslim lands. The struggle has many dimensions. Some see themselves fighting foreign domination; others are fighting against injustice, especially unjust state oppression. The term became known in the West in the early 1980s as the Afghan mujahidin battled against the Soviet invasion and occupation of Afghanistan.

4. Crusaders refers to the Christian warriors who participates in the Crusades (1096–1291), religious wars between Christians and Muslims for control of the holy sites considered sacred by both groups.

Finally, in Phase 3, after the declaration and subsequent rise of a caliphate, Islamist extremist, terrorist, and insurgent groups pledged allegiance to the self-proclaimed caliph, Abu Bakr al Baghdadi (Tran & Weaver, 2014), as leader of IS. IS military victories, territorial control, end-of-times narrative, and mastery of social media drew recruits, resources, and international attention toward the organization. In the current phase of global expansion, IS co-opting Islamist threat groups and setting up governorates (wilayats) in Asia, the Caucasus, Africa, and the Middle East.

In these three phases, *four ideologues* precipitated a generational fight by developing ideologies resonating with Muslims worldwide. Abdullah Azzam, Osama bin Laden, Aymen al Zawahiri, and abu Bakr al Baghdadi created a global movement that challenged the status quo of both the Muslim world and the international order. The genesis of the contemporary wave of global extremism, terrorism, and insurgency can be traced back to Abdullah Azzam and bin Laden's creation of Al Qaeda.

Al Qaeda: A Genesis of the Threat

Hailing from Silat al-Harithiya, near Jenin in the West Bank, Abdullah Azzam, a Palestinian-Jordanian, pioneered the doctrine of *perpetual combat* (Emerson, n.d.), an interminable war of jihad between Muslims and infidels. Sometimes referred to as the father of jihad, Azzam was a theologian. To fight the Soviets, he created MAK, the Afghan Service Bureau, in Pakistan in 1984 to support foreign fighter recruits who were traveling from around the world to join the anti-Soviet battle (Soufan, 2011). Azzam was supported in this venture by Osama bin Laden, an engineer and businessman at the time.

Preparing for the defeat of the Soviets in Afghanistan, the most dedicated and determined Arab commanders strove to unite the core of the fighters under one banner. As such, on August 11, 1988, six months before the Soviets withdrew from Afghanistan, Al Qaeda was created by bin Laden in Peshawar. The group drew on the vision of Azzam, who had conceptualized Al Qaeda as the "pioneering vanguard of the Islamic movements" (Gunaratna, 2002). Its stated global aims were to fight

> until every spot of the lands of Islam are liberated; and until the flag of victory and jihad is raised high and fluttering over Grozny, Kashgar, Bukhara, Samarkand, Kabul, Manila, Jakarta, Baghdad, Damascus, Mecca, Medina, Sana'a, Mogadishu, Cairo, Algeria, and Ceuta and Melilla; and until the Islamic conquests return, then it will liberate the

usurped Andalusia and the stolen Aqsa and restore them and the rest of all the usurped countries of the Muslims to the coming State of the Caliphate, Allah permitting. (Gunaratna, 2015, p. 25)

After Azzam was killed by Egyptian rivals in 1989, the leader of EIJ, the most ruthless Sunni terrorist group, Ayman al Zawahiri—who was widely suspected of masterminding the assassination—became an advisor to bin Laden. Zawahiri collaborated with Al Qaeda from its very inception, and in the 1990s, the EIJ merged with Al Qaeda, renaming the group Qaedat al-Jihad (Wright, 2006).

The success of the anti-Soviet multinational mujahidin campaign emboldened the Muslim fighters and inspired them to assist their Muslim brethren in other conflict zones, including Kashmir, Chechnya, Bosnia, Algeria, and Palestine. In the meantime, bin Laden fell out with Saudi Arabia following the Iraqi invasion of Kuwait in August 1990. Bin Laden's offer to bring the mujahidin to defend the country was rejected by the Saudi royal family. The Saudis preferred the presence of Western forces, which caused bin Laden, along with other activists and clerics, to protest these ambitions. Shortly afterward, bin Laden was placed under house arrest for creating dissent. He then left the country, against his family's instructions. In April 1991, bin Laden accepted an invitation from the National Islamic Front leader Hassan al Turabi to relocate to Khartoum in Sudan. During that period, Al Qaeda deepened its network in the Balkans, the Caucuses, and the Middle East by forging relations with African insurgent and terrorist groups.

In May 1996, bin Laden relocated from Sudan to Afghanistan, consolidating the collaboration of the Afghan Taliban with Al Qaeda. Mullah Mohammad Omar, the leader of the Islamic Emirate of Afghanistan who was designated the Amir al-Mumineen ("Commander of the Faithful"), gave permission to Al Qaeda to train the fighters in that country.

This development proved of considerable importance. By providing ideological indoctrination, training, weapons, and financing in Afghanistan and other theaters, Al Qaeda empowered insurgent and terrorist groups in Asia, Africa, the Middle East, the Caucuses, and the Balkans. Based on a 1998 fatwa[5] by bin Laden, Al Qaeda built an umbrella group, the World Islamic Front for Jihad against Jews and Crusaders, with the aim to attack

---

5. A fatwa is a ruling on a point of Islamic law given by a recognized authority ("Fatwa," n.d.).

the alleged distant enemies[6] of Islam (Lewis, 1998). In this connection, Al Qaeda conducted attacks targeting the US embassies in Kenya and Tanzania on August 7, 1998, killing 224 people and injuring 4,000. Other incidents included the *USS Cole* attack in Yemen's Aden harbor on October 12, 2000, which killed 17 and injured 39.

The US response to these provocations was weak,[7] and terrorist groups continued to plan other major attacks on US soil, particularly in two waves during October 2002 and May 2003. Of the attacks staged in Yemen, Kuwait, and Indonesia, on October 12, 2002, the worst, in which 202 people were killed, took place in Bali by Jemaah Islamiyah, a Southeast Asian Islamist terrorist group. Though Al Qaeda did not directly commit this act, they financed the operation ("12 October 2002 Bali Bombing Plot," 2012). There were five attacks staged in May 2003, but only the May 12 attack—a coordinated simultaneous assault on Western residence complexes in Saudi Arabia—was claimed by Al Qaeda. Associated groups in Chechnya, Pakistan, and Morocco were responsible for the four others. The high point for Al Qaeda came on September 11, 2001, with the attacks on US soil that killed 2,996 people and injured 6,000, while damaging close to $10 billion worth of property and infrastructure.

The September 2001 attacks targeted the United States' most iconic economic, military, and political landmarks. Moreover, this assault inspired and instigated 30 associated groups to mount attacks in the Global South against Western and local government targets within their own countries. Al Qaeda urged their associates to hit both "the US, the head of the poisonous snake shielding corrupt Muslim rulers and ungodly regimes at home" (Gunaratna & Woodall, 2005, p. 90).

Al Qaeda Transformation: From Organization to a Movement

In October 2001, when the United States launched its operations in Afghanistan, Al Qaeda's apex leadership relocated to Pakistan. Experiencing setbacks and depleted resources, the group transformed from an operational organization to an ideological one focused on training. From tribal areas of Pakistan, Al Qaeda worked with both the Pakistani and Afghan Taliban to

---

6. Distant enemies primarily refers to the United States and its Western allies.

7. There was no retaliation for the attack, merely a reconsideration of the rules of engagement by the US navy.

plan attacks on US and Afghan forces on Afghan soil. Some of these foiled plans included Richard Reid's attempt to blow up a US plane using a shoe bomb, Dhiren Barot's (alias Issa al Hindi) plans to launch attacks in the United Kingdom and the United States, and Rashid Rauf's airline liquid plot.[8]

The CIA continued to work with the counterterrorism directorate of Pakistan's Inter-Services Intelligence (ISI) to locate and annihilate Al Qaeda leaders and members. Most of the group's leaders who relocated to Pakistan or Iran are believed to have been killed or imprisoned. On March 1, 2003, an ISI team in Rawalpindi, the city adjacent to the capital of Pakistan, captured Khalid Sheikh Mohamed, the 9/11 mastermind. On May 2, 2011, bin Laden was located in Pakistan by the CIA and was killed in Abbottabad by a team of US Navy SEALs. After bin Laden's death, his deputy Aymen al Zawahiri, the former leader of the EIJ, became the head of Al Qaeda.

As the leader of the group, Zawahiri appointed bin Laden's former secretary, Nasir Abdel Karim al-Wuhayshi (alias Abu Basir), as the Yemeni leader of Al Qaeda in the Arabian Peninsula (AQAP) in 2013 (Lake, 2013). While AQAP grew, posing a threat both within and outside Yemen, the Al Qaeda core in Pakistan was by now an ideological organization focused on propaganda. Two years after 9/11, its military strength had diminished from about 2,500 to 3,000 fighters to less than 200. Al Qaeda branches, however, sprung up in various locations.

With the United States focused on eliminating Al Qaeda in tribal Pakistan, its associate groups in Asia, Africa, and the Middle East grew several times stronger than Al Qaeda itself. Nonetheless, due to its material wealth and a dense network of connections, the organization remained an influential voice in the jihadist movement, defining the global landscape of violence by mobilizing threat groups and galvanizing a segment of the Muslim community against the United States and its allies and friends.

Over its almost three decades of existence, Al Qaeda had managed to train thousands of fighters that fought in the Philippines, Indonesia, Thailand, Kashmir, Bangladesh, Pakistan, the Maldives, Tajikistan, Uzbekistan, Saudi Arabia, Yemen, Palestine, Iraq, Syria, Libya, Algeria, Sudan, and Chechnya. As a capacity builder in Afghanistan, Al Qaeda gave birth to an entire movement of radical and violent Muslims willing to fight, kill, and die for their beliefs. In the aftermath of the US and its allies' invasion of Afghanistan, Al Qaeda became operationally ineffective; however, its associated groups

---

8. Rauf planned to smuggle liquid bombs on board of several transatlantic flights in 2006.

ensured the continuity of the fight. The group's most enduring contribution toward sustaining the global jihad was to create a new generation of dedicated mujahidin.

Until Al Qaeda disowned IS in February of 2014 (as a consequence of doctrinaire differences in conducting jihad), the movement consisted of five organizations: (a) the Islamic State of Iraq (ISI), (b) Jabhat al Nusra, (c) al Shabab, (d) Al Qaeda in the Islamic Maghreb, and (e) AQAP. Several groups from the Philippines to Indonesia, Pakistan to Lebanon, and Nigeria to Mali also sought to follow Al Qaeda. The transformation of Al Qaeda from an operational group into a movement, drawing in leaders from Asia, the Middle East, and Africa, made it resilient to complete annihilation.

In the period since September 2001, the overwhelming majority of Islamist terrorist operations have not been conducted by Al Qaeda but rather by groups that it inspired and directed. A majority of these groups were groomed, financed, and trained by Al Qaeda in Afghanistan and other conflicts zones throughout the 1990s.

To compensate for the lack of its own operational capability, Al Qaeda worked together with these associated groups to shape its vision and purpose. Al Qaeda's ideologues transformed these group members' thinking to emphasize fighting both their near enemies (Muslim governments) and their distant ones (the United States and its allies). The group focused on investing in online propaganda and concentrated on ideological indoctrination to inspire and instigate the wider Muslim community to sustain this fight. In addition to Al Qaeda's main website, Al Qaeda supporters built a dozen websites urging Muslims to strike the West. Although the Internet is the mainstay of post-9/11 Al Qaeda propaganda, some influential imams[9] in the West (in the United States and the United Kingdom, among other countries) continue to openly support Al Qaeda causes. Some of these religious leaders declared the confrontation in Iraq between the US-led coalition forces and militant groups like Al Qaeda and the Islamic State of Iraq and Syria (ISIS) as a jihad and openly urged Muslim youth to travel to Iraq and Syria to join the fight.

Traditionally, Islamist groups fought secular Muslim governments in an effort to replace them and to form separate Islamic states. By infusing its ideology of a global jihad, Al Qaeda has successfully transformed the parochial thinking of these groups. Today, the latest generation of these associated groups has gone beyond narrow territorial confines to pursue a more

---

9. An iman is an Islamic leader usually charged with conducting prayers in a mosque.

pan-Islamic agenda. For instance, in January 2003, the Salafi Group for Call and Combat (GSPC), fighting the Algerian regime, produced the poison ricin in the United Kingdom (Johnson, 2005), though their plot to use it against Jewish targets was thwarted by the British security forces. Al Qaeda specialists also trained GSPC members to manufacture ricin in the Pankisi Valley in Georgia to target the "infidels."[10] Likewise, under Al Qaeda influence, the Eastern Turkistan Islamic Movement (ETIM) instead of simply rallying for the east, started a violent campaign for the liberation of both eastern and western Turkistan.

Reclaiming Afghanistan and Pakistan

Presently, in light of the US-led coalition's drawback of forces from Afghanistan in 2016, the Afghan Taliban and their associated groups—including Al Qaeda—are reconstituting the Afghan sanctuary.[11] Similar to the Soviets during the Afghan invasion, the Western forces failed to sustain and succeed against a long drawn-out insurgency. Despite the growing threat of terrorism to the United States, its allies, and its friends, the lack of US public will to commit forces to conflict zones made the drawdown inevitable.

Despite the delayed (and restricted) draw back of the US military from Afghanistan, a smaller footprint of its Special Operations Forces is still meant to remain there. In addition to mounting intelligence-led counterterrorism and insurgency operations, the United States will focus on providing trainers and advisors to support the Afghan National Army's (ANA) capacity to fight. Time will tell whether such limited support will be sufficient. It is evident, however, that without substantial international support the ANA cannot manage to prevail against a persistent and relentless adversary.

Whereas the Afghan Taliban comprises a highly motivated and battle-hardened 25,000 fighters, the ANA has far less experience and dedication (Mapping Militants Project, 2016). The Afghan Taliban fighters are followers of Deobandism, a puritanical sect of Sunni Islam, and its supporters include countless foreign warriors. As the news of the US drawdown emerges, these fighters and supporters are anxiously awaiting their re-entry into Afghanistan. According to experts, such return is highly likely.

---

10. *Infidels* is a term used to pejoratively describe nonbelievers in Islam.

11. This refers to the fact that the Taliban regime in Afghanistan provided shelter for a violent extremist organization, namely, Al Qaeda.

The Changing Capabilities of Al Qaeda and Its Global Influence

Upon Azzam's death in 1989, when his protégé and successor Osama bin Laden took over Al Qaeda, the group began to attack civilian targets, not just military ones. From February 1993, beginning with the attack on the World Trade Centre in New York and the Bojinka plot in the Philippines, Al Qaeda extended its targeting policy to include American civilians and civilian infrastructure. This strategy ultimately provoked the United States to a massive response that may have ultimately helped the jihadi cause, though its immediate consequence was the destruction of Al Qaeda as an operational force.

In the aftermath of the September 11, 2001 attacks, US intervention in Afghanistan and the US-led global coalition against terrorism led to the arrest or capture of at least three fourths of Al Qaeda's leadership. The loss of high-quality operatives and sustained global targeting weakened Al Qaeda gravely. As the group's key members have been arrested or killed, some generational exchange has been inevitable. Although new capable members are filling the positions of their mentors, it will take time before these fighters can fully establish themselves within the leadership's circle of trust. As their knowledge of the West is limited and considering the tough security measures imposed by Western nations, these new members will be exposed to a different nature and scale of threat. As long as the West maintains pressure, these members are unlikely to go down the road of spectacular operations in the West, consistent with Al Qaeda's doctrine, at least in the short term.

Changing Priorities and Strategies

The mainstay of terrorist strategy rests on the concept of *provocation*. While Al Qaeda and its leaders paid a dear price for the 9/11 attacks, it succeeded in provoking the United States to an enormous response, which helped convince thousands of Muslims that America is their archenemy. After the September 11, 2001 attacks, especially in light of the US intervention in Iraq, resenting the United States became an ideology that held significant resonance throughout the Muslim world.

Whereas Al Qaeda is a global network that wages a universal jihad, its associated territorial Islamist groups wage localized jihads. By closer association, post-9/11 Al Qaeda was able to influence the minds of the leaders of Al Qaeda's associated groups to wage fights at two different levels: at a local level against their domestic enemies—typically the opposing governments—and at an international level, against the United States and its allies.

Due to increased human vigilance, unprecedented security, intelligence, and military and law enforcement cooperation, targeting the United States mainland has become difficult (Brill, 2016). Al Qaeda's reduced operational capability combined with this hardening of strategic targets in the United States has prompted a shift in the target locations terrorist groups choose. Thus, the bulk of the targets attacked by Islamist groups since 9/11 has not been the interests of the United States but those of its allies and friends.

A shift in target classes has also taken place. With the terrorist threat moving from the United States to its allies and friends, the targets have shifted from hard to soft ("Soft Target," n.d.). The bulk of the targets attacked are not military (like army barracks or military installations) or diplomatic (e.g., embassies) but rather civilian including places of worship, residences, and hotels. The shift reflects a weakening of Al Qaeda's capabilities as well as the difficulties posed for the associated groups from striking hardened targets.

There has also been a shift in the types of weapons employed by terrorist groups. In light of enhanced government security measures and countermeasures—especially at land, sea, and air border crossings—terrorists are increasingly developing and acquiring dual-user technologies, that is, civilian technologies with military applications. They include fuel-laden commercial aircraft and explosives-laden land vehicles, boats, and ships that are employed as missiles and chemicals and commercial fertilizer purchased from chemist stores, pharmacies, and agricultural farms as well as liquid nitrogen or petroleum, used as explosive material. Terrorists have also made use of open, closed, and semiclosed scuba gear to access mobile and stationary maritime assets to plant underwater explosive devices and used radiological material from hospitals and industrial complexes in plots to create so-called dirty bombs.[12]

There has also been an increasing shift in terrorist tactics. Al Qaeda has demonstrated and repeatedly urged its associated groups to understand the value of employing suicide tactics (Al Zawahiri, 2001). More groups, particularly of the Islamist variety, have begun to use suicide bombings to strike more difficult targets. As it has proven cost-effective, suicide terrorism has grown in

---

12. A dirty bomb is an explosive device that could poison the area around the blast zone with toxic levels of radiation.

popularity among the core groups and their affiliates, and it is now employed often and in varied locations worldwide.

After 9/11, the propensity for extremist groups to engage in mass casualty violence has increased. The third and fourth generations of terrorists are likely to continue to develop and acquire mass casualty weapon systems, both conventional and unconventional. This is bound to lead to more brutal attacks with higher casualty numbers. Ideologically and operationally, 9/11 "raised their [i.e., the extremist groups'] potential" (for destruction) and "widened their horizons of what is possible" (A. Tan, personal communication, October 20, 2003).

The post 9/11 period also witnessed greater cooperation and coordination between Islamist groups. Dispersal of Al Qaeda members internationally affected greater interaction between different terrorist groups that embraced its program. Finally, and significantly, the center of gravity of global insurgency and terrorism shifted from the Pakistan–Afghanistan theater to the Iraq–Syria theatre.

The Theater of Jihad in Iraq and Syria

The Al Qaeda–associated group that outperformed all others in terms of training, weapons, and finance was Abu Musab al Zarqawi's Tawhid wal Jihad (Monotheism and Jihad). Abu Musab was a Jordanian criminal mentored into radical Islam by Abu Mohamed al Maqdisi, a Palestinian born in the West Bank (Teslik, 2008). After relocating to Afghanistan in 1999, Abu Musab received support from Al Qaeda to establish a training camp in Herat, Afghanistan, attended by Jordanian, Syrian, Lebanese, Palestinians, and Iraqi (including Kurdish) fighters from the Levant. Facing the US-led intervention in 2001, he relocated to Iran briefly and then to Iraq. With the help of another Al Qaeda–associated group, Ansar al Islam, he followed Al Qaeda's footsteps and established a base in the north of Iraq in 2002.

After the United States invaded Iraq in March 2003, Abu Musab pledged allegiance to Osama bin Laden and in October 2004 renamed his group al Qaidat al Jihad fi Bilad al Rafidayn (Al Qaeda in Mesopotamia/Al Qaeda in Iraq). Even when Osama bin Laden was still alive, many saw Abu Musab as his successor. The Abu Musab group, dominated by foreign fighters, fought against the US-led coalition and planned attacks overseas, alongside other Iraqi groups. His group's tactics of beheading captives and bombing Shia targets, including Shia shrines, were aimed at creating a sectarian conflict that heretofore Al Qaeda had avoided. Nonetheless, Abu Musab's group was highly visible and effective. It conducted the largest number of suicide attacks and produced the highest number of casualties. Although he did not live to witness its achievements, Abu Musab created the most successful second-generation group of jihadists that took the fight against the United States and its allies to a new level of intensity and brutality.

The US Intervention in Iraq

The US-led coalition's intervention in Iraq is generally considered as a strategic failure and tragic in its consequences. From 2003 to 2011, 4,475 US troops lost their lives in Iraq and another 32,225 were wounded in action (Boot, 2012). The US political experiment of regime change in Iraq, and other parts of the Middle East, resulted in a blow back. Comparable to Afghanistan in the 1980s and 1990s, culminating in the 9/11 attacks, the US intervention in Iraq raised the global threat level significantly. Arguably, the intervention in Iraq also deprived the United States of victory in Afghanistan.

In addition to originating in false intelligence,[13] hence lacking reasonable warrant, the intervention involved a number of strategic mistakes. As a result of these actions, the very infrastructure that ran the country and maintained order and security collapsed. This led to a failure to provide basic services to the public, including the supply of such necessities as water, electricity, and sanitation. In those circumstances, the Iraqi insurgency quickly took off. Although well-meaning, the US administrators failed to understand how best to manage Iraq and its people, fueling an impassioned opposition toward the occupation forces. Perhaps the gravest US strategic error was that of dismantling the Baathist regime and the Iraqi Army, which ultimately led to the recruitment of high-level military personnel to the insurgency's ranks and the considerable strengthening of what later was to become the Islamic State (IS).

In the background of these political developments, after joining with Iraqi groups, Abu Musab al Zarqawi created a short-lived Mujahidin Shura Council in January 2006. After his death in June 2006, Abu Umar al Baghdadi formed ISI. Shortly after ISI's formation, Abu Umar was killed, and he was succeeded by Abu Bakr al Baghdadi. Baghdadi dispatched Abu Mohamed al Julani from Iraq to Syria to strengthen the opposition to the Assad regime in the wake of the Arab Spring.

---

13. US intelligence services falsely believed that Saddam Hussein's regime possessed weapons of mass destruction.

Abu Mohamed al Julani operated in al Raqqah, Idlib, Deir ez-Zor, and Aleppo provinces until ISI merged with al Nusra in 2013, creating IS (Dawlah al Islamiyah fi al Iraq wal Sham or Da'ish; Ghosh, 2014). The merger did not last long. Though IS evolved from Al Qaeda in Iraq (AQI), Al Qaeda reprimanded IS for engaging in extreme violence and disowned it for disobeying its command to confine itself to operations in Syria. The Al Qaeda–IS infighting polarized radical and violent Muslim groups in the Middle East and beyond. While a segment of fighters supported IS, others remained loyal to al Nusra and fought both Baghdadi's IS and the Assad regime.

The weakening of Al Qaeda core in the Pakistan–Afghanistan region, coupled with the successes of the Islamic State, created a rivalry between the two organizations in which the IS challenged Al Qaeda's pre-eminent role in the jihadi movement. The divide between IS and Al Qaeda has affected jihadi threat groups in Asia, Africa, the Caucasus, and the Middle East. Multiple groups pledged allegiance to IS by raising its trademark black flag, but others reaffirmed their loyalty (baya) to Al Qaeda.

The discord between Aymen al Zawahiri and Baghdadi widened after IS declared an Islamic caliphate in May 2014. Although Zawahiri himself advocated an Islamic caliphate, he did not agree with the process that Baghdadi followed. In light of the conflict between the two groups, an Al Qaeda official, Muhammad bin Mahmoud Rabie al-Bahtiyti (alias Abu Dujana al-Basha), issued an audio speech warning Muslims against following the Islamic caliphate. The statement urged fighters in Syria to "rescue the ship of jihad, and reach it before it deviates from its course and settles on the path of the people of desires" (Joscelyn, 2014). Reflecting Al Qaeda's disappointment, he added:

> We call to restore the rightly-guided Caliphate on the prophetic method, and not on the method of deviation, lying, breaking promises, and abrogating allegiances—a Caliphate that stands with justice, consultation, and coming together, and not with oppression, infidel-branding the Muslims, killing the monotheists, and dispersing the rank of the mujahidin. (Joscelyn, 2014)

In many ways, IS was Al Qaeda's most extreme version. IS was one of the world's largest insurgent–terrorist groups with 60,000 fighters strong at the peak of its successes, including 30,000 foreign fighters. Straddling Iraq, Syria, and a global network, the organization was able to hold its own for an extended time against assaults by coalition forces and the Asad military assisted by Hizballah and Russia. In retaliation for coalition operations, the Islamic caliphate's worldwide network of groups, supporters, and sympathizers have been launching attacks against the United States and their allies.

Still, Al Qaeda and IS continue to compete for supremacy in the global arena. The IS–Al Qaeda discord, the IS rejection of Al Qaeda, and Baghdadi's proclamation of the caliphate has eroded the power and prestige of Al Qaeda in the Muslim world. The idea of the caliphate proclaimed in 2014 by al Baghdadi galvanized the imagination of Muslims worldwide. A bulk of the threat groups formerly allied with Al Qaeda have abandoned Zawahiri. These include the Bangsamoro Islamic Freedom Fighters and Abu Sayyaf Group (in the Philippines), Mujahidin Indonesia Timur and Jamaat Asharut Tawheed (in Indonesia), Sons of the Call for Tawhid and Jihad (in Jordan), Jamaat Ansar Bayt al-Maqdis (in Sinai), and the Majlis Shura al-Mujahedeen (in Gaza), to mention but a few examples.

Although not operationally associated with Al Qaeda, these groups were ideologically affiliated with it. To be sure, the trend away from Al Qaeda and toward IS has not been uniform. Despite the clash of the leaders, many members of IS admire Al Qaeda, and vice versa. Rather than wholly committing to IS, there have been multiple cases where given militant groups split between IS and Al Qaeda supporters. For example, the Al Qaeda in the Islamic Maghreb broke from Jund al-Khilafa in North Africa, pledging allegiance to IS. In the Middle East, AQAP split with Ansar Al-Dawlah Islamiyah in its support for IS. In South Asia, Tehrik-i-Taliban Pakistan split with Tehreek-e-Kalifat that supports IS. In some cases there were no formal splits though membership of an organization was divided in its support for IS and Al Qaeda. This was the case with Jamaah al Islamiyah in Southeast Asia, Boko Haram in Nigeria, and al Shabab in Somalia. In contrast to Al Qaeda building groups from the ground up, IS more or less hijacked existing groups that Al Qaeda had previously established.

Despite its waning influence and strength, Al Qaeda remains an influential player in the global jihadi movement. In September 2014, an Al Qaeda official Hossam Abdul Raouf commented in this connection:

So how then can Al Qaida have shrunken greatly and lost many of its senior leaders at a time when it is expanding horizontally and opening new fronts dependent on it? And it goes without saying that these new branches require a number of senior leaders, and that constant communication must be maintained with them for purposes of coordination, consultation, support, and so on. (Abd al-Raoof, 2014, p. 2)

Fighting the IS

The fight against IS includes several components. First, there is the US-led Western and Arab coalition (The Islamic Military Alliance to Fight Terrorism; IMAFT) that largely defeated IS in Iraq and Syria. Then, there is the Iranian contingent that works in tandem with Bashir al Assad's Syrian regime as of 2015 also with Russia to fight IS. Third, Kurdish, Iranian, and Iraqi Shia militias, as well as the Lebanese Hizzballah, have been fighting IS on the ground. Fourth, in August 2016, Turkey launched an offensive into Syria with the aim of fighting ISIS.

Coalition pressure on IS at its heartland in Iraq and Syria has led to significant losses of IS territory, including Fallujah, known as the gateway to Baghdad, the capital of Iraq. The coalition's drone attacks, airstrikes, and combat forces depleted IS rank and file; under this mounting pressure, IS was pushed into a defensive stance, and in July 2017 it lost Mosul, the city where the caliphate was pronounced only three years earlier. IS losses included the death of its most celebrated military commander, Umar al-Shishani, in the Iraqi city of Shirqat in July 2016. At the time of his death, the Chechen commander was tasked by Baghdadi to prepare the defenses of Mosul. The killing of al Adnani in the area of Aleppo in September 2016 was another major blow to IS, in particular, as concerns its global operations. All together, these combined pressures on IS wrested nearly 100% of its territory in Syria in Iraq by early 2018. Also, according to CNN, as many as 60,000 IS fighters were killed in Iraq and Syria (Starr, 2016).

The diverse political entities participating in the fight against IS have varied interests, creating considerable complications. For example, tensions between the United States and Russia have developed with respect to Russia's cooperation with Iran. In the meantime, the United States faces a dilemma with respect to the Syrian Kurds, who until recently were America's most effective ground force in the fight against IS. The United States has strongly encouraged Turkey's entrance into the fray, but Turkey uncompromisingly opposes the Syrian Kurds. No matter the feuds and the fault lines within the anti-IS coalition, with the fall of Raqqa, the caliphate's presumed capital, the IS lofty ambitions appear to be largely thwarted. Its possible global response, however, is cause for considerable concern.

IS Global Response

In reaction to the mounting setbacks that befell it, IS retaliated by reiterating its call to potential recruits to remain in their own countries and carry out attacks at home, rather than join the fight in Iraq and Syria. Abu Mohamed al Adnani, the (recently killed) spokesman of the Islamic State put out a message entitled "Your Lord Is Ever Watchful," released through al Furqan on September 21, 2014. In that message, Adnani encouraged Muslims to slaughter infidels, particularly those who participate in the fight against IS, wherever and however they can find them. In his words: "If you cannot [detonate] a bomb or [fire] a bullet . . . bash his [westerner] skull in . . . slaughter him with a knife, run him over with your car, throw him off a cliff, strangle him, or inject him with poison" (Middle East Media Research Institute, 2015, p. 1).

Similarly to the way that Al Qaeda transformed from an operational terrorist organization to an inspirational voice in the jihadi universe due to military pressure from the United States and its allies, so too IS, in response to setbacks on the ground, is gradually transforming from a caliphate-building concern to a global terrorist movement. After attacks in Paris in November 2015 and in Brussels in March 2016, IS dominated the global threat landscape by mounting attacks in North America, Europe, Africa, the Middle East, the Caucasus, and Asia.

The attacks were most pronounced during the Islamic month of Ramadan. Adnani designated the period from June 6 to July 5, 2016 a "month of conquest and jihad," launching it with the words: "Make it, with God's permission, a month of pain for infidels everywhere" (Hubbard, 2016). IS's "Ramadhan jihad" killed and injured over 1,000 people, mostly Muslims, in five of the six continents. Some of the most salient attacks were conducted in Orlando, Florida; Dhaka, Bangladesh; Kabul, Afghanistan; Mindanao, Philippines; Puchong, Malaysia; Solo, Indonesia; Lebanon; Iraq; and Syria. The spate of IS attacks were most intense during the last week of Ramadan, when an IS suicide bomber staged an attack on July 4, 2016 in the vicinity of the Prophet's mosque in Medina, Saudi Arabia, one of holiest sites in Islam.

As of mid-2018, the Islamic State, however weakened, is trying to recoup its strength and reenact its highly successful offensive of 2013 of targeting Iraqi police and government officials. There has been recent rise in targeted attacks of this kind, and in June 2018, IS fighters executed eight Iraqi security personnel and put the video of the assassination on Amaq, the group's media outlet. In response, the Iraqi government executed 12 convicted IS militants, and more is yet to come.

Threat Beyond the IS Heartland

Although IS remains capable of conducting mobile warfare in Syria and Iraq, as well as instigating terrorism worldwide, its mass appeal is slowly and steadily diminishing. There are early indications that the pace of recruits and the flow of foreign fighters to IS-controlled territories have suffered. Similarly, Syrians and Iraqis generally oppose IS rule and control over their territories.

With Turkey joining the fight against IS, the gateway to the IS theater previously used by many thousands of foreign fighters has been disrupted. Reciprocally, the country has become an IS target. While Turkey has continued to attack IS infrastructure on the ground, the country has suffered from half a dozen attacks in revenge. This response included the killing of 10 Germans in January 2016, which affected tourism and investment in the country. Moreover, on June 28, 2016, 47 people were killed and 230 injured when the IS bombed the Ataturk airport in Istanbul. Lebanon, another gateway to Syria, was similarly targeted by IS. Eight suicide bombers attacked the country in two waves in the Christian town of Al Qaa on June 27, 2016, killing 5 and wounding 11. To move its recruits into the heartland, IS will be forced to open new routes through Lebanon and operate clandestinely in Turkey; both actions will increase the difficulty of enabling foreign volunteers to join IS in Syria and Iraq.

As of June 2017, the IS threat to North America, Europe, Africa, the Middle East, the Caucasus, and Asia persists. Despite its losses, IS directs, instigates, and inspires attacks both on and off the battlefield. If the coalitions against IS can sustain their pressure over the long term, IS will continue to suffer defeats in Syria and Iraq. Nonetheless, IS also likely to compensate for its losses by directing and inspiring attacks worldwide. In preparation of these reprisals, IS operatives have been training foreign fighters to communicate, influence, and resource the proxies in their homelands to plan, prepare, and conduct attacks.

The somber forecast, unfortunately, is that global violence is likely to increase in the coming years. Moreover, contrary to public perception, IS does not constitute the only global terrorist movement. As mentioned earlier, Al Qaeda–centric groups remain active in the Sahel, Maghreb, Somalia, Yemen, Afghanistan, Pakistan, Bangladesh, India, the Maldives, Indonesia, the Philippines, and China. For instance, most Chinese Uighur jihadist fighters have served previously and are currently serving with al Nusra, the Al Qaeda branch in Syria, instead of with IS. In another instance, in March 2016, Al

Qaeda, mounted an attack in the Ivory Coast, at the Sahel, killing 15 civilians and 3 security forces personnel.

Seeding a Culture of Violence

At a global level, Al Qaeda and IS seeded a potent ideology in the late 20th and early 21st centuries. That ideology permeated the social fabric of Muslim society and crystalized into operational action and support for violence. Under the guise of spreading authentic Islam, Al Qaeda and IS challenged the moderate traditional and local versions of this religion. In the minds of those mobilized by Al Qaeda and IS, Muslims should defend the Islamic caliphate by attacking their enemies, namely, the West and its global and local allies. The IS and Al Qaeda strategy to seed a culture of extremism and violence within the world's Muslim community (the ummah), produced networks of Muslim extremists and swayed lone individuals to the IS cause, inducing in them the readiness to carry out attacks. Such readiness was instilled by ubiquitous IS propaganda products (e.g., as compiled by SITE Intelligence Group[14]), compellingly demonstrating the continuing threat from IS to states and communities worldwide.

IS Media Platforms: Jihadi Propaganda

Since the IS proclamation of the caliphate in June 2014, the IS phenomenon has spread largely through its media platforms. The IS strategy has been to build a vast global media network of supporters and sympathizers. To achieve this goal, IS has used coalition bombings and attacks in the caliphate territory as an excuse, portraying the attacks by IS supporters as ones of revenge and retaliation against aggression toward the caliphate. Every attack by IS supporters has been followed by considerable amplification of the event in the IS-controlled media, as are any killings of an important IS commander or official by IS detractors.

When the death of major IS commander Umar al-Shishani was announced by IS on July 13, 2016, the al-Samood media group showed his image next to the Eiffel Tower. To supplement the image, the following inscription was included: "The blood of our leaders is light and fire. Light to illuminate for the mujahideen the path, and fire upon the disbelievers and apostates to burn

---

14. https://siteintelgroup.com/

them wherever they are." Another image that referred to the November 2015 Paris attacks featured a picture of a Paris attacker, Abu 'Umar al-Baljiki, with an inscription stating, "As you kill you will be killed."

Following the July 14, 2016 Nice attack, IS also threatened Berlin. With a fighter in front of the Reichstag Building, an earlier image released by Furat Media read "Bald in Berlin" (Next in Berlin).[15] At that time, IS also released a French-language video chant of a child swearing revenge for massacres and destruction caused by coalition airstrikes. Two versions of that 3-minute, 40-second video, entitled "Blood for Blood" and produced by the group's al-Hayat Media Center, were released—one with Arabic subtitles and the other with English ones. IS also released the ninth issue of its French magazine *Dar al-Islam*, which included an article that called on lone wolves to kill a French imam in Bordeaux (*Dar al Islam Magazine*, 2016). On July 5, 2016, IS disseminated a French video chant, entitled "My Revenge," which hailed its supporters' attacks in France and Belgium and featured clips of the November 2015 Paris assailants and the two fighters involved in the March 2016 operation in Brussels.

In another video, American, French, Indonesian, Russian, and Uzbek fighters in the Furat province of Iraq lauded the Orlando nightclub gunman Omar Mateen and called upon Muslims to follow his example and kill "disbelievers." The 7-minute, 47-second, Arabic-subtitled video, titled "You Are Not Held Responsible Except for Yourself," was distributed on Telegram (an instant messaging app) and Twitter on June 19, 2016. Numerous additional examples exist of extensive IS media activity that applauds, encourages, and instigates attacks of its supporters in various corners of the world.

An Era of Increasing Threat

The IS strategy of targeting the far enemy is different from the Al Qaeda strategy. While Al Qaeda focused on planning and preparing few but high-impact attacks—the East Africa embassies in 1998, the *USS Cole* in 2000, and the 9/11 targets—IS has mounted two dozen small- to medium-scale off-the-battlefield attacks, aimed primarily at Western, Shiite, and Sunni targets (Paris, Brussels, Turkey, and Jakarta stand out). A dozen other attacks by the IS external operations wing have been detected and disrupted due to security and intelligence cooperation and collaboration. In light of its successes, IS

---

15. The message was a threat that Berlin would follow Nice as a site of a horrendous attack.

has remained relentless in its commitment to continued violence against its foes on their home turf. Accordingly, it encourages its supporters to hit major cities and launch attacks at high visibility, public events such as Euro2016 in Paris and the Olympics in Rio de Janeiro.

Thus, the threat from IS is no longer confined to IS central. IS has moved its experts to wilayats (or provinces) in various target countries, thus augmenting their capability of launching attacks. For instance, Boko Haram, known as IS West Africa, has expanded into parts of Niger, Chad, Mali, and Cameroon and has occasionally launched fights against military forces and law enforcement authorities. At least 100 groups worldwide have pledged allegiance to Baghdadi. In the Philippines, the Basilan-based Abu Sayyaf Group-led by Isnilon Hapilon (recently killed) was recognized by IS as its official branch, and other groups have joined the IS Philippines. IS support groups in the Philippines and Indonesia have copied the IS style of beheadings. In classic IS style, a victim is placed in an orange suit, and a photograph or a video is made of the beheading, which is then posted online.

In response to IS's rising tide of violence in varied world locations, governments are fighting back. In Malaysia, the Malaysian Special Branch Counter Terrorism Division dismantled al Kubro Generation and Kumpulan Gaga Hitam, a group planning and preparing attacks. In Indonesia, Detachment 88 prevented IS cells planning to attack Shiite targets to precipitate the Sunni–Shiite rivalry. In Bangladesh, both Ansarullah, an Al Qaeda affiliate, and Jamiatul Mujahidin Bangladesh, an IS affiliate, staged a wave of attacks targeting Bangladeshis as well as foreigners. In response, the newly created Counter Terrorism and Transnational Crime Unit mounted a series of effective operations to address the threat.

With IS vertical structures in Syria and Iraq coming under increasing threat, IS horizontal structures are expanding, primarily through IS cooperation and collaboration with its associated groups. There is increasing rivalry between Al Qaeda and IS and their affiliates in the Levant, Arabian Peninsula, Africa, South Asia, and Southeast Asia. In addition to its robust structures in the Levant, IS support groups in North Africa, Arabian Peninsula, Caucasus, South Asia, Southeast Asia, and Northeast Asia present a continuing threat. The international community has belatedly understood this development and is expanding its commitment, diverting its resources to target IS both at its core and in the periphery.

Although IS needs to be contained, isolated, and eliminated, to be effective the targeted state's response should not be focused on military measures alone. Otherwise, the world will continue to witness multiple IS-inspired attacks in the coming months and years. In such a scenario, there is grave need for both governments and communities to prepare for the day after the incident, especially in multireligious societies, where conflicts between Muslims and members of other denominations might well flare following a jihadist assault.

Furthermore, even though the world is currently focused on IS, there are other threat groups—both Muslim and non-Muslim—that present challenges at global, regional, and national levels. The momentum of IS activity is also creating an impetus for Al Qaeda and its associated to groups to revitalize and revive. IS activity spurred Al Qaeda in the Islamic Maghreb to mount a recent attack in the Ivory Coast and the Abu Sayyaf Group in the Philippines to perform several hostage-taking operations.

Although an arch rival to IS, Al Qaeda is fashioning its social media campaign along IS lines. The recent propaganda released by AQAP, al Shabab, and Afghan Taliban bear a remarkable similarity to IS productions. The long, boring ranting and poor-quality videos of Al Qaeda have been replaced by near-Hollywood quality and graphic productions of the IS style. With IS dominating the social media platforms, there is significant pressure on youth of Al Qaeda franchises to join the IS. Many spend their evenings watching IS videos on their mobile devices. The rivalry between Al Qaeda and IS has also resulted in sporadic clashes. For instance, Al Shabab killed its leaders who defected to IS. Similarly, in Afghanistan, the pro-IS and pro-Al Qaeda groups have often clashed.

The Future of Terrorism

It seems that the fight against IS and Al Qaeda, though both suffered substantial losses on the ground, isn't about to end anytime soon. Furthermore, whereas IS and Al Qaeda are currently in conflict, it is primarily a conflict between the leaders (al Baghdadi and al Zawahiri)—the groups themselves are slowly coming together (Johnson, 2018). Amidst discord and dissent, powerful and influential constituents of Al Qaeda are reconciling their relations with IS. If either Ayman al Zawahiri or Baghdadi were to be killed, the two groups would likely unite.

Under another scenario, IS and Al Qaeda could manage to resolve their dispute: If so, both IS- and Al Qaeda-affiliated groups would come together, posing an unprecedented threat not only to Syria but also to Israel, Jordan, Saudi Arabia, and beyond. The potential unification of IS and Al Qaeda would present a formidable and sustained threat throughout the world.

Furthermore, the drawdown of US-led coalition forces in Afghanistan open the space for a Taliban takeover of regions within the country. These regions could then possibly be used as launch pads for attacks against the perceived enemies of jihadism and for training grounds for recruits to the cause.

In short, the two epicenters of current violent extremism in the Iraq–Syria and the Pakistan–Afghanistan regions are likely to remain active in the foreseeable future. Furthermore, the inspirational capability of IS and Al Qaeda, and the presence of their affiliates in various world locations, make it likely that attacks on and off the battlefield will continue, as will the flow of new recruits to replenish those who have been killed. Like the Al Qaeda ideology that penetrated territorial, diaspora, and migrant communities, the IS vision too, and even more so, is affecting Muslims, creating a global network of groups, homegrown cells, and individuals willing to kill and die.

Conclusion

There has been an overall failure by the security community to recognize that the fight against the United States, its allies, and its friends is a multi-generational campaign by extremist organizations under the Islamist banner. Therefore, the government and societal responses to the Islamist groups and their support bases have been partially effective in the short-term and largely ineffective in the mid- and long-term. Cohort after cohort, the mujahidin have been reinventing themselves by adapting to changing political, geographic, and strategic realities. With the failure of one generation to achieve its political aims, a new generation emerged. Each time, the ideology has become more potent, the tactics increasingly lethal, and the global impact broader.

Dependent on the political and security environment facing them, the mujahidin invest in operational and ideological elements. When the environment is safe, they plan, prepare, and execute attacks, and when hostile, they lie low but recruit and build their strength through propaganda and ideological indoctrination. The death or incarceration of their leadership and severe losses to their membership is not terminal to their struggle. As their allegiance is to God, the essence of the struggle is passed down to the next generation to fulfill their objectives.

In 2004, Donald Rumsfeld, the US Secretary of Defense at the time, posed the question whether the ability of Islamist extremism to attract new recruits exceeded the US capability to kill or capture them. At this writing, the answer to this question appears to be unquestionably positive. It is becoming painfully obvious that military force alone is insufficient to defeat an ideologically fired-up adversary and that "we cannot kill our way out of this mess," as then-Governor Mitt Romney quipped during the 2012 US presidential campaign.

It is becoming obvious, too, that defeating the current wave of militant extremism requires more than brute force, namely, winning the battle for the hearts and minds of people who are currently willing to kill and die for the Islamist cause. To succeed in that battle, it is incumbent that we understand what engenders that incredible will—what prompts young Muslims and others to abandon current life pursuits, drop everything, and embark on a journey from which there may be no return. The present volume aims to advance such understanding by analyzing and explaining the psychological factors that produce this radicalization into violent extremism that threatens societies worldwide.

References

The 12 October 2002 Bali bombing plot (2012, October 11). *BBC News*. Retrieved from http://www.bbc.com/news/world-asia-19881138

Abd al-Raoof, S. H. (2014, September). And we are enraging them. *Jihadology*. Retrieved from https://azelin.files.wordpress.com/2014/09/shaykh-e1b8a5ussc481m-e28098abd-al-ra_c5abf-22in-remembrance-of-the-manhattan-raid-and-we-are-enraging-them22-en.pdf

Al Zawahiri, A. (2001, December 2–12). Knights under the prophet's banner. *Ash-Sharq al-ʾAwsaṭ*.

Baer, R. (2003). *Sleeping with the devil: How Washington sold our soul for Saudi Crude*. New York, NY: Crown.

Boot, M. (2012, September 28). A hard-won account of a hard-won victory. *Wall Street Journal*. Retrieved from https://www.wsj.com/articles/SB10000872396390443916104578020642839807834

Brill, S. (2016, September). Is America any safer? *The Atlantic*. Retrieved from http://www.theatlantic.com/magazine/archive/2016/09/are-we-any-safer/492761/

Gunaratna, R. (2003). Debriefing of Riduan Isamuddin alias Hambali. *Hudson Institute*. Retrieved from http://www.hudson.org/research/9868-the-ideology-of-al-jama-ah-al-islamiya

Dar al Islam Magazine. (2016). 9. Retrieved from https://azelin.files.wordpress.com/2016/04/dacc84r-al-islacc84m-magazine-9.pdf

Emerson, S. (n.d.). Abdullah Azzam. *International Association for Counterterrorism and Security Professionals*. Retrieved from https://www.iacsp.com/itobli3.html

Fatwa. (n.d.). *English Oxford Living Dictionaries*. Retrieved from https://en.oxforddictionaries.com/definition/fatwa

Ghosh, B. (2014, August 14). ISIS: A short history. *The Atlantic*. Retrieved from http://www.theatlantic.com/international/archive/2014/08/isis-a-short-history/376030/

Gold, D. (2003). *Hatred's kingdom: How Saudi Arabia supports the new global terrorism*. Washington, DC: Regnery.

Gunaratna, R. (2002). *Inside al Qaeda: The global network of terror*. New York, NY: Columbia University Press.

Gunaratna, R. (2011, July 15). Al Qaeda under Ayman Al Zawahiri: Still a lethal organization. *RSIS Commentary, 104/2011*. https://www.rsis.edu.sg/rsis-publication/rsis/1577-al-qaeda-under-ayman-al-zawahi/#.Wz9o4csaySM

Gunaratna, R. (2015). Al-Qaeda. In R. J. Bunker, J. P Sullivan, B. M. Jenkins, M. G. Devost, & J. T. Kirkhope (Eds.), *Counterterrorism: Bridging operations and theory* (pp. 20–29). Bloomington, IN: iUniverse.

Gunaratna, R., & Woodall, D. (2005). *Afghanistan after the Western drawdown*. Baltimore, MD: Rowman and Littlefield.

Hubbard, B. (2016, July 4). ISIS uses Ramadan as calling for new terrorist attacks. *New York Times*. Retrieved from http://www.nytimes.com/2016/07/04/world/middleeast/ramadan-isis-baghdad-attacks.html

Johnson, B. (2018, March 12). Are Al-Qaeda and ISIS about to form a terrorist supergroup? *Observer*. Retrieved from http://observer.com/2018/03/are-al-qaeda-and-isis-about-to-form-a-terrorist-supergroup/

Johnson, Z. K. (2005, January 25). Chronology: The plots. *PBS Frontline*. Retrieved from http://www.pbs.org/wgbh/pages/frontline/shows/front/special/cron.html

Joscelyn, T. (2014, September 27). Al Qaeda official warns against Islamic State in new speech. *Long War Journal*. Retrieved from http://www.longwarjournal.org/archives/2014/09/a_senior_al_qaeda_of.php

Kean, T. H., & Hamilton, L. H. (2004, July 22). *The 9/11 Commission 4eport*. Retrieved from http://www.9-11commission.gov/report/

Lake, E. (2013, September 8). Meet al Qaeda's new general manager: Nasser al-Wuhayshi. *Daily Beast*. Retrieved from http://www.thedailybeast.com/articles/2013/08/09/meet-al-qaeda-s-new-general-manager-nasser-al-wuhayshi.html

Lewis, B. (1998, November–December). License to kill: Usama bin Ladin's declaration of jihad. *Foreign Affairs*. Retrieved from https://www.foreignaffairs.com/articles/saudi-arabia/1998-11-01/license-kill-usama-bin-ladins-declaration-jihad

Mapping Militants Project. (2016, July 15). *The Taliban*. Retrieved from http://web.stanford.edu/group/mappingmilitants/cgi-bin/groups/view/367

Middle East Media Research Institute. (2015, November 16). *In the words of the Islamic State: Understanding the rationale behind the November 13 Paris attacks*. Retrieved from http://www.memrijttm.org/in-the-words-of-the-islamic-state-understanding-the-rationale-behind-the-november-13-paris-attacks.html

Mujahidin. (2003). *The Oxford Dictionary of Islam* (J. L. Esposito, Ed.). Oxford, England: Oxford University Press. http://www.oxfordreference.com/view/

10.1093/acref/9780195125580.001.0001/acref-9780195125580-e-1593?
rskey=rhrmkz&result=1

Schmitt, E. (2016, November 21). ISIS used chemical arms at least 52 times in Syria and Iraq, report says. *New York Times*. Retrieved from https://www.nytimes.com/2016/11/21/world/middleeast/isis-chemical-weapons-syria-iraq-mosul.html

Soft target. (n.d.). Wikipedia. Retrieved from https://en.wikipedia.org/wiki/Soft_target

Soufan, A. H. (2011). *The black banners: The inside story of 9/11 and the war against al-Qaeda*. New York, NY: Norton.

Starr, B. (2016, February 17). Estimate: More than 26,000 ISIS fighters killed by coalition. *CNN Politics*. Retrieved from http://edition.cnn.com/2016/02/17/politics/isis-fighters-killed-iraq-syria/

Teslik, L. H. (2008, August 8). Profile: Abu Musab al-Zarqawi. *Council of Foreign Relations*. Retrieved from http://www.cfr.org/iraq/profile-abu-musab-al-zarqawi/p9866

Tran, M., & Weaver, M. (2014, June 30). Isis announces Islamic caliphate in area straddling Iraq and Syria. *The Guardian*. Retrieved from https://www.theguardian.com/world/2014/jun/30/isis-announces-islamic-caliphate-iraq-syria

Wright, L. (2006). *The looming tower: Al-Qaeda and the road to 9/11*. New York, NY: Knopf.

3 SIGNIFICANCE QUEST THEORY OF RADICALIZATION

The so-called global war on terror,[1] in its 17th year in 2018, beginning with the US-led response to the September 11, 2001 attacks, is far from over. As described in Chapter 2, rampant Islamist violence is spreading now to an increasing number of world locations. Unquestionably, radicalization is on the rise and is posing serious threats to the security and stability of nations worldwide. What accounts for these disturbing trends? Scholars from a range of disciplines attempted to address this question. Political scientists theorized about failed states as a condition that fosters radicalization (Piazza, 2008) or argued that occupation by foreign powers or political oppression lead to extremism (Pape, 2006); economists hypothesized that poverty may create extremism (Berrebi, 2007); sociologists focused that anomie[2] (Gupta, 2004) or social stress may cause it; and psychiatrists inquired whether terrorists are mentally disturbed.

Major prior attempts to understand violent extremism are reviewed in Chapter 4. They illuminate important aspects of the radicalization problem. Yet, ultimately, radicalization boils down to individual decisions and consequent behavior. It is the individual, after all, who decides to join a terror organization, take up arms, don a suicide belt, or travel thousands of miles to kill people who did him or her no harm. The mechanisms that produce radicalization must be, therefore, ultimately, psychological.

---

1. The war on terror was actually waged primarily against Islamist terror groups like Al Qaeda, ISIS, and their affiliates who target the US and its allies.

2. Anomie is defined as "condition in which society provides little moral guidance to individuals" ("Anomie," n.d.).

From this perspective, macro-level factors identified by social scientists (e.g., poverty, oppression, anomie, etc.) would produce radicalization only if they activated those psychological processes and not otherwise. After all, countless people who experience poverty, oppression, and/or social stress do not turn to violent extremism (cf. Krueger & Malečková, 2002; Kruglanski & Fishman, 2006). The theory featured in this book aims, therefore, to identify the psychological core factors that drive extremism and the broader societal conditions that induce them. But, first, we offer a psychological perspective on *extremism* as a general phenomenon, subsequent to which we examine *violent* extremism as its special case.

We view violent extremism as merely one of different possible extremisms, including extreme diets, extreme sports, extreme (fatal) attractions a variety of addictions (e.g., substances, behavior patterns), or selfless humanism or asceticism, all of which fit our conception of extremism. We assume that despite their vastly different contents, the various extremisms share a psychological core in common. What might this core consist of?

Two Meanings of Extremism

In everyday language the label *extreme* has two connotations. First, it denotes a high intensity or magnitude of an attribute or a process. For example, *extreme heat* connotes a highly elevated temperature; *extreme destruction*, a near total destruction; and *extreme pleasure*, an intense pleasure. Second, it indicates something rare or unusual, as in the extremes of a statistical distribution. For example, an *extreme case* describes a case that is infrequent or rare, and the same applies to the expression *extreme circumstances* or *extreme conditions* ("Extreme," n.d.).

One might wonder why the same term is used to describe what appears to be two unrelated phenomena. After all, high intensity or magnitude need not be necessarily related to infrequency, and it is possible to envisage a circumstance where high magnitude is the rule rather than the exception (e.g., the average temperature in a given location may be high, as may be the average real estate prices in a given location; the average wealth of residents of a given county may be considerable; the majority in a given population may suffer from a disease; etc.). Our psychological model of extremism explains why, in the realm of human behavior, extremity and infrequency typically coincide. And, the concept that underlies their convergence is that of *motivational imbalance* as explained next.

Moderation and Extremism

In the behavioral domain, *extremism* is often contrasted with *moderation*. Moderation, in turn, assumes a state of *motivational balance* characterized by a harmonious satisfaction of the individual's basic biological and psychogenic needs.

The existence of basic needs, universal to all humans, is stressed by major psychological theories of motivation (e.g., Deci & Ryan, 2000; Fiske, 2009; Higgins, 2012; Maslow, 1943). Some basic needs pertain to fundamental biological concerns, including nutrition, hydration, rest, etc. It is generally agreed that satisfaction of those needs is indispensable to biological health and ultimately to survival.

Other basic needs are *psychogenic*: These are the needs for safety, love/belonging, esteem, and self-actualization (Maslow, 1943); needs for autonomy, competence and relatedness (Deci & Ryan, 2000); needs for value, truth, and control (Higgins, 2012); or needs to belong, understand, control, enhance, and trust (Fiske, 2009). Whereas psychological theorists differ somewhat in how they parse the universe of basic psychogenic needs, they concur nonetheless that such needs exist and that their deprivation causes suffering and distress.

Humans are assumed to strive for fulfillment of their basic psychogenic needs, much as they do with respect to their physiological needs. All of people's specific goals are traceable, ultimately, to their basic needs. The goal of cooking a meal may derive from the need for nutrition; rebellion against oppression, from the need of autonomy; competition, from the need for competence; formation of intimate ties, from the need of relatedness; and so on. In other words, the myriad of people's specific goals that vary widely across cultures and societies may be thought of as culturally specific *means* to the same universal *ends*: satisfaction of people's basic biological and psychogenic needs.

Balance and Constraint

The differ basic needs constrain one another such that behaviors that gratify only some of those needs while undermining others tend to be avoided. For instance, one's hunger may co-exist with concerns about health and taste; as a consequence, foods that are unhealthy or foul-tasting would be avoided. One's need for intimacy and relatedness may temper one's need for achievement and competence, thus promoting a work–family balance. One's need for admiration may be tempered by one's need for safety so that highly dangerous athletic exploits or heroics (that could beget admiration) would be generally shunned.

Imbalance and Release

At times, however, a motivational imbalance may occur in which a given need is appreciably elevated, thus overriding the others. At the extreme, this state may be described as one of *prepossession*, in which one's mind is predominantly absorbed with a given concern and is oblivious to all else (Bélanger, Lafrenière, Vallerand, & Kruglanski, 2013; Shah, Friedman, & Kruglanski, 2002). The mere shifting of motivational priorities is in fact commonplace and part of everyday experience. A specific circumstance may elevate the urgency of a given goal, thus interrupting other ongoing pursuits: A parent may cancel a professional obligation on learning that her or his child is ill; a physician may interrupt a family vacation to attend to an emergency; and a police officer might forego an uninterrupted night's sleep to hurry to a crime scene. In general, our motivational system is highly pliant and flexible, and our goals, interests, and priorities are capable of changing on the spot in response to new information.

An interesting thing happens when a given need becomes acutely dominant in a given situation. Because our mental (attentional) resources are limited, investing them in the dominant need withdraws them from other needs. The latter are (temporarily) suppressed. They fade away as it were. As a consequence, the constraints they normally exercise on behavior are released or removed. This liberates formerly constrained behavior, and extremism is the result. For instance, whereas under normal circumstances what we eat when hungry is constrained by concerns of diet, health, and taste when extremely starved, we would eat anything at all, even if tasteless, fattening, or disgusting. Whereas normally we observe the norms and mores of our social group and behave rationally, when "in love," we may throw caution to the wind and behave like "a fool in love," "lose one's head," and proclaim to be "crazy" about one's sweetheart.

The dynamics of constraint and release are illustrated in Panels A and B of Figure 3.1. Panel A demonstrates *constraint*. Specifically, it depicts two goals, X and Y along with several behavioral means (1 through 4) pertinent to those goals. As can be seen, means 2 and 3 are *multifinal* (Kruglanski et al., 2002; Kruglanski et al., 2015) in that they serve both goals X and Y. Means 1 and 4 while serving (+) one of the goals (X and Y, respectively) are detrimental

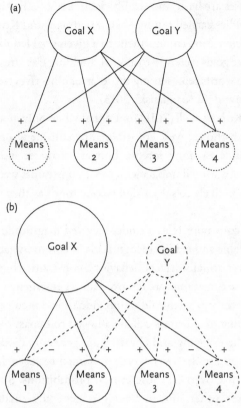

FIGURE 3.1. Constraint (a) and release (b).

to the other goal (Y and X, respectively). We refer to them as *counterfinal*. As can be seen in Panel A, the two goals constrain the behaviors exhibited in their pursuit such that only the multifinal means (2 and 3) are considered whereas the counterfinal means (1 and 4) are eliminated from consideration (indicated by the interrupted line).

Consider now Panel B of Figure 3.1, which demonstrates *release*. As can be seen, goal X is now dominant, and goal Y recedes in its importance. For that reason, all the behavioral links that lead to goal Y are now much weaker (i.e., less salient). Consequently behavior 1 that was negatively related to Y (i.e., behavior 1 assumed to undermine it) is now released from the constraint that (the desire to attain) Y was imposing. That behavior that formerly was barred from consideration now constitutes a legitimate option for the pursuit of goal X and is likely to be selected by some individuals at least.

These processes are basic and readily demonstrable. For instance, in a set of laboratory studies carried out by Shah, Friedman, and Kruglanski (2002), experimentally increasing commitment to a given goal led to relative inhibition of alternative goals (referred to as goal shielding), as attested to by slower reaction times to words representing those latter objectives (see also Bélanger, Lafrenière, Vallerand, & Kruglanski, 2013).

In addition, Köpetz et al. (2011) found that when only moderately hungry, individuals' lunch choices were constrained by consideration of caloric content, whereas under a more intense hunger (stronger motivation to eat, hence greater motivational imbalance), those constraints were removed, and individuals were as likely to select high caloric foods as they were low caloric foods for lunch.

The logic of constraint release under elevated magnitude of a given need is broadly applicable and readily recognizable in commonplace examples. For instance, whereas normally drivers' behavior is constrained by speed limits and traffic lights, these constraints are removed under emergency conditions such that ambulances rushing to the aid of individuals in a medical crisis or police vehicles responding to a distress call are allowed to bypass those restrictions. Alternatively, whereas lying and cheating are generally disallowed, they are allowed to spies and undercover agents presumed to serve the vital interests of their nation that override those ethical prohibitions. Similarly, whereas aggression against other human beings is generally disallowed in most cultures and religions and tempered by the needs for relatedness and empathy, it is permitted in wartime conditions where existential threat catapults individuals' need for survival to utmost dominance.

Degrees of Radicalization

From the present perspective, different instances of extremism or radicalization lie on a continuum and are a matter of degree. Any given location on this continuum reflects the extent of deviation from the motivational balance wherein people's needs are harmoniously gratified. The greater the imbalance, the greater the inhibition of alternative concerns and hence the more complete the release of constraints those were imposing on allowable behaviors. Thus, the greater the imbalance the larger the set of behavioral options for gratifying the dominant need. For instance, when one's need for a given intoxicating substance (e.g., alcohol, crack, heroin) is particularly intense, it may permit behaviors destructive to the self and others (e.g., foregoing healthy nutrition, neglecting one's work obligations, engaging in criminal behavior) whose sole purpose is to obtain the object of one's desire. Such behaviors are *extreme* in that they derive from a highly intense need that causes a motivational imbalance. And because people in general strive to maintain balance, extreme behavior is infrequent. In this sense, the enactment of extreme behaviors combines the intensity sense of extremism (stemming from an intense need) with its infrequency or rarity.[3] But how do these general dynamics of extremism manifest themselves specifically in the case of violent extremism? This question is addressed in the remainder of this chapter.

Violent Extremism

A major challenge in understanding extremism is to explain why *some* individuals support and enact behaviors that most *others* eschew or reject. In the context of violent radicalization, the question is why would anyone in their right mind—and hardly anyone believes these days that *all* violent extremists are insane—commit acts that so clearly violate pervasive human concerns such as health, wealth, comfort, and pleasure, let alone norms and injunctions that prohibit murderous aggression against innocent human beings who did one no harm.

Recall that the underlying cause behind the readiness to condone or embrace radical behaviors is a particularly intense commitment to goals those behaviors serve. In the case of violent extremism, those goals are to advance some collective cause (e.g., of religious, nationalistic, or social nature), and the overriding commitment to such cause proportionately reduces their concern about other matters (e.g., professional development, safety, or cultural injunctions against causing harm to others).

Through their propaganda and rhetoric, radical organizations attempt to induce in individuals a motivational imbalance of this kind through appeals to values these persons hold sacred—such as honor, dignity, or duty—and through enhancement of individuals' commitment to those cherished values

---

3. Whereas typically extremism characterizes a minority of individuals (thus, converging with statistical extremism), under special circumstances it may apply also to a *majority* of persons within a given population. Consider by analogy the concept of *health*. Normally, most people are (more or less) healthy, and their bodily systems function appropriately. Occasionally, however, entire populations might fall sick, owing to a plague, mass starvation, or poisoning. Similarly, whereas societies are relatively peaceful and nonviolent much of the time (Pinker, 2011), there are circumstances (at times of war) where most members are required to mobilize and fight (i.e., employ violence) for a common cause. In short, whereas generally the intensity and frequency conceptions of extremism are in sync, they may occasionally diverge, in the sense that a majority of people in a given population may exhibit an extreme behavior.

via group pressure, charismatic leadership, and emotional appeals (Atran, 2010). The results of such a process can be striking. Consider the words of a Black Tamil Tiger, a member of the elite suicide cadre of the Liberation Tigers of Tamil Eelam (LTTE), one of the most vicious terrorist organizations in history, (active for 30 years from 1979 to 2009, when it was defeated by the Sri Lanka military) whom we interviewed recently in northeastern Sri Lanka:

> Family and relationships are forgotten in that place. There was no place for love. That means a passion and loyalty to that group, to those in charge, to those who sacrificed their lives for the group. Then I came to a stage where I had no love for myself. I had no value for my life. I was ready to give myself fully, even to destroy myself, in order to destroy another person.

As this statement vividly demonstrates, the readiness to commit to the ultimate sacrifice in service of a cause is strongly coupled with a complete suppression of other concerns in different life domains. It is such circumstance that liberates behavior from the latter concerns thus enabling extremism that would have been prohibited otherwise. But the foregoing description and others like it, though perhaps striking, leave the ultimate questions unanswered: *Why* (for what psychological reasons) do individuals make such a commitment, and what specific circumstances may prompt them to do so? We address these issues in what follows.

The 3Ns of Radicalization: Need, Narrative, and Network

The Need

As we noted earlier, any goal that people may set for themselves derives, at the end of the chain, from one of the basic human needs. Which prompts the question: Which of those needs is served by commitment to a culturally hallowed cause? The literature on terrorists' motivations (e.g., Bloom, 2005; Gambetta, 2005; Stern, 2004) lists a variety of constructs as potentially underlying terrorists' behavior including honor, vengeance, religion, loyalty to the leader, perks in the afterlife, and even feminism. All these may be valid descriptions of specific cases. But, underlying them, there seems to exist a more general motivating force that we have called the *quest for significance*. The quest for significance is the fundamental desire to matter, to be someone, to have respect (Kruglanski, Chen, Dechesne, Fishman, & Orehek,

2009; Kruglanski et al., 2013). Psychological theorists have long realized that this quest constitutes a universal, human motivation variously labeled as the need for *esteem, achievement, meaning, competence, control,* etc. (Deci & Ryan, 2000; Fiske, 2009; Frankl, 2000; Higgins, 2012; Maslow, 1943; White, 1959). Harre (1979), for instance, wrote, "The pursuit of reputation in the eyes of others is the overriding preoccupation of human life" (p. 3). The philosopher Axel Honneth suggested that the *struggle for recognition* is the underlying motivation in social conflicts (Honneth, 1995). Arthur Miller (1949), in his essay "Tragedy and the Common Man" commented on "the tragic feeling . . . in the presence of a character who is ready to lay down his life, . . . to secure on thing—his sense of personal dignity." And in his essay on "Honor," the anthropologist, Julian Pitt-Rivers (1968) observed that across cultures "the withdrawal of respect dishonors . . . and . . . inspires the sentiment of shame" (p. 503).

From the present perspective then, the various specific motivations mentioned in the terrorism literature are *special cases* of significance quest. Consider feminism, for example. In the context of terrorism, feminism refers to the motivation to prove that women matter, that they are as worthy as are men, as committed to the cause, and as willing to undertake sacrifices in its behalf—in short, as deserving of significance.

Alternatively, take loyalty to the leader often mentioned as a motivation for terrorism. In our conversations with detained members of the LTTE and with Sri Lankan intelligence officers tasked with the interrogation of captured Black Tamil Tigers, members of the elite squads of LTTE's suicide bombers, it turned out that the love of Velupillai Prabhakaran, the all-powerful leader of the LTTE, often was the major motivation underlying the cadres' readiness to die for the cause.[4] Psychologically speaking, however, such love and worship of the leader translate into the quest for his or her approval, which endows Prabhakaran with the ultimate authority in matters of personal significance.[5]

For a final example, consider *revenge,* the desire to reciprocate harm against those who did harm to oneself or one's group. Beyond any material costs that deliberate harm from another entails, it constitutes an unwelcome invasion into one's life that renders one powerless and reduces one's esteem

---

4. Establishment of an Independent Tamil State in the northeastern part of the Sri Lankan island.

5. It has been reported that before each suicidal mission, the Black Tamil Tiger tasked with its implementation was granted the honor of dining with Prabhakaran, or one of his major lieutenants, clearly representing a major significance bestowing event.

in the eyes of self and others and, hence, is humiliating and significance reducing.[6] Revenge levels the playing field and restores the balance of power by dealing a humiliating blow to one's enemy, the source of one's humiliation, thus redeeming one's lost significance. In summary, the seeming heterogeneity of motives underlying engagement in terrorism boils down to a major underlying motivation—the quest for personal significance.

Arousing the Significance Quest

For the significance quest to induce behavior, it must first be activated. After all, we do not invariably seek significance; often we invest our energies in alternative pursuits related to comfort, survival, or health, for example (cf. Kruglanski et al., 2013). Activation of the significance quest can happen in one of three major ways: (a) through a *loss of significance* or humiliation of some sort, corresponding to the psychological construct of *deprivation*; (b) through an anticipated (or threatened) significance *loss*, corresponding to the psychological construct of *avoidance*; or (c) through an opportunity for *significance gain*, representing the psychological construct of *incentive*.

Significance loss: Personally based. Significance loss can happen due to a personal failure or humiliation or as an affront to one's social identity that one shares with others in one's group. Personal humiliation unrelated to one's social identity is illustrated by Palestinian women who volunteered for suicide missions after they had suffered some kind of stigma in their lives caused by, for example, infertility, divorce, accidental disfiguration, an extramarital affair (Pedahzur, 2005). All these individuals suffered from a significance loss, which they were apparently motivated to eradicate through volunteering for a socially venerated cause.

Or consider the Tsarnaev brothers, Dzokhar and Tamerlan, the perpetrators of the Boston Marathon bombing of April 2013. It appears that at least the older brother, Tamerlan, was poorly assimilated and feeling rather marginalized in America: his family on welfare, his parents on the verge of divorce, himself unemployed and supported by his wife, a college dropout (ostensibly to pursue a boxing career), and in feud with his successful uncles, Alvi and Ruslan, who viewed the Boston Tsarnaevs as "losers." In response,

---

6. Robert Pape (2006) argued that suicide attacks are generally attributable to the presence on one's soil of foreign occupation. Whereas scholars (e.g., Kiras, 2007) have questioned the exclusive place of foreign occupation as a motivator of suicidal bombings, from the present perspective there is no doubt that occupation, the presence of foreign check points in one's own land, searches in the middle of the night, etc. can be highly humiliating and in this sense significance reducing.

Tamerlan may have entertained dreams of glory (e.g., as an Olympic boxer?) whose realization appeared possible by becoming a hero or a martyr according to the extremist ideology that he adopted.[7]

Often, personal humiliation could be a direct consequence of violent conflict with some outgroup and could arise out of personal losses perpetrated by the enemy. This characterization applies, for example, to Chechen "black widows" who were rendered powerless and thus demeaned and humiliated by having their significant other wrested from them by the Russian forces (Speckhard & Akhmedova, 2006). A similar dynamic applies to some Palestinian terrorists. Hanadi Jaradat (see Chapter 6), a 29-year-old lawyer from Jenin, a town in the West Bank, is a case in point. Hanadi blew herself up (on October 4, 2003) in the Maxim restaurant in Haifa, killing 21 people (Jews and Arabs) and wounding 51 others. This was in response to the killing by the Israeli military of her fiancé and her beloved brother. In an interview with the Jordanian daily *Al Arab al-Yum*, Hanadi sworn revenge: "Your blood will not have been shed in vain," she is reported to have said. "The murderer will yet pay the price and we will not be the only ones who are crying."

Individual significance loss can be the result of general, economic, social, and political conditions prevailing in a given state including internecine conflict, instability, insecurity, and the government's failure to provide order. Such conditions define a state of *anomie* (Durkheim, 1893), the sense that the state is unable to provide the means for its citizens to attain their goals. On the individual level this could translate into a feeling of helplessness and, hence, of personal insignificance, arousing a significance quest that may be potentially taken advantage of by a terrorist organization.

The use of violence in the name of significance restoration is hardly limited to politically or religiously motivated aggression exhibited by terrorists. James Gilligan, a psychiatrist who devoted his career to the study of violent criminals found *shame* caused by *disrespect* of oneself by others is a universal underlying reason for assaults against them. As he put it, "the word 'disrespect' is so central in the vocabulary, moral value system, and psychodynamics of these chronically violent men that they have abbreviated it into the slang term, 'he dis'd me' (Gilligan, 1997, p. 106). And in his session with a particularly violent inmate (Chester T.) in answer to the question "What do you

---

7. A note captured in the location where Dzokhar was finally apprehended indicates that he perceived his brother as a martyr and a hero and that he too craved a similar recognition (Woolf, 2015).

want so badly that you would sacrifice everything else in order to get it?" the inmate responded without hesitation: "Pride. Dignity. Self Esteem" (p. 106).

Socially based significance loss. Often, experience of significance loss relates to one's social identity that is disparaged by others. This type of loss may be acutely felt by Muslim immigrants to Europe who often encounter disrespect, if not rabid "Islamophobia" from native residents in their host countries (Sageman, 2004; Kruglanski, Crenshaw, Post, & Victoroff, 2008). The humiliation of one's group and the trampling of its sacred values (Atran, 2010) may engender a considerable significance loss felt by all its members (e.g., all Muslims); this is often skillfully exploited by terrorist propagandists of Al Qaeda and its affiliates (Cohen, Kruglanski, Gelfand, Webber & Gunaratna, 2018). Consider the following excerpt from one of Al Qaeda's most eloquent communicators, the late Yahia Al Libi (killed in 2012) that he directs at Muslim audiences worldwide in a video:

> Jihad in Algeria today is YOUR hope with permission from Allah in redemption from the hell of the unjust ruling regimes whose prisons are congested with YOUR youths and children if not with YOUR women; [regime] which thrust its armies, police, and intelligence to oppress YOU, for which they opened the doors to punish YOU . . . So join YOUR efforts to theirs, add YOUR energies to theirs . . . and know that their victory is YOUR victory . . . Their salvation is YOUR salvation . . .

As can be seen, Al Libi addresses here the listeners' own identity as Muslims and alleges their humiliation by oppressive deeds committed toward other members of their religion in a faraway land.

Avoidance of significance loss. A mere *threat* of significance loss can motivate actions intended to prevent it. A striking example is that of the Japanese Kamikaze of World War II. Their letters to their loved ones (see Ohnuki-Tierney, 2006) reveal that they did not want to die, nor did they expect heavenly rewards for their sacrifices. Yet had they refused the mission, unbearable shame and humiliation would have befallen them and their families, and it is such avoidance of significance loss that apparently motivated them to crash their planes into US vessels.

Opportunity for significance gain. Often, pursuit of violence and terrorism seem to afford an individual an *opportunity* for an untold significance gain, a place in history, and the status of a hero or a martyr in one's community. Sprinzak (2001) wrote about this connection, referring to such individuals as "megalomaniacal hyper terrorists," including Muhammad Atta, Bin Laden, Ramzi Yussuf, Ayman Zawahiri, and others of greater-than-life stature. According to Sprinzak, these individuals engaged in terrorism primarily because they saw in it an opportunity for tremendous significance gain as a reward for their engagement. An opportunity for a significance gain underlies what Post (2006) has called the "breeding in the bone" of suicide bombers in kindergartens and summer camps of the Palestinian Hamas and the Lebanese Hizballa, which inculcates them the notion that they should all become shahids and thus earn vast glory and significance.

Loss of Significance, Need for Closure, and Radicalism

It is of interest to consider the path whereby a loss of significance propels individuals toward radical, fundamentalist ideologies. We assume, and research described in Chapter 5 suggests, that a humiliating, significance reducing experience creates a sense of painful confusion, arousing an individual's need for cognitive closure (Kruglanski, 2004) and a motivation to restore the feeling of certainty. Cognitive closure (i.e., need for closure [NFC]) is defined as the desire for firm, unambiguous world views. It is this desire for certainty that fosters a preference for simplistic black-and-white, us-versus-them narratives. Since holding positive self-regard constitutes a fundamental human motivation, self-doubt and uncertainty engender considerable negative affect that fuels a motivation to remove it, thus elevating one's NFC. In turn, NFC arousal may motivate the proclivity to embrace radical, imbalanced points of view that privilege the ingroup's narrative and justify aggression against the outgroup. Such ideologies not only offer individuals coherence and closure but also simple ways of asserting one's significance by coming to the ingroup's defense. The creation and propagation of such Manichean narratives are thus effective in radicalizing individuals who crave certainty and significance.

The Narrative

Obviously, the quest for significance as such is insufficient for producing violent extremism. A person may exhibit a high ambition, a craving to be respected, famous, and recognized yet channel it in various constructive, nonviolent directions (e.g., as a scientist, physician, inventor, or athlete) that do not harm and often benefit others. For the need for significance to be served by violence a credible link between the two must be forged.

Striking out aggressively in response to personal or group humiliation is a direct and primordial way of restoring a person's sense of significance.

By hurting others, people demonstrate their power to be effective (Higgins, 2012) to have an impact and demonstrate their power to retaliate and harm their perceived detractors. Yet, blind aggression (against innocent others) is frowned upon and is strictly prohibited in most cultures and societies; hence, it may elicit widespread social opprobrium. Substantial and enduring significance gain through violence requires societal license and authorization. Such endorsement is afforded by a violence-justifying ideology.

By *ideology*, we mean a prescriptive belief system shared by members of a group (e.g., a nation or a religion) and articulated in the group's narrative. Typically, such narratives uphold the group's protection from its enemies as a preeminent task (Zartman & Anstey, 2012), whose undertaking merits glory and veneration. The group's continued existence and welfare are among the most *sacred values* to group members (Atran, 2010; Graham & Haidt, 2010; Haidt & Graham, 2007), and their protection by any means necessary is hailed as members' utmost duty.

Whereas some authors (e.g., Sageman, 2004, 2008) have questioned the role of the ideological narrative in producing violent extremism, viewing it as an after-the-fact rationalization and highlighting its alternative determinants (e.g., networks, traumas), other investigators (Atran, 2010; Gunaratna, 2000) insisted on narratives' importance. To understand whether the narrative matters and, if so, why and under what conditions, its functions in promoting extremism need to be delineated and how it interacts with alternative conditions for radicalization needs to be identified.

Typically, a violence-justifying narrative is designed to accomplish two functions. First, it arouses the exposed individuals' quest for significance by highlighting and dramatizing the humiliation one's group may have suffered. For instance, Al Libi's sermon cited earlier poignantly depicts the humiliation of Muslims in Algeria and the dishonor it bestows upon Muslims worldwide. Second, it forges the critical link between violence and significance, suggesting that engagement in the former will bring about the latter, as exemplified in Al Libi's plea to his listeners to join the struggle against Islam's alleged enemies. Implicitly or explicitly, the narrative suggests that violent actions on the group's behalf will earn an individual the group's everlasting gratitude and accord her or him a coveted hero and/or a martyr status. In other words, the considerable (and arguably sacred) value attached to the cause is transferred to individuals who are willing to make sacrifices on the cause's behalf.

An important implication of this analysis is that it is not the cultural value as such, nor even the defense of the cultural value as such, that produces violent extremism. Rather, it is the individual's belief that does so, namely, the belief that defense of an important cultural value would gratify the individual's burning desire for significance aroused by her or his special circumstances. In other words, demonstrated devotion to a value turns out not to constitute an *end* in itself but rather to represent a *means* to satisfying a basic human motive for mattering and significance.

Prosocial Ideological Narratives

When the quest for significance is aroused, individuals may support violence to gain significance in accordance with the ideological script that links the two. Clearly, however, not all ideologies promote violence. In fact, some are emphatically humane and prosocial. They affirm that significance is earned by kindness, tolerance, and empathy toward others, and they are firmly and decidedly anti violence.

The Christian lore, for instance is replete with sinners-to-saints accounts in which individuals who committed despicable acts—likely to have occasioned considerable loss of significance—embraced the religious ideology with particular passion. They then engaged in a life of purity and self-sacrifice that earned them the gratitude of their community, culminating in the attainment of *sainthood*. St. Paul, for example, was responsible for killing many Christians before his dramatic conversion experience on the road to Damascus. Also, prior to devoting his life to Christianity, St. Augustine of Hippo led a life of arrogant pride and sexual immorality; Mary Magdalene was reputed to have been a repentant sinner; St. Angela of Foligno lived a life of wealth, sex, and vanity before her conversion; and St. Callixtus was a former thief and embezzler. Anecdotes abound.

Thus, it is not the quest for significance *as such* that drives violence. An ideology may inspire individuals to perform acts that are benevolent and unselfish. Work carried out under the auspices of terror management theory suggests that making one's *mortality* salient (known as the MS manipulation[8]) conveys the prospect of one's fundamental insignificance; this, in turn, strengthens individuals' tendency to embrace the *values* embedded in their world view (Greenberg, Simon, Pyszczynski, Solomon, & Chatel, 1992). Often, the strengthened tendency increases the likelihood of prosocial, value-affirming behaviors.

---

8. The typical MS manipulation consists of having participants imagine their being dead (lying in the coffin, etc.) and responding to a brief questionnaire as to their feeling in response to thoughts about their death.

In this vein, Rothschild, Abdollahi, and Pyszczynski (2009) found in a Christian American sample that although high levels of fundamentalism was *generally* associated with greater support for military force, exposure to Jesus' compassionate teachings—embodied in dictums such as "Love your neighbor as yourself"—plus an MS manipulation led fundamentalists to drop their support for violence to a level equivalent to that of mainstream (i.e., less fundamentalist) Christians. Similarly, for Shiite Muslims in Iran, death reminders generally led to more aggressive anti-Western attitudes. However, priming group members with compassionate verses from the Koran, like "Do goodness to others because Allah loves those who do good," redirected the response to MS and led to reduced hostility against the United States.

In other words, when the quest for significance is activated, whether a prosocial or antisocial behavior is enacted depends on the ideological narrative that identifies the means that may lead to significance attainment. Effecting a shift from a terrorism-justifying ideology to one that identifies alternative routes to significance seems essential to eradicating violence. This shift redirects the motivation to matter and to have respect in a prosocial direction.

The Role of Education

Some researchers have suggested that a lack of education is a contributing factor to terrorism (e.g., Peters, 2015). There are findings that lower education tends to promote terrorism in a cluster of countries where socio-economic, political, and demographic conditions are unfavorable, while higher education reduces terrorism in a cluster of countries where conditions are more favorable (Brockhoff, Krieger, & Meierrieks, 2015). However, there is no clear consensus on this topic, because other researchers have published data suggesting that there is no connection between education and terrorism (Krueger & Malečková, 2002; Richardson, 2011) or that higher education is linked to a greater likelihood of engaging in terrorism (Berrebi, 2007; Testas, 2004).

From the present perspective, low education might reduce individuals' chances of finding a respectable place in society that proffers a sense of significance. In this sense, low education may constitute a contributing factor that increases individuals' acceptance of narratives that promise individuals significance through the engagement in violence. That said, education as such is no guarantee against engagement in or support of violent extremism. Whether education would discourage or encourage extremism should depend on its contents and the moral values that it highlights. For instance, whereas Western liberal education may contain antiviolence as one of its core values, socialization (and in this sense education) that stresses the values of honor and ingroup morality (Haidt & Graham, 2007) may encourage violence against the group's enemies. For example, a religious education that advocates a fight against infidels (violent jihad) may promote rather than discourage aggression against the infidels. Thus, no direct link between education and violent extremism is to be expected. Whatever indirect effects education may have on extremism should strongly depend on its implications for individuals' sense of significance and on the values that it highlights.

The Network

Terrorism researchers (e.g., Weinberg & Eubank, 1987; Sageman, 2004, 2008) have long recognized the importance of social networks in promoting violent extremism. These serve as conduits through which individuals get acquainted with, and embrace, the ideological narrative that the network espouses and that guides their attempts to earn or restore their sense of significance.

Individuals are typically exposed to violence-justifying ideological content through social contact with friends and relatives. Individuals are generally motivated to agree with those who are close to them, such as their friends, relatives, and teachers (e.g., Chaiken, Wood, & Eagly, 1996; Cialdini & Goldstein, 2004). These social sources are generally regarded as trustworthy and authoritative, and their opinions are taken seriously. Because eloquent clerics, charismatic leaders, and intimate friends are respected and trusted, the radical ideologies that they may espouse are accepted on faith and aren't carefully scrutinized. In such situations, individuals have little motivation to use their critical skills to assess the ideologies or question their validity, as they are coming from trusted and admired sources.

It follows that endowing individuals with *critical skills* (Francis, 2015) alone may not counteract the impact of radical ideologies or make a serious dent in radical beliefs. Critical skills may be useful in counteracting extremist rhetoric where one's overriding motivation was the desire for the Truth. They may not be as useful where one's dominant motivation was to agree with such rhetoric and to embrace it (Bélanger et al., 2014, 2015; Dunning, 1999; Kunda, 1990).

The social process underlying radicalization isn't limited to social networks of relatives and friends with whom an individual has concrete, face-to-face encounters. Exposure to charismatic persuaders in Internet chat rooms, via propaganda videos, or through radical sermons at mosques or madrasas are also part of the process. Farouk Abdelmutaleb, the notorious "underwear bomber," accused of planning to detonate an explosive device on a commercial flight to Detroit, was radicalized through his correspondence with Al Awlaki, the fiery Al Qaeda preacher operating out of Yemen. So was Malik Nidal Hassan, the US army major who killed 13 persons in Fort Hood, Texas. The Indonesian Bali bomber Ali Ghufron was exposed to radical Islamic values in the madrasa (pesantren[9]) that he attended. Later, he became a preacher and served as a role model to his brothers and co-conspirators Amrozi and Ali Imron. Another co-conspirator in the Bali attack, Imam Samudra, was inspired to join militant struggle via a book by Abdullah Azam, *Signs of God's Power in the Jihad in Afghanistan* (Milla, Ancok, & Anock, 2013).

Mujahidin fighters returning from the battlefields of the Afghan–Russian confrontation (1979–1989) are believed to have exerted a considerable radicalizing influence on Muslim youth, who were excited and inspired by the fighters' war stories of courage, sacrifice, and toughness (Gunaratna, 2011). All of this suggests that commitment to radical ideologies cannot be fully understood without appreciating the process of group dynamics within kinship and friendship networks. Charismatic leaders and persuasive communicators play an essential role in radicalization as they skillfully manipulate their listeners' motivations and convince them to embrace radical messages extolling the legitimacy and desirability of violence in service of a cause.

The Role of Families

In recent years, the public has become increasingly aware that family members may form close-knit radical networks that collaborate in the perpetration of violent attacks. The Kouachi brothers, for example, were involved in the Paris attacks of November 2015; the Bakraqui brothers were among the perpetrators of the March 2016 attacks in Brussels; the Tsarnaev brothers carried out the Boston marathon massacre in April, 2013; and Syed Rizwan Farook and his wife Tashfeen Malik carried out the San Bernardino killings in December 2015. By some estimates as many as 30% of "Western fighters have a familial connection to jihad, whether through relatives currently fighting in Syria or Iraq, marriage, or some other link to jihadists from prior conflicts or attacks" (Bergen, Schuster, & Sterman, 2015, p. 3). Especially in cultures where families constitute particularly cohesive social groupings, they may be able to form firm shared realities centered on the extremist ideology.

---

9. *Pesantren* is the Indonesian term for an Islamic religious school, known elsewhere as the *madrasa*.

From the standpoint of clandestine terrorist organizations, family networks offer a number of strategic advantages. The siblings often are in constant communication with each other, which facilitates mutual radicalization as well as the coordination of eventual attacks. They are also typically highly committed to each other, forming a tight impenetrable group, from which defection is unlikely. Relatedly, they are likely to feel tightly bound by their joint decision and are therefore unlikely to abort the plot they have agreed on. For all these reasons, siblings or other family networks are highly useful in carrying out high-risk operations and have been increasingly visible in terrorist attacks around the globe.

For pretty much the same reasons, family networks have constituted an important tool in the enterprise of *deradicalization*. The shared reality (Hardin & Higgins, 1996; Higgins, 2018) that family members subscribe to, and the motivation to agree with one's loved ones, can make families a formidable vehicle for getting former extremists to return to moderation. Of course, the successful use of families in the deradicalization process presupposes their moderation and the eschewal of extremism. Otherwise, the outcome of relying on families—those that may follow radical ideologies—might backfire and be the opposite to the desired result.

The Saudi deradicalization program (initiated in 2004 by the Saudi Ministry of the Interior) shows how families have been used to successfully pull members back from immersion in radicalism. In this program, families were made responsible for their formerly radicalized members and were entrusted with preventing their recidivism. Attention to militants' families also characterized the successful Singaporean deradicalization program, initiated in 2001 after arrests of suspects in a plot to explode bombs in embassies of the United States, Israel, and Australia, where the Taman Bachaan organization provided extensive care and aftercare to families of detained militants.

Networks, Narratives, and Rewards

We already alluded to the intimate relation between the social network and the ideological narrative that makes the connection between violence and significance. Obviously, a social network would promote violent extremism only if its members embraced such a narrative and not otherwise. In fact, connection to networks that embrace a moderate narrative incompatible with violence is known to facilitate individuals' exit from violent movements (Kruglanski, Webber, & Koehler, in press).

As implied earlier, the present notion of the social network is intended here in its basic sense as a reference group, rather than necessarily a membership group (Merton & Kitt, 1950).[10] A reference group is one that serves as an *epistemic authority* for individuals. It defines for individuals the factual (how things are) and the normative (how things should be) reality and hence serves as a basis for shaping their beliefs and attitudes. In other words, the network's *epistemic authority* (Kruglanski et al., 2005) validates its narrative for deferential members.

Beyond its epistemic function, however, the social network also fulfills a *rewarding* function in dispensing respect and appreciation to individuals who implement its narrative in action. Extremist organizations seem well aware of their members' significance motivation, and they tend to bestow considerable honor and recognition on individuals who sacrificed everything for the cause. Suicide bombers in Palestine and Iraq, for instance, are treated as future martyrs in the premission period and are celebrated with great pomp and circumstance after their death (Perry & Hasisi, 2015). As a token of their importance to the organization, the Sri Lankan members of the Black Tigers suicide squad were typically invited, on eve of their mission, to a one-on-one dinner with Velupillai Prabhakaran, their venerated leader, or with one of his top lieutenants.

A particularly appealing token of significance used by some terror organizations is access to attractive sexual partners. The Islamic State (IS), for example, was known for its clever use of sex as an accolade to its fighters. The primordial aspect of this coupling is striking. In the animal kingdom, males often gain access to females through their aggressive domination over their rivals (Buss & Duntley, 2011). Sexual access is the most primitive token of significance (in humans and beasts), and it is often attainable through aggressive dominance over rivals (Buss & Kenrick, 1998). IS has strategically turned the sexual rewarding of violence into a well-oiled machine that delivers results.

Young, often sexually frustrated, men are promised a sexual Shangri La for their bravery: There are brides eager to marry the fighters for Islam, rape of nonbelievers is legitimized and encouraged, sexual slaves can be purchased (through IS mediation), and fatwas are issued proclaiming a "sexual jihad," forcing girls to marry militants. There have been reports of IS marriage centers (e.g., in al Bab in the Syrian Aleppo province) where women register to be

10. Often though not invariably, a membership group is also a reference group. There are cases, however, where one defers to the opinions and attitudes of a group to which one does not belong but which one perceives as of superior wisdom and expertise compared to the group to which one does.

wed to fighters, and captured Iraqi women are reportedly forced into brothels run by female jihadists ("ISIS Fighters," 2014). Moreover, should they die in battle or in a suicide attack, fighters are promised the shahid status, whose ultimate reward is marrying beautiful virgins on entry into Paradise.

Though many Westerners might view IS's sexual strategies as a horrific, cynical, and exploitative, not all women see it quite that way. According to *The Guardian* (Sherwood et al., 2014), for example, some young women find appeal in the prospect of marrying a hero and raising future fighters for the glory of Islam. Women who volunteer for suicide attacks are promised that they will become beautiful and sexually attractive in the afterlife and to wed heroic Muslim warriors who await them in heaven (Berko, 2007).

In his momentous study, *Civilization and Its Discontents,* Freud (1930) described how cultures, through the creation of moral systems, restrain the primitive urges of aggression and sex, thus allowing societies to function and thrive. By removing those restraints and legitimizing these primordial instincts, the IS propaganda, in an intriguing tour de force, transmutes the profane into the sacred, unleashing considerable motivational forces and turning killers into martyrs in their own eyes and those of others committed to their creed.

In summary, the *need*, or the motivational element, that comes from the quest for personal significance defines the end that the individual strives to attain. The ideological *narrative* identifies the means to that end (i.e., how significance may be gained) and legitimizes it, and the social network validates the violence–significance nexus and dispenses significance for those who implement the dictates of the narrative in actual practice.

Relations between the 3Ns

Although the elements of need, narrative and network are typically involved in the phenomenon of violent extremism, their relative degree of impact may vary across instances. People differ, after all, on a variety of dimensions that may be relevant to extremism and these differences determine the influence that each of the 3Ns has in the process. For example, individuals may be more or less ambitious (or significance focused), and the more ambitious they are, the more attuned to and convinced they may be by a narrative that identifies a given means (of violence in this case) to the significance end.

Some individuals may be more socially dependent than others (Merari, 2010). They may, therefore, give more weight to the network support that a narrative receives and be less likely to pay critical attention to the narrative's contents. Other persons may be more reliant on their own rather than the group's perceived epistemic authority (Kruglanski et al., 2005). They may concoct, therefore, their own narrative that ties violence to significance with lesser deference to others' opinions. Lone-wolf terrorists such as Ted Kaczynski and Andres Breivik created their own narratives that justified their violent activities by tying them to lofty causes they aimed to serve (thus gaining significance). In the case of Kaczynski, the cause was protection of the environment, and in the case of Breivik, defense of the European culture against Muslims and feminists. It is of interest that even in such extreme cases of social isolationism as those of Kaczynski and Breivik, there was a reference (however faint) to a group on whose behalf purportedly the violence was carried out. In the case of Kaczynski, it was fellow environmentalists, who Kaczynski presumably hoped would appreciate the value of his actions, and in the case of Breivik, the imaginary Knights Templar organization that he claimed to represent.

Persons who are high on trait aggressiveness and/or in the habit of asserting their social standing by brute force may be more likely to accept a narrative that links violence to significance and to be less likely to require an extensive validation of such a narrative via a social network. For instance, criminals, gang members, and members of the military may be accustomed to, and skilled in the use of, violence; hence, they may be particularly readily persuaded, all else being equal, to pursue violence in their quest for significance.

Also, these individual differences may be stable and trait-like or be driven by situational circumstances: A personal failure or humiliation may activate the individual's quest for significance and increase her or his attunement to significance-promising narratives, the experience of social exclusion may render individuals susceptible to social influence by networks that offer acceptance.

A Model of Radicalization

Radicalization and its determinants are schematically depicted in Figure 3.2. The left portion of this figure depicts individual significance loss and its possible sources: stigma, personal failure (e.g., of loved ones, property, or position), and humiliation (e.g., through insults or torture), as well as political, economic, and social *anomie* (Durkheim, 1883/1964, as mentioned in Marks, 1974)—wherein individuals feel a lack of means to pursue their ends—resulting in a sense of reduced significance. According to our theory, *individual* significance loss induces the goal of significance restoration and is

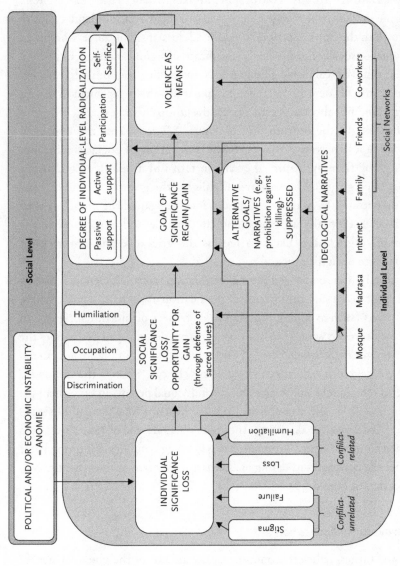

FIGURE 3.2. Determinants of radicalization. Adapted with permission from "The Psychology of Radicalization and Deradicalization: How Significance Quest Impacts Violent Extremism," by A. W. Kruglanski, M. J. Gelfand, J. J. Bélanger, A. Sheveland, M. Hetiarachchi, & R. Gunaratna, 2014, *Political Psychology*, 35, 69–93.

one of the two sources of attunement to the ideological narrative concerning the social significance loss. The second source is the sense of *collective* discrimination (e.g., Islamophobia), foreign occupation (Pape, 2004, 2006), and collective humiliation (e.g., via a blasphemous depiction of one's religious icons as in the Danish cartoons of the prophet Muhammad or in the *Charlie Hebdo* magazine in Paris, which was subjected to a terrorist attack in January 2015). As shown in the central section of Figure 3.2, loss of significance, whether of individual or social origin, is tied to the means of significance gain or restoration. At times of real or imagined intergroup conflict, the ability to earn significance may be identified in the ingroup narrative as engagement in violent struggle (and possibly terrorism) against the group's nemeses.

Accordingly, the bottom part of Figure 3.2 represents the impact of the ideological narrative that fuels the perception of social significance loss (e.g., by framing historical events in terms of a humiliating injustice against one's group). The narrative highlights the group's profound grievance perpetrated by a known culprit. Violence against the culprit is then identified as a morally warranted and effective method of response to the presumptive grievance, likely to redress the grievance and restore one's group's sense of significance.

Crucially, if the end of significance restoration is of a sufficient magnitude, it can result in the suppression and/or devaluation of alternative goals, values, or concerns (such as killing prohibition or respect of individual rights). In turn, the degree to which the latter concerns are downplayed determines the *degree of radicalization*, depicted at the upper right part of Figure 3.2. A relatively low degree of radicalization represents the case wherein the alternative concerns remain relatively active and the individual persists in his or her pursuit even as he or she is concerned to some degree about the end of significance (Kruglanski et al., 2014). The individual's degree of radicalization is assumed to increase proportionately to a growing commitment to the latter end and the concomitant fading of alternative concerns as shown in the central portion of Figure 3.2.

Pathways to Radicalization

As noted earlier, radicalization assumes the arousal of the quest for significance, which motivates the search for, and hence attention to, possible means of attaining significance. Typically, these means are found in the collective ideology of one's group that enshrines specific paths to that objective. If such ideology sanctifies violence and terrorism and portrays them as justifiable and effective pathways to significance, individuals may endorse them and commit to their pursuit.

Individuals might encounter these ingredients of the radicalization process in different temporal orders defining *distinct pathways* to terrorism. In some cases, the terrorism justifying narrative may be highly salient in the individual's informational environment. In other cases, the push to embrace extremism may originate in a personal significance loss that, as discussed earlier, might predispose the individual to pay close attention to a violence-justifying narrative. In other cases, social contact with a violence supporting networks may come first (Weinberg & Eubank, 2006) and precede individuals' exposure to a violence justifying narrative.

In yet different instances, individuals may encounter the narrative through various communication media (e.g., at an Internet chat room or by exposure to extremist sermons by charismatic clerics). From the present perspective, the specific pathway to violence does not matter much and is largely irrelevant to the ultimate strength of individuals' commitment to the cause or the degree of their radicalization. The latter depends, instead, on the extent of significance loss ultimately experienced by the person, her or his readiness to completely commit to the end of significance restoration, and her or his readiness to implement to that goal via violent means, even if this entails considerable personal sacrifice.

Summary

In this chapter, we outlined a psychological theory of radicalization that progresses toward violent extremism. We assumed that extremism (of any kind) derives from a motivational imbalance in which a given basic need is elevated disproportionately to other needs, which are then correspondingly inhibited. As a consequence, constraints that the latter needs normally exert upon behavior are weakened or removed. This process expands the set of behavioral options for addressing the dominant need, including violent activities generally prohibited by societal norms.

We also identified the quest for personal significance (mattering, respect, etc.) as the fundamental human need that typically underlies violent extremism. We assumed that the linkage between violence and significance and, hence, the selection of violence as the means to significance is often spelled out by an (ideological) narrative that invokes a cultural (sacred) value whose defense legitimizes violence. That narrative is typically validated by a referential social network that rewards members with respect and admiration for implementing the narrative's dictates. Finally, we addressed the relations between the 3Ns of our model—the need, the narrative, and the network—and identified the conditions that determine the degree of their relative influence in fostering radicalization.

References

Al-Libi, A. Y. (2009, June 23). Algeria between the sacrifices of our fathers and the loyalty of our sons [Videofile; translation of speech from As Sahab video]. *SITE Intelligence Group Services*. Retrieved from http://sitemultimedia.org/video/SITE_Sahab_AYL_Algeria_Sacrifices.wmv

Anomie. (n.d.). *Wikipedia*. Retrieved from https://en.wikipedia.org/wiki/Anomie

Atran, S. (2010). *Talking to the enemy: Violent extremism, sacred values, and what it means to be human*. London, UK: Penguin.

Bandura, A. (1999). Moral disengagement in the perpetration of inhumanities. *Personality and Social Psychology Review, 3*, 193–209.

Bélanger, J. J., Kruglanski, A. W., Chen, X., & Orehek, E. (2014). Bending perception to desire: Effects of task demands, motivation, and cognitive resources. *Motivation and Emotion, 38*(6), 802–814.

Bélanger, J. J., Kruglanski, A. W., Chen, X., Orehek, E., & Johnson, D. J. (2015). When Mona Lisa smiled and love was in the air: On the cognitive energetics of motivated judgments. *Social Cognition, 33*(2), 104–119.

Bélanger, J. J., Lafrenière, M. A. K., Vallerand, R. J., & Kruglanski, A. W. (2013). When passion makes the heart grow colder: The role of passion in alternative goal suppression. *Journal of Personality and Social Psychology, 104*, 126–147.

Bergen, P., Schuster, C., & Sterman, D. (2015, November). ISIS in the West: The new faces of extremism. *New America*. Retrieved from https://static.newamerica.org/attachments/11813-isis-in-the-west-2/ISP-Isis-In-The-West-v2.b4f2e9e3a7c94b9e9bd2a293bae2e759.pdf

Berko, A. (2007). *The path to paradise: The inner world of suicide bombers and their dispatchers*. Westport, CT: Greenwood.

Berrebi, C. (2007). Evidence about the link between education, poverty and terrorism among Palestinians. *Peace Economics, Peace Science and Public Policy, 13*(1). https://doi.org/10.2202/1554-8597.1101

Birnbaum, M., & Mekhennet, S. (2016, March 24). Anti-terrorism crackdowns may have spurred attackers. *The Washington Post*, p. A11.

Bloom, M. (2005). *Dying to kill: The allure of suicide terror*. New York, NY: Columbia University Press.

Brockhoff, S., Krieger, T., & Meierrieks, D. (2015). Great expectations and hard times: The (nontrivial) impact of education on domestic terrorism. *Journal of Conflict Resolution, 59*(7), 1186–1215.

Buss, D. M., & Duntley, J. D. (2011). The evolution of intimate partner violence. *Aggression and Violent Behavior, 16*, 411–419.

Buss, D. M., & Kenrick, D. T. (1998). Evolutionary social psychology. *The handbook of social psychology* (Vol. 2, pp. 982–1026). New York, NY: Random House.

Chaiken, S., Wood, W., & Eagly, A. H. 1996. Principles of persuasion. In E. T. Higgins & A. W. Kruglanski (Eds.), *Social psychology: Handbook of basic principles* (pp. 702–744). New York, NY: Guilford.

Cialdini, R. B., & Goldstein, N. J. (2004). Social influence: Compliance and conformity. *Annual. Review of Psychology, 55*, 591–621.

Cohen, S. J., Kruglanski, A. W., Gelfand, M. J., Webber, D., & Gunaratna, R. (2018). Al-Qaeda's propaganda decoded: A psycholinguistic system for detecting variations in terrorism ideology. *Terrorism and Political Violence, 30*, 142–171.

Deci, E. L., & Ryan, R. M. (2000). The "what" and "why" of goal pursuits: Human needs and the self-determination of behavior. *Psychological Inquiry, 11*, 227–268.

Dunning, D. (1999). A newer look: Motivated social cognition and the schematic representation of social concepts. *Psychological Inquiry, 10*(1), 1–11.

Durkheim, E. [1893] 1964. *The division of labour in society*. New York, NY: Free Press.

Extreme. (n.d.). *Oxford living dictionaries*. Retrieved from (https://en.oxforddictionaries.com/definition/extreme)

Fiske, S. T. (2010). *Social beings: Core motives in social psychology*. New York, NY: Wiley.

Francis, M. (2015, June 30). Teachers on the frontline against terror: what should schools do about radicalisation? *The Conversation*. Retrieved from http://theconversation.com/teachers-on-the-frontline-against-terror-what-should-schools-do-about-radicalisation-43942

Frankl, V. E. (2000). *Man's search for ultimate meaning*. New York, NY: Basic Books.

Freud, S. (1930). *Civilization and its discontents*. London, UK: Hogarth.

Gambetta, D. (2005). *Making sense of suicide missions*. Oxford, UK: Oxford University Press.

Gilligan, J. (1997). *Violence: reflections on a national epidemic*. New York, NY: Vintage.

Graham, J., & Haidt, J. (2010). Beyond beliefs: Religions bind individuals into moral communities. *Personality and Social Psychology Review, 14*, 140–150.

Greenberg, J., Simon, L., Pyszczynski, T., Solomon, S., & Chatel, D. (1992). Terror management and tolerance: Does mortality salience always intensify negative reactions to others who threaten one's worldview? *Journal of Personality and Social Psychology, 63*, 212–220.

Gunaratna, R. (2000). Suicide terrorism: A global threat. *Janes Intelligence Review, 12*(4), 52–55.

Gunaratna, R. (2011, July 15). Al Qaeda under Ayman Al Zawahiri: Still a lethal organisation, *RSIS Commentary, 104/2011*. https://www.rsis.edu.sg/rsis-publication/rsis/1577-al-qaeda-under-ayman-al-zawahi/#.Wz9o4csaySMs

Gupta, D. K. (2004). Exploring roots of terrorism. In T. Bjorgo (Ed.), *Root causes of terrorism* (pp. 34–50). London, UK: Routledge.

Haidt, J., & Graham, J. (2007). When morality opposes justice: Conservatives have moral intuitions that liberals may not recognize. *Social Justice Research, 20*, 98–116.

Hardin, C. D., & Higgins, E. T. (1996). Shared reality: How social verification makes the subjective objective. In R. M. Sorrentino & T. E. Higgins (Eds.), *Handbook of motivation and cognition* (Vol. 2, pp. 28–84). New York, NY: Guilford.

Harre, R. (1979). *Social being: A theory for social psychology*. Oxford, England: Basil Blackwell.

Higgins, E. T. (2012). *Beyond pleasure and pain: How motivation works*. Oxford, England: Oxford University Press.

Higgins, E. T. (2018). *Shared reality: What makes us strong and tears us apart*. New York, NY: Oxford University Press.

Honneth, A. (1995). *The struggle for recognition: The moral grammar of social conflicts*. Cambridge, MA: Polity.

Institute for Economics and Peace. (2015). *Global terrorism index 2015: Measuring and understanding the impact of terrorism*. Retrieved from http://economicsandpeace.org/wp-content/uploads/2015/11/Global-Terrorism-Index-2015.pdf

ISIS fighters open "marriage bureau." (2014, July 28). *Al Arabiya*. Retrieved from http://english.alarabiya.net/en/variety/2014/07/28/Marry-me-ISIS-fighters-open-marriage-bureau-.html

Kiras, J. D. (2007). Dying to prove a point: The methodology of dying to win. *Journal of Strategic Studies, 30*, 227–241.

Köpetz, C., Faber, T., Fishbach, A., & Kruglanski, A. W. (2011). The multifinality constraints effect: How goal multiplicity narrows the means set to a focal end. *Journal of Personality and Social Psychology, 100*(5), 810.

Krueger, A. B., & Malečková, J. (2002). Education, poverty and terrorism: Is there a causal connection?. *Journal of Economic Perspectives, 17*(4), 119–144.

Kruglanski, A. W. (2004). *The psychology of closed mindedness*. New York, NY: Psychology Press.

Kruglanski, A. W., Bélanger, J. J., Gelfand, M. G., Gunaratna, R., Hetiarrachchi, M., Reinares, F., . . . Sharvit, K. (2013). Terrorism, a (self) love-story: Redirecting the significance-quest can end violence. *American Psychologist, 68*, 559–575.

Kruglanski, A. W., Chen, X., Dechesne, M., Fishman, S., & Orehek, E. (2009). Fully committed: Suicide bombers' motivation and the quest for personal significance. *Political Psychology, 30*, 331–357.

Kruglanski, A. W., Chernikova, M., Babush, M., Dugas, M., & Schumpe, B. (2015). The architecture of goal systems: Multifinality, equifinality, and counterfinality in means-end relations. In A. J. Elliot (Ed.), *Advances in motivation science* (pp. 69–98). Cambridge, MA: Academic Press.

Kruglanski, A. W., Crenshaw, M., Post, J. M., & Victoroff, J. (2008). Talking about terrorism. *Scientific American Mind, 19*, 58–65.

Kruglanski, A. W., & Fishman, S. (2006). The psychology of terrorism: "Syndrome" versus "tool" perspectives. *Terrorism and Political Violence, 18*, 193–215.

Kruglanski, A. W., Gelfand, M. J., Bélanger, J. J., Sheveland, A., Hetiarachchi, M., & Gunaratna, R. (2014). The psychology of radicalization and deradicalization: How significance quest impacts violent extremism. *Political Psychology, 35*, 69–93.

Kruglanski, A. W., Raviv, A., Bar-Tal, D., Raviv, A., Sharvit, K., Ellis, S., . . . & Mannetti, L. (2005). Says who? Epistemic authority effects in social judgment. *Advances in experimental social psychology, 37*, 345–392.

Kruglanski, A. W., Shah, J. Y., Fishbach, A., Friedman, R., Chun, W. & Sleeth-Keppler, D. (2002). A theory of goal systems. In M. P. Zanna (Ed.), *Advances in experimental social psychology* (Vol. 34, pp. 331–378). San Diego, CA: Academic Press.

Kruglanski, A.W., Webber, D. & Koehler, D. (in press). *Radicals' Journey: German Neo-Nazis' Voyage to the Edge and Back*. New York, NY: Oxford University Press.

Kunda, Z. (1990). The case for motivated reasoning. *Psychological bulletin, 108*(3), 480.

Marks, S. R. (1974). Durkheim's theory of anomie. *American Journal of Sociology, 80*, 329–363.

Maslow, A. H. (1943). A theory of human motivation. *Psychological Review, 50*, 370–396.

Merari, A. (2010). *Driven to death: Psychological and social aspects of suicide terrorism.* Oxford, England: Oxford University Press.

Merton, R. K., & Kitt, A. S. (1950). Contributions to the theory of reference group behavior. *Continuities in Social Research*, 40–105.

Milla, M. N., Ancok, F., & Anock, D. (2013). The impact of leader–follower interactions on the radicalization of terrorists: A case study of the Bali bombers. *Asian Journal of Social Psychology, 16*, 92–100.

Miller, A. (1949, February 27). Tragedy and the common man. *New York Times.* Retrieved from https://www.nytimes.com/1949/02/27/archives/tragedy-and-the-common-man-notes-on-tragedy-and-the-common-man.html

Mini-manual of the urban guerilla (n.d.). *Wikipedia.* Retrieved from https://en.wikipedia.org/wiki/Minimanual_of_the_Urban_Guerrilla

Ohnuki-Tierney, E. (2006). *Kamikaze diaries: Reflections of Japanese student soldiers.* Chicago, IL: University of Chicago Press.

Pape, R. A. (2004). True worth of air power. *Foreign Affairs, 83*, 116–130.

Pape, R. A. (2006). *Dying to win: The strategic logic of suicide terrorism.* New York, NY: Random House.

Pedhazur, A. (2005). *Suicide terrorism.* Cambridge, England: Polity.

Perry, S., & Hasisi, B. (2015). Rational choice rewards and the jihadist suicide bomber. *Terrorism and Political Violence, 27*(1), 53–80.

Peters, M. A. (2015). *Education, globalization and the state in the age of terrorism.* New York, NY: Routledge.

Piazza, J. A. (2008). Incubators of terror: Do failed and failing states promote transnational terrorism?. *International Studies Quarterly, 52*, 469–488.

Pinker, S. (2011). *The better angels of our nature: The decline of violence in history and its causes.* Penguin, UK.

Pitt-Rivers, J. (1968). Honor. In W. A. Darity (Ed.), *International encyclopedia of social science* (pp. 503–511). Detroit, MI: Thomson.

Post, J. M. (2006). *The mind of the terrorist: The psychology of terrorism from the IRA to al-Qaeda*. New York, NY: Palgrave Macmillan.

Rothschild, Z. K., Abdollahi, A., & Pyszczynski, T. (2009). Does peace have a prayer? The effect of mortality salience, compassionate values, and religious fundamentalism on hostility toward out-groups. *Journal of Experimental Social Psychology*, *45*, 816–827.

Sageman, M. (2004). *Understanding terror networks*. Philadelphia, PA: University of Pennsylvania Press.

Sageman, M. (2008). *Leaderless jihad: Terror networks in the twenty-first century*. Philadelphia, PA: University of Pennsylvania Press.

Shah, J. Y., Friedman, R., & Kruglanski, A. W. (2002). Forgetting all else: On the antecedents and consequences of goal shielding. *Journal of Personality and Social Psychology*, *83*, 1261–1280.

Sherwood, H., Laville, S., Willsher, K., Knight, B., French, M., & Gambino, L. (2014, September 29). Schoolgirl jihadis: the female Islamists leaving home to join Isis fighters. *The Guardian*. Retrieved from https://www.theguardian.com/world/2014/sep/29/schoolgirl-jihadis-female-islamists-leaving-home-join-isis-iraq-syria

Speckhard, A., & Akhmedova, K. (2006). Black widows: The Chechen female suicide terrorists. *Female suicide bombers: Dying for Equality*, *84*(1), 63–80.

Sprinzak, E. (2001). The lone gunmen: The global war on terrorism faces a new brand of enemy. *Foreign Policy*, *1127*, 72–73.

Stern, J. (2004). *Terror in the name of God: Why religious militants kill*. New York, NY: Harper Perennial.

Testas, A. (2004). Determinants of terrorism in the Muslim world: an empirical cross-sectional analysis. *Terrorism and Political Violence*, *16*, 253–273.

Weinberg, L., & Eubank, W. L. (1987). *The rise and fall of Italian terrorism* (p. 155). Boulder, CO: Westview Press.

Weinberg, L., & Eubank, W. L. (2006). *What is terrorism? The roots of terrorism*. New York, NY: Chelsea House.

White, R. W. (1959). Motivation reconsidered: The concept of competence. *Psychological Review*, *66*, 297–333.

Woolf, N. (2015, April 27). Dzhokhar Tsarnaev's older brother was driving force, Boston bombing jury told. *The Guardian*. Retrieved from https://www.theguardian.com/us-news/2015/apr/27/dzhokhar-tsarnaev-brother-tamerlan-boston-marathon-bombing

Zartman, W. I., & Anstey, M. (2012). The problem: Preventing identity conflicts and genocide. In W. I. Zartman, M. Anstey, & P. Meerts (Eds.), *The slippery slope to genocide: Reducing identity conflicts and preventing mass murder* (pp. 3–34). New York, NY: Oxford University Press.

4 OTHER THEORIES OF RADICALIZATION

The topic of radicalization has been a long-standing interest to so-cial scientists and several theories have been put forth to explain the phenomenon. In this chapter, we review major such theories and discuss their relation to our own model of radicalization described in Chapter 3. Radicalization theories are diverse, though not nec-essarily antagonistic to each other. Rather, each model addresses a somewhat different aspect of radicalization or depicts it from a distinctive disciplinary perspective at a different level of analysis. In what follows, we describe five approaches to understanding rad-icalization: root cause explanations, psychological models, rational actor model, social network theory, and social movement theory.

Root Cause Explanations

The root cause explanation of terrorism is based on the idea "that certain conditions provide a social environment and widespread grievances that, when combined with certain precipitant factors, result in the emergence of terrorist organizations and terrorist acts" (Neuman, 2006, p. 750). Wilkinson (1986), for instance, suggested that the causes of political violence—such as ethnic, religious, and ideological conflicts—are similar to those related to terrorism. Root causes cover a very large scope of issues. In his 2004 book, *The Psychology of Terrorism*, John Horgan compiled 14 root causes or grievances commonly discussed by terrorism experts:

- Lack of democracy, civil liberties, and the rule of law;
- Failed or weak states;
- Rapid modernization;
- Extremist ideologies of a secular or religious nature;
- Historical antecedents of political violence, civil wars, revolutions, dictatorships, or occupation;

- Hegemony and inequality of power;
- Illegitimate or corrupt governments;
- Powerful external actors upholding illegitimate governments;
- Repression by foreign occupation or by colonial powers;
- The experience of discrimination on the basis of ethnic or religious origins;
- Failure or unwillingness by the state to integrate dissident groups or emerging social classes;
- The experience of social injustice;
- The presence of charismatic ideological leaders; and
- Triggering events.

Other, commonly identified root causes include poverty and the lack of sufficient education (e.g., Fearon & Laitin, 2003; Kennedy, 1998; Stern, 2001). Implicit in the identification of root causes is the belief that addressing them would constitute an effective counterterrorism strategy (Newman, 2006). Despite this enticing proposition, a direct causal link between the proposed causal factors and violent extremism is unlikely (Hafez & Mullins, 2015; Horgan, 2004; Krueger & Malečková, 2002; 2003). Indeed, it does not seem to be the case that poverty or lack of sufficient education inevitably results in radicalization to violent extremism. Consistent with this notion, a number of large-scale empirical studies have found no relationship between poverty and terrorism, both at the level of individual terrorists and at the aggregate level of their country of origin (e.g., Krueger & Malečková, 2003). In the same vein, Sageman's (2004) research on the Salafi jihad movement uncovered that its leadership and its largest membership cluster had come mostly from the upper and middle classes. Pape's (2006) study of suicide bombers' demographic profile indicated that only 17% in their midst were unemployed or part of the lower classes, considerably less than their fair share representation in their societies, of which they make up about one-third overall.

On the aggregate level, in the late 1990s and 2000, when terrorism against Israeli citizens was soaring, the average Palestinian was reporting an optimistic economic forecast and unemployment was declining. Berrebi (2003) performed a time-series analysis in efforts to find a relationship between economic conditions in the West Bank and Gaza Strip and the number of terrorist incidents but found that there was none. Nor does lack of formal education appear to constitute a root cause of terrorism. Sageman's 2004 examination of the central staff of the global Salafi jihad found that 88% had finished college and 20% had doctorate degrees. In fact, only a quarter of his sample could be considered unskilled workers with few prospects. Similar results can be found in other empirical studies looking at education, occupation, and terrorism (Pape, 2006; Stern, 2003).These studies imply that poverty and lack of education are neither necessary nor sufficient causes of terrorism.

Some recent data hint at the possibility that many of today's terrorists originate in countries that suffer from political repression (Krueger & Laitin, 2003). But there are reasons to doubt a general causal link here as well. Recall that Western democracies such as Germany, Italy, Spain, France, Canada, and the United States have all seen instances of indigenous terrorism, whereas Stalin's Soviet Union, for example (a repressive regime by all criteria), or Hitler's Nazi Germany saw none.

Presumably, the logic underlying the root cause notion is that conditions of absolute or relative deprivation—due to poverty, political oppression, discrimination, and low social status—are frustrating; hence, they foment aggression against others that translates into terrorism (Gurr, 1970; Victoroff, 2005). But in scientific psychology, the simple frustration–aggression hypothesis has long been discarded (Berkowitz, 1993). Just because someone is frustrated does not necessarily mean that he or she would aggress against others. Frustration could lead to withdrawal, depression, escape, or aggression against the self rather than outwardly. Frustration could also motivate the search for alternative means to one's objectives, not necessarily violent ones.

Indeed, studies have shown that terrorism may constitute a strategy of last resort, used when all other means have been exhausted (Laqueur, 1987; Merari & Friedland, 1985; Sidanius & Pratto, 1999; Victoroff, 2005). In this vein, Sageman (2004) argues that relative deprivation is a probable necessary condition for terrorism but not a sufficient condition: Many individuals are frustrated in their own lives or feel economic deprivation, but very few become terrorists.

In short, the root cause notion seems to have garnered little empirical support or conceptual grounding. This doesn't mean, however, that various personality traits or motivations fueled by such conditions as poverty or political oppression or by feelings of injustice, discrimination, or relative deprivation are irrelevant to terrorism. In fact, as *contributing factors*, they can play a major role.

Root Causes versus Contributing Factors

In contrast to root causes, contributing factors may be correlated with a given variable of interest *under specific circumstances*. In this vein, Silke (2003) describes how the vast majority of terrorists neither suffer from mental disorders nor can be classified by a certain personality characteristic; instead "their involvement in political violence is a result of a series of understandable factors which combined result in a process of deepening involvement in violent extremism" (p. 94). In other words, none of these factors is a sufficient or a necessary cause of terrorist behavior; however, under *certain conditions* and in the right combination, they may contribute to an individual's support of, or enrollment in, a terrorist organization. Indeed, scholars generally agree that root causes are facilitative factors that set the stage for terrorism (e.g., Bjørgo, 2005, Horgan, 2008).

According to the present analysis, the contributing factors at issue pertain to the need factor in the 3N model of radicalization described in Chapter 3— the motivational state of frustration and loss of significance produced by oppression, lack of professional opportunities due to insufficient education, and a general sense of grievance and deprivation that the identified root causes, as well as other factors, may induce. And the certain conditions under which a sense of insignificance may lead to violent extremism are the remaining two Ns in our equation, that is, exposure to the ideological narrative and the network elements. As explained in Chapter 3, it is the ideological narrative that links the goal of significance to the appropriate means, whether violent or nonviolent. The network element is typically important in providing support for the shared ideological narrative and in affirming that violence is the means by which important ends are best accomplished, bestowing significance on those who engage in it for the collective cause.

Consider finally Gurr's (1970) influential volume titled *Why Men Rebel*, in which he advances the argument that *relative deprivation* is the root cause of radicalization. Gurr defined relative deprivation as the "perceived discrepancy between men's value expectations and their value capabilities" (p. 13) whereby "value expectations are the goods and conditions of life (to which) people believe they are rightfully entitled" and "value capabilities are the goods and conditions they think they are capable of attaining or maintaining, given the social means available to them" (p. 13). Gurr's work suggests that frustration with regard to one's relative standing leaves one vulnerable to radicalization and political violence.

Taken at face value, Gurr's (1970) relative deprivation hypothesis might be open to criticism applicable to all root cause notions on grounds of their insufficiency. As Newman (2006) observed "the vast majority of the millions of people who suffer from these grievances do not become terrorists" (p. 756). In fairness to Gurr's theory, however, it is important to note that he incorporated elements of the ideological narrative in his analysis. Specifically, Gurr discussed the *normative* and *utilitarian* justifications for political violence. Both justifications may serve to overcome the general prohibitions against violence present in most cultures and religions. The normative justification suggests that violence is normally acceptable under the circumstances, whereas the utilitarian justification conveys that violence is likely to work and bring victory and glory to its users. As combined with the loss of significance element representing the need element of our model and implicit in the concept of relative deprivation, the justification element refers to the narrative element, which is presumably embraced by the community at issue, hence implying our network element. In this sense, Gurr's theory comes close to the present portrayal of radicalization's major ingredients.

Psychological Models

Psychological models provide a unique viewpoint on radicalization by highlighting micro-level processes related to personality, attitudes, beliefs formation, and motivations of potential recruits to radical groups. There are a wide variety of psychological models of radicalization; in the following discussion, we briefly survey some of the more influential ones, including psychoanalytic theories, psychological profiling notions, and social psychological theories of radicalization.

Psychoanalytic Theories

Psychoanalytic theories of radicalization assume that human behavior is strongly influenced by unconscious forces and unresolved childhood conflicts (Gabbard, 2000). Three major psychoanalytic theories are often invoked in relation to terrorism: identity theory, narcissism theory, and paranoia theory. *Identity theory* posits that the consolidation of identity constitutes a formal stage of personal development (Erikson, 1959). In line with this perspective, embracing an ideology or joining radical groups, especially those with charismatic leaders (representing love objects in Freudian terms), are adequate means to assuage identity-related crises (Böllinger, 1981) and obtain a sense of purpose and self-worth (Taylor & Quayle, 1994). It should be readily apparent that these psychoanalytic notions are intimately related to the concept of significance quest. In those terms, identity crises do not pertain exclusively to the informational question "Who am I?" but rather importantly touch on the deeply motivational issue of "Whether I matter" and, if so, why.

According to *narcissism theory*, damage to the self by chronic abuse or humiliation during early childhood precludes the child from fully developing its sense of morality and empathy (Crayton, 1983; Kohut, 1972, 1978; Morf, 1970). When experiencing a "narcissistic injury," or ego-threat, individuals undergo a "narcissistic rage" (Akhtar, 1999), which drives them to eliminate the source of injury. Again, the conceptual kinship of these notions to *significance loss* is striking. However, whereas the concept of narcissism pertains to a stable dimension of personality, the notion of significance loss is broader in its implication that this state of affairs could befall anyone in the appropriate circumstances, rather than being reserved specifically for given personality types.

Lastly, proponents of *paranoia theory* (e.g., Robins & Post, 1997) suggest that paranoid personality disorder is common among terrorists. This would predispose them to project hateful motives and be suspicious of others. Thus, attacking others is rationalized as self-defense against the "oppressor." In present terms, a paranoid personality leads individuals to perceive others as motivated to subjugate and humiliate them and in that sense to constitute threats to their sense of their power and significance.

In summary, although the occurrence of elaborate unconscious intrapsychic conflicts during childhood is debatable, virtually all psychoanalytic theories refer to some perceived frustration or disappointment with one's self. Whether it is an identity crisis, narcissistic injury, or self-defense against an aggressor, the theme of ego-threat is pivotal to psychoanalytic conceptions, recalling the concept of significance loss. It is important to note, however, that whereas the frustration and lowered self-worth portrayed by psychoanalytic theories of terrorism is assumed to stem from a defective psychological development, largely unrelated to the social and political conditions in which the individual is embedded, our quest for significance notion, while allowing for intrapsychic sources of feelings of inferiority, also recognizes external factors in the individuals' situation that might induce it (such as oppression, discrimination, and subjugation imposed by an outgroup).

Psychological Profiling

The assumption of personality differences in susceptibility to ego-threat inspired the psychological profiling of violent extremists. This practice, popularized in the 1970s, posited that terrorists shared common characteristics that correlated with various psychological and demographic variables, including personality traits, age, sex, and education. In this vein, based on case histories of right-wing Italian terrorists, Ferracuti and Bruno (1981) concluded that terrorists possessed an "authoritarian-extremist personality" (p. 209). They identified nine characteristics of this personality: (a) ambivalence toward authority, (b) defective insight, (c) adherence to convention, (d) emotional detachment from the consequences of their actions, (e) sexual role uncertainties, (f) magical thinking, (g) destructiveness, (h) low education, and (i) adherence to violent subculture norms and weapons fetishes. Note that eight of those characteristics are psychological in nature. However, critical examination of the evidence brought forth by Ferracuti and Bruno suggests that their conclusions were only germane to a small minority of right-wing terrorists (for a discussion, see Silke, 1998).

Over the years, scholars generally came to agree that profiling, and the notion that terrorists suffer from some sort of psychopathology, are untenable (e.g., Atran, 2003; Post et al., 2009; cf. Lankford, 2013). As Post (1985) noted in this connection, "behavioral scientists attempting to understand the psychology of individuals drawn to this violent political behavior have not succeeded in identifying a unique 'terrorist mindset'" (p. 103). Instead, it appears now that people attracted to terrorist organizations come from all walks of life, as well as different cultures, nationalities, ideological backgrounds, and socioeconomic statuses—they are "as diverse as the general population" (Atran & Sageman, 2006, p. 68). As a result, many have called into question the search for a terrorist personality and the utility of trait measures as indicators of the propensity toward violent extremism (e.g., Horgan, 2003, 2008).

These conclusions should not be taken to suggest that stable personality traits are irrelevant to violent extremism. They may be better thought of as *contributing factors* to extremism. For instance, personal aggressiveness and anger might predispose individuals to accept the tactic of violence as legitimate. Sensitivity to rejection (Downey, Mougios, Ayduk, London, & Shoda, 2004; Horney, 1937) or the culture of honor (Nisbett & Cohen, 1996) may dispose individuals to react with particular upset to perceived affronts and insults. Conformism and dependence might render persons more susceptible to social influence and hence to peer influence that in some contexts may be supportive of violence (Merari, 2010). Or sensation-seeking may dispose individuals to embark on violent extremism because of the inherent challenge and excitement that a terrorist career may offer (Zuckerman, 1979, 2002).

Thus, a variety of personality characteristics may be relevant to violent extremism and enhance the likelihood that an individual will find it appealing.

From the present perspective, such characteristics may be relevant to violent extremism in so far as they relate to the needs, narrative, and network elements of our theory. For instance, rejection sensitivity may augment the significance loss felt in response to an affront or an insult; dependency and conformism may augment the tendency to embrace one's network's shared reality, and sensation-seeking may be prompted by the challenge of dangerous exploits whose accomplishment will beget admiration and respect of one's peers.

The Radicalization Process

Horgan (2004, 2008) proposed to move the inquiry of radicalization "from profiles to pathways" by shifting it from *who* may be susceptible to radicalization to *how* individuals may radicalize. Horgan's pathway approach partitions the radicalization process into three phases: becoming a terrorist, being a terrorist, and disengaging from terrorism.

According to Horgan (2008), "becoming a terrorist" (i.e., the phase that concerns radicalization) is facilitated by a series of risk factors such as:

- emotional vulnerability (e.g., anger, alienation and disenfranchisement);
- dissatisfaction with current political or social activity and the perception that conventional political actions won't do much to change things;
- an identification with the victims of a grievance (perceived or real);
- belief that engaging in violence against the state or its symbols is *not inherently immoral*;
- belief that they can achieve more in death than they ever could in life; and
- kinship or strong social ties with people experiencing similar issues or who are already involved in radical activities.

As with the other analyses of terrorism discussed in this chapter, Horgan's (2004, 2008) model overlaps substantially with the present 3N classification. Specifically, emotional vulnerability, dissatisfaction with the status quo, and identification with the victims relate to the significance loss (i.e., the need) portion of our model; similarly, a belief that violence is not inherently immoral and that one could achieve more status, glory, or prestige in death than in life pertain to the ideological narrative part; finally, having kinship or social ties with people involved in or supporting radical activities pertains to the network aspect of the model.

Social Psychological Mechanisms of Radicalization

Somewhat similarly to Horgan (2008), McCauley and Moskalenko (2008) approach the issue of radicalization through the listing of 12 psychological mechanisms that may promote the process. These are:

- personal victimization;
- political grievance;
- the power of love (attachment to ingroup);
- the slippery slope, characterized by progressive self-persuasion into increasingly violent actions;
- extremity shift in like-minded groups, which is the tendency for groups to polarize their opinions by considering more congruent arguments in favor of a given position;
- cohesion under isolation and threat, which fosters behavioral compliance and value consensus;
- competition for the same base of support, resulting in groups progressively choosing more radical means to gain status and supporters;
- condensation, in which activists abandon radical groups because of state repression, thus causing the group to increasingly be made up of radical members;
- fissioning, in which radical groups splinter into more radical ones because they disagree over the means to reach their goals;
- jujitsu politics, in which terrorists provoke disproportionate and violent repressive actions from the government to gain new sympathizers;
- hate, whereby the enemy is increasingly seen as less than human, thus legitimizing the use of violence (see Bandura, 1990, 1999); and
- martyrdom, which relies on the perception of selflessness for the cause and on continuing the fight so those that sacrificed themselves have not died in vain.

McCauley and Moskalenko's (2008) items are readily classifiable within the 3N framework. Thus, personal victimization and political grievance belong with the significance loss part of our model, whereas the power of love, group polarization, cohesion under isolation, and competition pertain to group dynamics that represent the network component. Persuasion by cogent arguments alludes to the narrative part of our model, and the slippery slope depicts increasing persuasion by the violence-justifying narrative.

In summary, the various psychological models of radicalization contain elements of our 3N conceptualization; they invariably address the need component through mention of grievances and deprivations; they contain the narrative component through mention of persuasion and perception (e.g. a paranoid view of the world); and they bring in the network element through a discussion of cohesion, group polarization, and social influence. In a sense then, our present framework constitutes an integration of prior psychological proposals concerning the nature of radicalization. We affirm the essential role of individual *needs* and the ideological narratives that identify and justify the *means* to addressing those needs. Those narratives are then validated by the social context of network interaction. Lastly, rewards are dispensed in the form of status and significance to those who put the narrative's injunctions into action.

Rational Actor Model

The view that violent extremism isn't necessarily prompted by psychopathology (e.g., Atran, 2003, Post et al., 2009) raises the question of whether or not extremists' actions may be considered *calculated* decisions geared toward reaching specific sociopolitical goals. The rational actor model, derived from economics, postulates that "choices made by a terrorist group are the result of an economic optimization process [...] where terrorist group uses its scarce resources to maximize its expected utility" (Enders & Su, 2007, p. 35). To be sure, this means that violent extremists engage in a cost and benefit analysis to strategically utilize their limited resources—financial assets, weapons, buildings, and personnel—to attain their goals.

Former CIA agent Michael Scheuer argues that terrorist organizations (e.g., Al Qaeda) are *calculating* adversaries whose activities aim to achieve specific political outcomes (Scheuer, 2004, see also Crenshaw, 1990), such as eradicating US military presence in the Arabian Peninsula and ending US exploitation of energy sources in Muslim-dominated countries. Similarly, in his influential book titled *Dying to Win*, Pape (2006) asserts that "modern suicide is best understood as an extreme strategy for national liberation against democracies with troops that pose an imminent threat to control the territory the terrorists view as their homeland" (p. 23). Pape provides data to support the claims that suicide terrorism is mainly a strategic, as compared to an irrational, phenomenon. He observes that suicide attacks tend to occur in coordinated, versus isolated and randomly timed, campaigns aimed at making political gains by attacking democracies.

The rational actor model has also been used by Perry, Berrebi, Brown, Hollywood, and Jaycocks (2013) in predicting the location of suicide attacks—precious information to be sure. These authors concluded

> Attackers would trade off between risk (of carrying out the attack) and reward (numbers of casualties). Suicide bombers targeted accessible crowds . . . attackers were not simply targeting groups of people at random. First, they were very repetitive in making target decisions . . . attacks most often targeted not just places where people congregate but places that were *well known*. (pp. 54–55; emphasis in original)

In support of the idea that terrorism is a rational strategy, scholars have also noted that terrorism is often effective in reaching its goals. Pape (2006), for example, reports that 7 out of 13 suicide bombing campaigns between 1983 and 2003 led to political concessions from the state. Among these successful campaigns was that of the Irish Republican Army that precipitated accommodations leading to the Irish Free State (established in 1922) and Hizballah's suicide bombing campaign of 1983–1985, which directly led to the American, French, and Israeli withdrawal from Lebanon and establishment of a Shi'a-controlled society in major parts of this country. In sum, radicalized groups looking for a way to change the political status quo are likely to engage in terrorism because it represents an effective means at their disposal.

In discussing the rational model, it may be helpful to distinguish between the organizational and the individual levels of analysis. For example, at the organizational level, it may seem quite rational to dispatch suicide attackers, a relatively inexpensive and effective strategy, but it is more difficult, perhaps, to understand the rationality of individuals' sacrificing their lives in service of an organization. From the present perspective, however, all individual actions are momentarily and subjectively "rational" as well, in the sense that they constitute (subjectively) the best means to an individual's goals (Kruglanski & Orehek, 2009). According to our theory, the individuals' personal goal that underpins their radicalization is the attainment of personal significance. The individual may see suicidal attack and self-sacrifice, on behalf of a cherished cause, as a superior way to personal significance. In that sense, not only organizational strategies but also members' acts of self-sacrifice may be considered rational.

Consistent with the foregoing notions, Scott Atran and colleagues have developed an impressive cross-cultural research program evincing that individuals motivated to defend sacred values display formidable willingness to engage in extremely costly forms of self-sacrifice. Defined as "non-negotiable preferences whose defense compels action beyond evident reason . . . regardless of risks or costs" (Atran & Sheikh, 2015, p. 401), sacred values encompass a wide range of religious ideological beliefs (e.g., Islam, Christianism, or ancestral land) and secular ideological beliefs (e.g., human rights or democracy). Atran and colleagues refer to people adhering to sacred values as "devoted actors" (Atran 2016; Atran, Axelrod, & Davis, 2007). According to their research, devoted actors are deontic, meaning that they behave based on what feels morally right, as opposed to following an utilitarian cost and benefit calculus. Notably, devoted actors are vehemently opposed to trading off their sacred values for material incentives. Proposing such a compromise often backfires, resulting in devoted actors becoming even more willing to use violence to defend their values (Dehghani et al., 2010; Ginges Atran, Medin, & Shikaki, 2007). This intransigence and iron will to protect sacred values have been put forward to explain how, across history, revolutionary movements have been able to triumph over more potent and organized foes such as the military or the police (e.g., Arreguin-Toft, 2001; Atran & Ginges, 2012).

It is through their group membership that people become devoted actors (Atran & Sheikh, 2015). When they are psychologically invested in a group, their identity *fuses* with that of the group—the two collapse into one. As this process unfolds, ties between group members become stronger, family-like, making people more susceptible of adhering to the group's values, norms, and beliefs (Swann et al., 2014). Because the individual's identity is attached to the group, the group's values become sacred—nonnegotiable and upheld at all cost (Atran & Sheikh, 2015). From this standpoint, defense of sacred values bestows personal significance and glory through the group's recognition.

The devoted actor hypothesis has received substantial empirical support. In one particular study, Moroccans who considered the imposition of sharia a sacred value reported greater willingness to die for sharia and support militant jihad in comparison to those that did not believe in such value (Sheikh, Gomez, & Atran, 2016). This effect was even stronger for individuals' whose identity was fused with a kin-like group of friends. In a subsequent study, the interaction between sacred values and group-identity fusion was stronger for individuals whose democratic values were considered under threat (e.g., Spaniards considering the imposition of sharia in Spain). In this context, individuals considered violence and self-sacrifice as the best means to defend their ideological beliefs.

From perspective of means–end rationality, a successful counterterrorism strategy would consist of increasing the costs associated with committing an act of terrorism, and/or reducing its perceived benefits. At the level of the individual, this would amount to convincing potential radicals that extremism not only will not advance their quest for significance but is also likely to bring about shame and ignominy. In so far as glory partially depends on the organization's success in attaining its goals, to which the individuals may have considered contributing, defeating the organization and causing it to fail may dim the luster that joining it may have possessed. For instance, defeating the Islamic State (IS) and reversing its conquests may decrease its appeal to potential recruits and lessen the perception that fighting on its behalf would bring honor and respect.

Compelling arguments from revered authorities that the actions the organization demands are contrary to sacred values and moral dictates (e.g., of Islam as a religion) may undermine the recruits' conviction that carrying out those acts will result in enhanced significance. Finally, offering alternative ways to significance (e.g., by providing the means to become a respected and contributing member of society) may also decrease individuals' dependence on extremist violence as a route to significance.

Critiques of rational actor theories of violent extremism impose external criteria of rationality on others' behavior. Behavior of violent extremists is deemed "irrational" because they are prepared to sacrifice needs that most of us deem essential, including the readiness to give up one's life for a cause that most people cannot identify with. But such analysis commits the "objectivist fallacy" in that it assumes that the perceiver's ends and needs are universal and whoever does not subscribe to them is, therefore, irrational.

Major theorists of rationality—notably, the German sociologist Max Weber, the French sociologist Emile Durkheim, or the American psychologist Herbert Simon—defined rationality as the choice of effective means to one's own ends that might not be the ends of others (for discussion, see Kruglanski & Orehek, 2009). This conception does not prejudge what those ends are and what means are effective to advancing them. From the present perspective, both ends and means are subjective and idiosyncratic. Sacrificing one's life for the glory of martyrdom may strike us as contrary to *our* specific ends and hence irrational. But for an individual in pursuit of significance— one who believes self-sacrifice is a superior means to that end—martyrdom is wholly rational and sensible.

Social Network Theory

At the heart of the social network theory of extremism is the idea that radicalization and collective political action are intimately related to interpersonal relationships and connections to others who are already radicalized (e.g., Dean, 2007; Ressler, 2006). This notion, central to several radicalization models, is studied via a unique analytical strategy derived from the mathematical principles of graph theory (Harary, 1969; Harary & Norman, 1953), referred to as the *social network analysis*. By investigating members of radical organizations, represented by intersecting lines on a graph or "nodes," and the social ties that unite them, such analysis aims to discover the workings of terrorist organizations. Aspects of ties in social networks may represent several relationship characteristics such as their directionality (e.g., asymmetry of influence), frequency, and intensity. Collectively, connections between nodes serve to quantify the amount of interrelatedness among its constituents, known as the *density* of the network, and *centrality* of actors, or hubs of influence, within the organization.

In the last decade, observations guided by social network analysis have revealed that a growing proportion of violent attacks from political groups were largely orchestrated by small, informal, dynamic social groups, rather than by rigid hierarchal paramilitary organizations (McAllister, 2004; Raufer, 2003; Sageman 2004). Commenting on the radicalization of young Muslims in the West, Sageman (2007) noted that often this happens in "small groups of friends and relatives, who spontaneously self-organize into groups that later turn to terrorism" (p. 1). Subsequently, Sageman (2008) used the term "leaderless jihad," and Michael (2012) used the term *leaderless resistance* to describe decentralized homegrown Islamist terrorist organizations of the 21st century.

In support of this approach, Sageman (2008) reported that for Al Qaeda "about two thirds of the people in the sample were friends with other people who joined together or already had some social connection to people engaged in terrorism" (p. 66). In her research with the Brigate Rosse, della Porta (1988) reaches a similar conclusion. She reports that 69% (843 out of 1,214) of Italian left-wing militants who joined an underground group had been friends with at least one member before joining. One reason brought forth by social network theorists to explain the relevance of social ties to violent extremism is that friends and family members share strong social bonds that foster trust and organizational commitment (Krebs, 2002; Lin, 2001; Qin, Xu, Hu, Sageman, & Chen, 2005; Sageman, 2004), so essential to clandestine organizations. With these factors in place, social contagion and the probability of engaging in risky behaviors become more acute (Centola & Macy, 2007). This could potentially explain why terrorists have repeatedly appeared in pairs of intimates, siblings in particular: for example, the Tsarnaev brothers of the Boston bombings, the Kouachi brothers of the Paris Charlie Hebdo attacks, and the Bakraoui brothers of the Brussels attacks, not to mention that 6 of the 19 9/11 hijackers were also brothers.

Espousing a different view, Scott and Carrington (2011) proposed that close-knit organizational structures are not necessarily optimal for terrorists as radical groups are inherently confronted with a trade-off between efficiency and security. Specifically, these authors concur that "dense cohesive networks facilitate coordination within the group, increase group compliance, are less likely to be infiltrated by outsiders, and are difficult to destabilize" (p. 259). Nonetheless, dense social networks can also compromise the security of the organization. If one member is captured, he or she can release vital information about all the others (Xu, Marshall, Kaza, & Chen, 2004). In contrast, loosely connected networks are more susceptible to betrayal by other members, but betrayal may be less devastating in its consequences for the group because the members don't know as much information about each other as they would if there were in a close-knit group and therefore cannot provide that information to authorities (Scott & Carrington, 2011).

To explain how individuals radicalize, Sageman (2007) proposed a bottom–up radicalization process that, in its application to Islamist extremism, is characterized by four stages, which do not necessarily happen in a uniform sequence:

- a sense of moral outrage;
- the outrage interpreted as a "war against Islam";
- the resonance of moral outrage with personal experience; and
- mobilization through networks, resulting in further radicalization due to intra-group dynamics.

Sageman's (2007) analysis shares important elements in common with our present conceptualization. Specifically, the resonance of moral outrage with personal experience is reminiscent of the individual's experience of significance loss, whether through personal humiliations or through dishonor suffered by one's group. Interpretation of the humiliation in terms of the "war on Islam" pertains to the ideological narrative element, and the mobilization through group dynamics pertains to the network element of our theory.

More generally, to the extent that social network analyses bear on the rad-icalization process (rather than addressing issues of group effectiveness, etc.), they coincide with the present theory that assigns the network element an important function in cementing individuals' acceptance of the violence–significance link that in our view epitomizes radicalization.

Networking through Media

Social networks are critical to radicalization given the current importance of social media and the wealth of radical information readily available on the Internet (e.g., bomb recipes, radical preaching, tactical information). According to Gabriel Weimann, a communication expert at Haifa University, terrorist groups have predominantly moved their propaganda efforts to cy-berspace. His research focused on the monitoring of terrorists' Web activi-ties over the last decades, revealing that in 1998 there were approximately 12 radical websites, whereas today their number exceeds 9,800 (Weimann, 2014; also see Luxner, 2014). Virtually all radical movements around the world have joined the bandwagon—including IS, Al Qaeda, the Colombian National Liberation Army, the Japanese Red Army, the Kurdish Workers' Party, Boko Haram, and more—and are making pervasive use of varied social media platforms.

To propagate their message and attract new recruits, some terrorist groups have even started their own online magazines. One of the most notorious is *Inspire*, Al Qaeda's English-language online publication. In one of its issues, jihadists in the United States are encouraged to initiate a new wave of terror using car bomb attacks in metropolitan areas. Attesting to the popularity of this magazine, several jihadists and lone wolves have been arrested while in its possession, including Dzhokhar Tsarnaev, Jose Pimentel, and Naser Jason Abdo. Alongside digital propaganda calling to jihad on American and British soil, Al Qaeda has also published the *Lone Mujahid Pocketbook*, a weapon tutorial similar to the *Anarchist Cookbook*, which provides detailed how-to instructions for creating a deadly arsenal using common household objects. For example, a segment of this document that received wide media attention describes "how to make a bomb in the kitchen of your mom" using a pressure cooker—that recipe was followed to a T by the Tsarnaev brothers in their preparations for the Boston Marathon bombings.

Although websites, forums, and online magazines are an important part of radicalization, Weimann (2014) notes that terrorist groups have concentrated their efforts on popular online platforms such as YouTube, Facebook, Twitter, and Instagram. These highly interactive platforms are easy to access, free, and mostly unregulated. Across these platforms, anyone can follow their "favorite" radical groups by reading their press releases (e.g., eulogy of "martyrs"), commenting on their photos, and watching their propaganda videos. When used wisely, social media can constitute an enormously effective recruitment tool. Terrorist organizations such as IS have been conspicuously successful at drawing massive attention to their message. In August 2014, they widely disseminated the videotaped execution of the American journalist James Wright Foley. Their film, edited in a professional style, was posted on YouTube and within minutes became "viral" and spread to numerous online platforms worldwide. IS released this video proclaiming that other American journalists would die if the United States did not stop using airstrikes over their positions in Iraq. Soon thereafter, IS militants published another video featuring the execution of the American journalist Steven Joel Sotloff and made similar demands, this time directly addressed at President Barack Obama.

Unquestionably, the appeal of social media as a tool of radicalization stems partly from the organizations' ability to use them as a way of reaching young, technology-savvy audiences. Additionally, however, social media allows for "narrowcasting"—the antonym of broadcasting—whereby terrorist organizations "aim messages at specific segments of the public defined by values, preferences, demographic attributes, or subscription" (Weimann, 2014, p. 3). Thus, terrorist organizations can carefully tailor their messages to their varied audiences as any political party or company would do to advertise a message or a product. If used appropriately, the receiver is more likely to be attuned to the sender's message, which will have been tailored narrowly to her or his specific characteristics, increasing its recruiting mobilization potential.

The interactive nature of social media contributes to the development of a strong emotional bond, a sense of shared reality, and a communion with members of terrorist organizations. Connecting psychologically with extremist networks is substantially facilitated by these social platforms, thus overcoming the many difficulties involved in physically meeting radically minded individuals and recruiters to radical organizations. Ultimately, the shared reality that the social media afford serves to validate the narrative that touts violence as a means to significance as well as dispensing rewards of admiration and respect to those who implemented the narrative by fighting and dying for the cause that it sets forth.

Social Movement Theory

Societies are characterized by an ebb and flow of conflicts and reforms: a perpetual battle between groups espousing different ideological beliefs. Social movement theory defines social movements as "networks of individuals and organizations that have common identities and conflictual aims that use unconventional means" (della Porta 2013, p. 14; see della Porta, 2006, Chapter 1) such as marches, boycotts, occupations, roadblocks, violent protest, and bombings.

According to this approach, "political violence can be explained as an outcome of the interactions between social movements and their opponents" (della Porta, 2013, p. 15). It further proposes that "when feeling excluded from the political system, social movements tend to escalate their demands, both elaborating radical frames of meaning and taking on a revolutionary rhetoric" (della Porta, 2013, p. 207). In her 2013 book, *Clandestine Political Violence*, della Porta proposes a model of radicalization characterized by three mechanisms that foster radical violence (onset factors) and four mechanisms that maintain it (persistence factors). A brief look at della Porta's factors provides a further understanding of the social movement theory and how it relates to our 3N framework.

Onset Factors

Escalating Policing

Based on her extensive research on radical groups, della Porta (2013) notes that "violence develops as a reaction to hard and indiscriminate repression, considered by the challengers as brutal and deeply unjust" (p. 30). To retaliate, protesters use more radical means to have their voices heard. Importantly, the willingness to fight back is moderated by protesters' identification with their group (Davenport, 2005; della Porta & Piazza, 2008). When protesters use more radical means, the police adopts harsher means of repression. Progressively, a *danse macabre* unfolds between protesters and the police, thus promoting the escalation of violence and fostering the perception that there is no other way out and that, therefore, violence is inevitable.

Whereas della Porta's account is descriptive, it hints at the essential factors that promote radicalization. The "hard," "indiscriminate," and "deeply unjust" repression suggests the humiliation of those who are its targets, and the use of violent means to have one's voice heard suggests the development of a narrative that ties violence to significance. Finally, the emphasis on identification with the group suggests importance of the network and its narrative in facilitating members' radicalization.

Competitive Escalation

Violence often develops in situations of competition both within and between social movements. When social movements compete for limited resources and supporters, outbidding competing organizations by using more radical tactics becomes a means to capture these resources while impressing and potentially gaining future supporters. As a consequence, individuals radicalize through progressive exposure to violent political actions. Competition can also occur within the organization due to personal and ideological conflicts that can cause the group to split and adopt more radical actions.

From the present perspective, outbidding and competition via increasingly radical tactics may signal the group's commitment to the cause and willingness to undergo ever greater sacrifices on its behalf, thus espousing a narrative that promises ever greater significance to the group's members.

Activation of a Militant Network

As mentioned earlier, della Porta (1988) reports that 69% of Italian left-wing militants that joined an underground group had at least one friend who was also a member. Sageman (2008) reported similar numbers for Al Qaeda. These observations clearly support the importance of social networks and the contention that people are socialized into violence (e.g., Bandura, 1990).

Persistence Factors

Organizational Compartmentalization

Increasing repression and decreasing popular support may alter the structure and dynamic of social movements. Under these circumstances, social movements tend to become compartmentalized into small cells isolated from outside influence. As a consequence, individuals have fewer opportunities to debate radical violence or be exposed to divergent opinions, keeping them radicalized. Eventually, these small cells may have divergent opinions concerning the best means for pursuing the struggle, potentially splintering into even more radicalized groups. These observations underscore the importance of shared reality in violent political networks and factors that may undermine it, thus affecting the size of the network and its ability to consensually validate a given, violence-supporting, narrative.

Action Militarization

As the spiral of violence continues, the conflict reaches a tipping point where the number of comrades that have fallen into the hands of the enemy is too great and adhering to nonviolent means becomes inconceivable. Ultimately, the group resorts to assassinations, bombings, and other war-like actions to attain its goal (della Porta, 2006, 2013). These developments describe the gradual evolution of the group's (or movement's) narrative as to what means may ultimately afford significance (e.g. by avenging the fallen comrades) and illustrate the seemingly inevitable descent into violence, the most primordial means of asserting one's dominance over others through causing them physical harm.

Ideological Encapsulation

In fact, della Porta (2013) explicitly discusses the evolution of radical narratives as the conflict unfolds. Specifically, through repression and isolation from outside influence, social movements' narratives tend to become Manichean and categorical, lacking in nuance and portraying reality in stark black and white, good and evil contrasts. Progressively, outgroup members are dehumanized, and ingroup members are perceived as morally superior. These ideological developments serve to justify violence as a means of asserting significance through courageous protection of the good from the evil.

Militant Enclosure

The last mechanism of radicalization discussed by della Porta (2013) is militant enclosure. It suggests that in social movements individuals' emotional lives tend to be fulfilled exclusively through other group members. These strong affective bonds foster conformism and alter members' belief system because other members are their sole reference points.

Connection to the 3N Framework

In summary, social movement theory has significant overlap with the 3N framework. First, the initial sense of grievance and disgruntlement that may motivate individuals to start a protest movement represent a felt significance loss—the need element—that is exacerbated by the brutal repression by the state.

Second, competitive escalation relates to the idea that the increasingly radical means adopted by some groups in competition with others signify greater commitment to the cause, presumably conveyed by embarking on extreme actions, affording greater significance to those who exhibit such commitment. Third, encapsulation and enclosure of the militant group ensure that its ideological narrative isn't questioned by different views and hence that it is consensually validated within the group. The network element concerns the friends and acquaintances that introduce the individual to the group and influence her or him to embrace the group narrative.

Beyond the 3N elements that it contains, an important contribution of social movement theory to understanding radicalization is its emphasis on the *unfolding process*, including the spiraling escalation of commitment to the group and the accelerating gravitation to violence as consequence of the group's interaction with other entities in its social environment, specifically law enforcement agencies and competing extremist groups.

Indeed, one strength of social movement theory is that it conceptualizes radicalization as a multilevel process involving an interplay between macro, meso, and micro factors. Accordingly, it offers a comprehensive analysis of how individual dynamics are influenced by their social contexts, a common shortcoming of other approaches.

Though the case study methodology adopted by social movement researchers allows for rich descriptions of radicalization and political violence, it lacks control conditions that would allow the isolation of critical variables from the variety of attributes present in any specific case. Another problematic aspect concerns the representativeness of cases selected for analysis: Larger samples of cases would allow for more systematic comparisons and improve the generalizability of a social movement's findings. In short, though social movement theory is conceptually appealing, its main weakness concerns reliance on qualitative data and a lack of a firm empirical basis for its assertions.

Summary

Social scientists have approached the issue of radicalization from diverse angles and perspectives. In this chapter, we reviewed major social science theories of this phenomenon and related them to our present 3N model. Throughout the discussion, it was apparent that previous conceptualizations of radicalization shared important elements in common with our analysis; in that sense, the latter builds on past insights and connects the dots contributed by other scholars.

Whereas prior models offer interesting insights into an unfolding process of radicalization (e.g., outbidding and splintering of groups, the slippery slope toward elevated violence), our model offers an integrative conception of the essential parameters of the process. Such parameters are seen to underlie numerous more detailed analyses offered in prior theories. For instance, whereas some previous psychological theories focused on problematic personality development reducing individuals' sense of self-worth, we view developmental issues as one among several possible sources of experienced insignificance. Also, whereas some models highlighted one element in particular (e.g., the network element or the ideological element), our model suggests that all three elements are typically involved in radicalization to some degree.

To reiterate our analysis suggests that to radicalize: (a) the individual typically commits to the attainment of significance and is ready to sacrifice to this end other common needs and concerns; (b) that he or she embraces an ideological narrative that sanctions and justifies violence and terrorism as ways of attaining significance; which typically is facilitated by (c) the individual's embeddedness in a social network whose shared reality reinforces the primacy of the significance goal and of violence as means to that goal's attainment. Whereas prior theories typically identified some specific ways in which these ingredients may come together, our 3N model identifies what they essentially consist of.

References

Akhtar, S. (1999). The psychodynamic dimension of terrorism. *Psychiatric Annals, 29,* 350–355.

Arreguin-Toft, I. (2001). How the weak win wars: A theory of asymmetric conflict. *International Security, 26,* 93–128.

Atran, S. (2003). Genesis of suicide terrorism. *Science, 299,* 1534–1539.

Atran, S. (2016). The devoted actor: unconditional commitment and intractable conflict across cultures. *Current Anthropology, 57,* S000.

Atran, S., Axelrod, R., & Davis, R. (2007). Sacred barriers to conflict resolution. *Science, 317,* 1039–1040.

Atran, S., & Ginges, J. (2012). Religious and sacred imperatives in human conflict. *Science, 336,* 855–857.

Atran, S., & Sageman, M. (2006). Connecting the dots. *Bulletin of the Atomic Scientists, 62,* 68.

Atran, S., & Sheikh, H. (2015). Dangerous terrorists as devoted actors. In V. Zeigler-Hill, L. Welling, & T. Shackelford (Eds.), *Evolutionary perspectives on social psychology* (pp. 401–416). New York, NY: Springer.

Bandura, A. (1990). Mechanisms of moral disengagement. In W. Reich (Ed.), *Origins of terrorism: Psychologies, ideologies, theologies, states of mind* (pp. 161–191). Cambridge, England: Cambridge University Press.

Bandura, A. (1999). Moral disengagement in the perpetration of inhumanities. *Personality and Social Psychology Review*, 3, 193–209.

Berkowitz, L. (1993). *Aggression: Its causes, consequences, and control.* New York, NY: McGraw-Hill Book Company.

Berrebi, C. (2007). Evidence about the link between education, poverty, and terrorism among Palestinians. *Peace Economics, Peace Science and Public Policy 13*(1), art. 2. https://doi.org/10.2202/1554-8597.1101

Bjørgo, T. (Ed.). (2005). *Root causes of terrorism: Myths, realities and paths forward.* London, England: Routledge.

Böllinger, L. (1981). Die entwicklung zu terroristischem handeln als psychosozialer prozess: begegnungen mit beteiligten. In H. Jäger, G. Schmidtchen, & L. Süllwold (Eds.). *Analyzen zum terrorismus 2: Lebenslaufanalysen*, (pp. 175–231), Darmstadt, Germany: DeutscherVerlag.

Centola, D., & Macy, M. (2007). Complex contagions and the weakness of long ties. *American Journal of Sociology*, 113, 702–734.

Crayton, J. W. (1983). Terrorism and the psychology of the self. In L. Z. Freedman & Y. Alexander (Eds.), *Perspectives on terrorism* (pp. 33–41). Wilmington, DE: Scholarly Resources.

Crenshaw, M. (1990). Questions to be answered, research to be done, knowledge to be applied. In W. Reich (Ed.), *Origins of terrorism: Psychologies, ideologies, theologies, states of mind* (pp. 247–260). Cambridge, England: Cambridge University Press.

Davenport, C. (2005). Repression and mobilization: Insights from political science and sociology. In C. Davenport, H. Johnston, & C. Mueller (Eds.), *Repression and mobilization: Social movements, protest, and contention* (pp. vii–xxxi). Minneapolis, MN: University of Minnesota Press.

Dean, G. (2007). Criminal profiling in a terrorism context. In R. Kocsis (Ed.) *Criminal profiling: International perspectives in theory, practice & research* (pp. 169–188). Totowa, NJ: Humana.

Dehghani, M., Atran, S., Iliev, R., Sachdeva, S., Medin, D., & Ginges, J. (2010). Sacred values and conflict over Iran's nuclear program. *Judgment and Decision Making, 5*, 540–546.

della Porta, D. (1988). Recruitment processes in clandestine political organizations: Italian left-wing terrorism. *International Social Movement Research, 1*, 155–169.

della Porta, D. (2006). *Social movements, political violence, and the state: A comparative analysis of Italy and Germany.* Cambridge, England: Cambridge University Press.

della Porta, D. (2013). *Clandestine political violence.* Cambridge, England: Cambridge University Press.

della, Porta, D., & Diani, M. (2006). *Social movements: An introduction.* Malden, MA: Blackwell.

della Porta, D., Piazza, G. (2008). *Voices of the valley, Voices of the straits: How protest creates community.* Oxford, England: Berghahn.

Downey, G., Mougios, V., Ayduk, O., London, B. E., & Shoda, Y. (2004). Rejection sensitivity and the defensive motivational system: Insights from the startle response to rejection cues. *Psychological Science, 15,* 668–673.

Enders, W., & Su, X. (2007). Rational terrorists and optimal network structure. *Journal of Conflict Resolution, 51,* 33–57.

Erikson, E. H. (1959). Identity and the life cycle. *Psychological Issues, 1,* 1–171.

Fearon, J. D., & Laitin, D. D. (2003). Ethnicity, insurgency, and civil war. *American Political Science Review, 97,* 75–90.

Ferracuti, F., & Bruno, F. (1981). Psychiatric aspects of terrorism in Italy. In I. Barak-Glanatz, & C. R. Huff (Eds.). *The mad, the bad and the different: Essays in honour of Simon Dinitz* (pp. 199–213). Lexington, MA: Lexington Books.

Gabbard, G. O. (2000). Psychoanalysis. In B. J. Sadock & V. A. Sadock (Eds.), *Kaplan and Sadock's comprehensive textbook of psychiatry* (7th ed., pp. 563–607). Philadelphia, PA: Lippincott Williams & Wilkins.

Ginges, J., Atran, S., Medin, D., & Shikaki, K. (2007). Sacred bounds on rational resolution of violent political conflict. *Proceedings of the National Academy of Sciences, 104,* 7357–7360.

Gurr T. R. (1970). *Why men rebel.* Princeton, NJ: Princeton University Press.

Hafez, M., & Mullins, C. (2015). The radicalization puzzle: A theoretical synthesis of empirical approaches to homegrown extremism. *Studies in Conflict and Terrorism, 38,* 958–975.

Harary, F. (1969). *Graph theory.* Reading, MA: Addison Wesley.

Harary, F., & Norman, R. Z. (1953). *Graph Theory as a mathematical model in social science.* Ann Arbor, MI: University of Michigan Press.

Horgan, J. (2003). The search for the terrorist personality. In A. Silke (Ed.), *Terrorists, victims and society: Psychological perspectives on terrorism and its consequences* (pp. 3–27). Chichester, England: Wiley.

Horgan, J. (2004). *The psychology of terrorism.* London, England: Routledge.

Horgan J. (2008). From profiles to pathways and roots to routes: Perspectives from psychology on radicalisation into terrorism. *Annals of the American Academy of Political and Social Science, 618,* 80–94.

Horney, K. (1937). *The neurotic personality of our time.* New York, NY: W. W. Norton.

Kennedy, M. (1998). The 21st century conditions likely to inspire terrorism. In H. W. Kushner (Eds.), *The future of terrorism: Violence in the new millennium* (pp. 185–207). London, England: SAGE.

Kohut, H. (1972). Thoughts on narcissism and narcissistic rage. *Psychoanalytic Study of the Child, 27,* 360–400.

Kohut, H. (1978). *The search for the self.* New York, NY: International Universities Press.

Krebs, V. E. (2002). Mapping networks of terrorist cells. *Connections, 24,* 43–52.

Krueger, A. B., & Laitin, D. D. (2003). Kto kogo? A cross-country study of the origins and targets of terrorism. In P. Keefer & N. Loayza (Eds.), *Terrorism, economic development, and political openness* (pp. 148–173). Cambridge, England: Cambridge University Press.

Krueger, A. B., & Malečková, J. (2002). Does poverty cause terrorism? *New Republic, 226,* 27–33.

Krueger, A. B., & Malečková, J. (2003). Education, poverty and terrorism: Is there a causal connection? *The Journal of Economic Perspectives, 17,* 119–144.

Kruglanski, A. W., & Orehek, E. (2009). Toward a relativity theory of rationality. *Social Cognition, 27,* 639.

Lankford, A. (2013). *The myth of martyrdom: What really drives suicide bombers, rampage shooters, and other self-destructive killers.* Basingstoke, England: Palgrave Macmillan.

Laqueur, W. (1987). *The age of terrorism.* Boston, MA: Little, Brown.

Lin, N. (2001). Building a network theory of social capital. In N. Lin, K. Cook, & R. S. Burt (Eds.), *Social capital: Theory and research* (pp. 3–29). New York, NY: Aldine De Gruyter.

Luxner, L. (2014, May 7). Expert talks Islamic inspired cyberterrorism. *Washington Jewish Week.* Retrieved from http://washingtonjewishweek.com/12104/expert-warns-of-islamic-inspired-cyberterrorism/

McAllister, B. (2004). Al Qaeda and the innovative firm: demythologizing the network. *Studies in Conflict & Terrorism, 27,* 297–319.

McCauley, C., & Moskalenko, S. (2008). Mechanisms of political radicalization: Pathways toward terrorism. *Terrorism and Political Violence, 20,* 415–433.

Merari, A. (2010). *Driven to death: Psychological and social aspects of suicide terrorism.* Oxford, England: Oxford University Press.

Merari, A., & Friedland, N. (1985). Social psychological aspects of political terrorism. *Applied Social Psychology Annual, 6,* 185–205.

Michael, G. (2012). *Lone wolf terror and the rise of leaderless resistance.* Nashville, TN: Vanderbilt University Press.

Morf, G. (1970). *Terror in Quebec: Cases studies of the FLQ.* Toronto, ON: Clarke, Irwin.

Newman, E. (2006). Exploring the "root causes" of terrorism. *Studies in Conflict & Terrorism, 29,* 749–772.

Nisbett, R. E., & Cohen, D. (1996). *Culture of honor: The psychology of violence in the south.* Boulder, CO: Westview.

Pape, R. (2006). *Dying to win: The strategic logic of suicide terrorism.* New York, NY: Random House.

Perry, W. L., Berrebi, C., Brown, R. A., Hollywood, J., & Jaycocks, A. (2013). *Predicting suicide attacks: Integrating spatial, temporal, and social features of terrorist attack targets.* Santa Monica, CA: Rand.

Post, J. M. (1985). Individual and group dynamics of terrorist behavior. In P. Pichot, P. Berner, R. Wolf, & K. Thau (Eds.), *Psychiatry* (pp. 93–106). Boston, MA: Springer.

Post, J. M., Ali, F., Henderson, S. W., Shanfield, S., Victoroff, J., & Weine, S. (2009). The psychology of suicide terrorism. *Psychiatry, 72,* 13–31.

Qin, J., Xu, J. J., Hu, D., Sageman, M., & Chen, H. (2005). Analyzing terrorist networks: A case study of the global Salafi jihad network. In P. Kantor, F. Roberts,

F. Y. Wang, & R. C. Merkle (Eds.) *Intelligence and security informatics* (pp. 287–304). Berlin, Germany: Springer

Radicalization of global Islamist terrorists before the Senate Committee on Homeland Security and Government Affairs, 110th Congr. 1st sess. (2007) (Testimony of Marc Sageman). Retrieved from http://www.hsgac.senate.gov/download/062707sageman

Raufer, X. (2003). Al Qaeda: A different diagnosis. *Studies in Conflict & Terrorism, 26,* 391–398.

Ressler, S. (2006). Social network analysis as an approach to combat terrorism: Past, present, and future research. *Homeland Security Affairs, 2.* art. 8. https://www.hsaj.org/articles/171

Robins, R. S., & Post, J. M. (1997). *Political paranoia: The psychopolitics of hatred.* New Haven, CT: Yale University Press.

Sageman, M. (2004). *Understanding terror networks.* Philadelphia, PA: University of Pennsylvania Press.

Sageman, M. (2008). A strategy for fighting international Islamist terrorists. *The Annals of the American Academy of Political and Social Science, 618,* 223–231.

Scheuer, M. (2004). *Imperial hubris: Why the West is losing the war on terror.* Washington, DC: Potomac Books.

Scott, J., & Carrington, P. J. (2011). *The SAGE handbook of social network analysis.* London, England: SAGE.

Sheikh, H., Gómez, Á., & Atran, S. (2016). Empirical evidence for the devoted actor model. *Current Anthropology, 57,* S204–S209.

Sidanius, J., & Pratto, F. (1999) *Social dominance: An intergroup theory of social hierarchy and oppression.* Cambridge, England: Cambridge University Press.

Silke, A. (1998). Cheshire-cat logic: The recurring theme of terrorist abnormality in psychological research. *Psychology, Crime and Law, 4,* 51–69.

Silke, A. (2003). Becoming a terrorist. In A. Silke (ed.) *Terrorists, victims and society: Psychological perspectives on terrorism and its consequences,* (pp. 29–53). Chichester, England: Wiley.

Stern, J. (2001, September 15). Being feared is not enough to keep us safe. *Washington Post,* p. A27.

Stern, J. (2003). *Terror in the name of God: Why religious militants kill.* New York, NY: Ecco.

Swann, W. B., Jr., Gómez, A., Buhrmester, M. D., López-Rodríguez, L., Jiménez, J., & Vázquez, A. (2014). Contemplating the ultimate sacrifice: Identity fusion channels pro-group affect, cognition, and moral decision-making. *Journal of Personality and Social Psychology, 106,* 713–727.

Taylor, M., & Quayle, E. (1994). *Terrorist lives,* London, England: Brassey.

Victoroff, J. (2005). The mind of the terrorist: A review and critique of psychological approaches. *Journal of Conflict Resolution, 49,* 3–42.

Weimann, G. (2014). *New terrorism and new media. Wilson Center*. Retrieved from: https://www.wilsoncenter.org/sites/default/files/new_terrorism_v3_1.pdf

Wilkinson, P. (1986). *Terrorism and the liberal state* (2nd ed.). New York, NY: New York University Press.

Xu, J., Marshall, B., Kaza, S., & Chen, H. (2004). Analyzing and visualizing criminal network dynamics: A case study. In H. Chen, R. Moore, D. D. Zeng, & J. Leavitt (Eds.), *Intelligence and security informatics proceedings* (pp. 359–377). Berlin, Germany: Springer.

Zuckerman, M. (1979). *Sensation seeking: Beyond the optimal level of arousal*. Hillsdale, NJ: Erlbaum.

Zuckerman, M. (2002). Genetics of sensation seeking. In J. Benjamin & R. P. Ebstein (Eds.), *Molecular genetics and human personality* (pp. 193–210). Washington, DC: American Psychiatric Publishing.

5 EMPIRICAL EVIDENCE FOR SIGNIFICANCE QUEST THEORY

Our conceptual framework presented in Chapter 3 suggests that radicalization comprises an interwoven chain of processes commencing with the arousal of the significance quest. This search for significance typically results from a perceived loss of it, either due to personal circumstances or perceived humiliation of the group of which one sees oneself as a member. Significance loss arouses the feelings of self-uncertainty and activates or enhances the individual's need for cognitive closure (NFC); in turn, the latter fosters the adoption of a group-centric orientation (Kruglanski, Pierro, Mannetti, & De Grada, 2006) and of a categorical ingroup narrative that vilifies the outgroup. Such fusion with the group (Swann, Gómez, Seyle, Morales, & Huici, 2009) is both empowering and obliging: It increases the individual's readiness to undergo self-sacrifices on the group's behalf and in defense of its sacred values (Atran, Sheikh, & Gomez, 2014).

Over the last decade, we have collected several types of empirical evidence relevant to the significance quest theory. We have employed different data gathering methodologies, including surveys that have yielded correlations among variables and laboratory and field experiments affording greater degree of control and warranting stronger inferences about causality. Our investigations have taken place in various world locations, including the Middle East, South and Southeast Asia, Europe, and the United States. They have addressed different aspects of our theory of radicalization and tapped different populations representing diverse ethnic and national communities, as well as detained terrorism suspects held in prisons or other detention facilities. An individual does not become radicalized overnight: The process, starting with a feeling of a loss of significance (LoS), is somewhat gradual. To understand this progression, this chapter briefly presents our empirical studies concerning the different relations in the chain leading from significance loss to violent extremism.

Significance Loss and "Collectivistic Shift"

When the significance quest is aroused, people look for ways to gratify it. This search typically entails seeking guidance from a group and its shared values and beliefs. We call this phenomenon a "collectivistic shift," representing a transition from one's individual identity to one's social identity as the member of some group. This shift has two consequences: First, it gives individuals a sense of *empowerment* that comes from identifying with a stronger, more robust, and enduring entity whose existence transcends the fragile lives of the individual members, and, second, it promotes individuals' *attunement* to the group's needs and values that, if fulfilled, would bring them significance.

The pivot to the collective sensitizes members to their obligations vis-à-vis the group and augments their readiness to serve it, undertaking sacrifices on its behalf should the need arise. An occasion to do so may present itself at times of severe conflict between the group and its perceived enemies. In those circumstances, standing up and fighting for the group by unleashing violence against its detractors may be seen as a sacred duty. Fulfilling this duty bestows great honor upon individuals, thus boosting their sense of personal significance. In what follows, we review studies that bear on those various links in the significance quest chain, starting with the hypothesized link between significance loss and collectivism.

Life Failures and Collectivism

In an Internet survey of 12 Arab countries, Pakistan, and Indonesia, carried out by Maryland's National Consortium for the Study of Terrorism and Responses to Terrorism (START), participants indicated their agreement with the statement, "I have been successful in achieving my personal and individual goals." In reviewing the survey, we found that participants who reported *lower life success* and, hence, had presumably experienced a significance loss, tended more to self-identify as *members of collectives* (i.e., their nation or religion) rather than as individuals (Kruglanski, Gelfand, & Gunaratna, 2012; Orehek & Kruglanski, 2018). Specifically, they tended more to agree with the statements "A parent's major goal should be ensuring that their children serve their nation" and "A parent's major goal should be ensuring that their children serve their religion." Similarly, participants who reported lower life success tended to agree less with the statement "A parent's major goal should be ensuring that their children have good education and a chance to succeed in life," revealing their individualistic orientation.

These findings were replicated in research using representative samples of respondents from Egypt, Indonesia, and Pakistan. We also conducted a study in the United States with university students at the University of Pittsburgh. In the latter study, participants were 47% less likely to self-identify as members of their nation, compared to self-identifying as an individual, for each unit increase in personal success, and they were 45% less likely to self-identify as adherents of their religion rather than as an individual for each unit increase in personal success.

Our findings *do not* imply that religion/nationalism and failure are generally correlated, nor that religious/nationalistic individuals generally fail in their life pursuits. The research, however, does suggest that people who report lower success in attaining their goals experience a sense of insignificance and are thus disposed to embrace a collective identity, whether it be a nationalistic, social, or religious one. This identity promises significance by virtue of its strength, the touted "strength in numbers" concept. Intriguing evidence shows that individuals whose sense of personal control has been lost or reduced turn to a benevolent God or the government as a vicarious way of regaining control has been adduced by psychologist Aaron Kay and his associates (Kay, Shepherd, Blatz, Chua, & Galinsky, 2010).

Evidence consistent with the notion that lowering individuals' personal significance promotes a collectivistic orientation was also obtained in several *experimental* studies carried out at the University of Maryland (Orehek & Kruglanski, 2018). Experimental evidence is important because survey findings are correlational and, hence, indeterminate as to the causes of obtained effects. Our theory suggests a specific causal direction, namely, that it is failure that prompts individuals to execute the collectivistic shift and embrace the broader religious and national identities. But the correlational nature of the results also allows the interpretation that it was the collectivistic identity of individuals that invited failure. For example, perhaps they didn't care enough to invest in their individualistic pursuits, resulting in failure to reach their desired goals? A third variable explanation of correlational findings is also possible: Perhaps the same general factor—such as gullibility or conformity—underlies both failure and collectivistic identification, thus accounting for their correlation. Experiments manipulating failure and measuring identification are, therefore, needed to decide among these possibilities. To that end, we carried out several studies investigating the notion that LoS, instigated by the experience of failure in one's life pursuits, is associated with a collectivistic shift, measured by greater salience of one's social rather than individual identities.

In one study, participants wrote an essay describing an experience of either personal failure or success. Subsequently, we assessed their national identification as Americans by having them indicate their agreement with the statements "I am proud to be an American," "I am emotionally attached to America," and "The fact that I am American is an important part of my identity." Individuals' degree of agreement with each statement was recorded on a seven-point scales appropriately anchored at the end with the statements "very much agree" (1) and "very much disagree"(7). Individuals' responses to these measures were then averaged, and the resulting average was assumed to indicate the strength of identification as Americans. Consistent with our analysis, participants in the failure condition reported a significantly stronger identification as Americans than participants in the success condition. These findings support the notion of a *shift* to a collective identity under a lowered sense of personal significance occasioned by the recalled failure.

In another experiment, participants were given positive (success) or negative (failure) feedback concerning their performance on an experimental task involving remote semantic associations[1]; their interdependent self-construal was then assessed via Singelis's self-construal scale (1994). An interdependent self-construal refers to thinking of oneself *relationally*, in terms of connections with others, and thus reflects a collectivistic orientation. Just as predicted, participants in the negative feedback condition professed a more *interdependent* self-construal than participants in the positive feedback condition (see Figure 5.1).

In a follow-up study, participants wrote about a time in their lives when they attained an important personal goal, defining a *success* condition, or a time when they had failed to attain their goal, defining a *failure* condition. As in the prior experiment, participants then completed self-report measures, but this time of both interdependent *and* independent self-construals (Singelis, 1994). Consistent with the prior results, participants in the failure condition scored significantly higher on the *interdependence* dimension. In

1. This test typically consists of 30 to 40 questions each of which consists of three common stimulus words that appear to be unrelated. The person being tested must think of a fourth word that is somehow related to each of the first three words. For instance, the three stimulus words could be *bass, sleep* and *complex* (to which the related fourth word is *deep*).

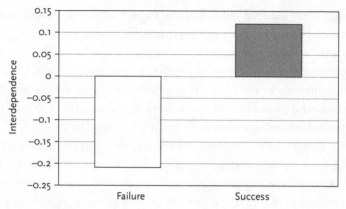

FIGURE 5.1. The effect of failure versus success condition on interdependence predominance.

addition, they also scored significantly lower on the *independence* scale than participants in the success condition.

Another experimental study in Orehek, Vazeou-Nieuwenhuis, and Kruglanski's (2017) research program investigated whether participants would prefer to work in a group rather than alone after they had experienced some type of failure. To test this prediction, participants first engaged in a computer video game. They were told that their performance on this task is a reliable predictor of their intelligence and future life success. The video game was rigged so that participants were made to either succeed or fail. Subsequently, participants were informed that they would engage in another task that offered them a chance to win a reward (a chocolate bar). They were told that they had the option of working alone on this task or working in a group. Participants in the *success* condition preferred significantly more to work *alone*, as compared to in a group, than participants in the *failure* condition.

Whereas failure may induce a sense of insignificance, as we had hypothesized, it may also induce anxiety, which is known to induce the tendency to affiliate with others (Schachter, 1959). Our next study, therefore, aimed to examine whether the psychological process that underlies our findings is indeed mediated by people's sense of personal significance. To that end, we experimentally induced perceptions of personal success versus failure through feedback on an experimental task. We then measured the extent to which participants felt that their existence was significant, as well as their sense of collectivism and individualism. The results of that study replicated the finding that failure instigated a tendency toward collectivism, whereas success induced individualism. Importantly, it was also found that the relation between the experimental conditions and a shift away from individualism in the failure condition toward individualism in the success condition was mediated by a sense of significance (measured by the Meaningful Existence subscale of the Need–Threat Scale; Williams, 2006). Specifically, individuals who scored low on the measure of "meaningful existence" tended more toward collectivism than individuals who scored high.

All in all, the evidence supports the notion that failure shifts the individuals' mindset from an independent way of thinking to an interdependent way of thinking, paving the way to engagement in collective *action*. Moreover, these tendencies are mediated in part by the sense of personal significance as it is impacted by various life experiences. In joining a group, an individual may gain feelings of empowerment, which are further supported by action on behalf of the group, that would earn her or him the group's appreciation and respect and, hence, the coveted sense of significance.

Collectivist Empowerment and Readiness for Sacrifice

Empowerment

Self-identification as a member of a larger social entity can have a buffering effect against life's failures and increase one's sense of personal empowerment and significance. Consistent with this notion, advanced by terror management theorists, is evidence that activating or making salient one's collective identity reduces one's *fear of death* (Arndt, Greenberg, Solomon, Pyszczynski, & Simon, 1997; Greenberg, Pyszczynski, Solomon, Simon, & Breus, 1994). In this context, death is nonexistence, which arguably represents the ultimate form of insignificance (Becker, 1962; Rousseau, 1762/1968).

In one relevant study (Orehek, Sasota, Kruglanski, Dechesne, & Ridgeway, 2014, Study 1) participants circled either singular first-person pronouns (i.e., I, me, and my) or collective pronouns (i.e., we, us, and ours). In prior research (Brewer & Gardner, 1996; Oyserman & Lee, 2008), this manipulation effectively instilled in participants individualistic versus collectivistic orientations, respectively: Repeatedly circling "we," "us," and "our" primes, or activates, in the individual a sense of collective identity. In contrast, repeatedly circling "I," "me," and "my" activates the person's individual identity. Consistent with the empowerment hypothesis, we found that participants exposed to the collectivistic priming scored lower on a scale of death anxiety, a measure tapping the individual's fearful preoccupation with death (Templer, 1970; see Figure 5.2).

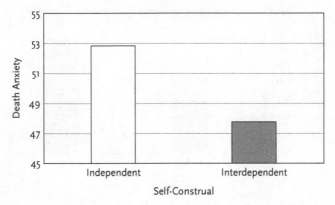

FIGURE 5.2. Experimental evidence that strengthening collective identity reduces individuals' fear of death.

Another study (Orehek et al., 2014, Study 5) used a joystick methodology (Fishbach & Shah, 2006) to implicitly assess participants' attitudes toward death under individualistic versus collectivistic priming, through the first-person plural versus singular pronouns method previously described. Prior research established that the speed of *pulling* a joystick toward oneself is proportionate to one's tendency to *approach* a stimulus, whereas the speed of *pushing* the joystick away from oneself is proportionate to individuals' tendency to *avoid* a stimulus. We found that under collectivistic, versus individualistic, priming, participants pulled the joystick faster toward themselves and pushed it away more slowly in response to death-related words flashed on the computer screen. This action indicated a stronger approach and/or lesser avoidance of death, as predicted by the empowerment effect hypothesized in our theory (see Figure 5.3).

Identical results concerning the approach and avoidance of death-related stimuli were obtained using a different manipulation of collective versus individualistic identity. In this case, participants were requested to think of what made them similar to their family and friends—known to induce an *interdependent* or collectivistic orientation—or about what made them different from their family and friends—known to induce an individualistic orientation (cf. Orehek et al., 2014, Study 2; Trafimow, Triandis, & Goto 1991, Study 2).

In another conceptual replication (Orehek et al., 2014, Study 3), we used a different operationalization of self-construal. Participants read two different versions of a story about a Sumerian warrior. In the *independent* condition, the warrior was interested in personal reward and prestige. In the

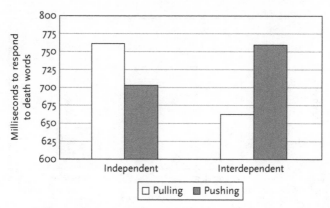

FIGURE 5.3. Milliseconds to respond to death-related words by experimental condition: action (pulling vs. pushing) and self-construal (independent vs. interdependent).

interdependent condition, he was interested, instead, in loyalty to the group. In the *no-prime* condition, participants did not read either story, nor were they presented with reading materials of any sort. It was found that whereas participants in the independent and control (no-prime) conditions did not significantly differ, those in the interdependent—in this sense collectively minded—condition exhibited significantly lower death anxiety as measured by the Templer (1970) scale, specifically designed to measure this particular emotion.

Sacrifice

Having one's collective identity activated may not only result in a sense of empowerment and a reduced fear of death but also in greater readiness to undertake risks and sacrifices on behalf of one's group. In a study by Orehek et al. (2014, Study 4), participants primed with *plural* versus *singular* pronouns exhibited high group identification, expressing greater readiness to sacrifice their lives for fellow group members—in this case, throw themselves in front of a trolley to save others in a hypothetical scenario—though not for strangers (see Figure 5.4).

Convergent evidence consistent with the hypothesized relation between collective identity and the readiness to undertake sacrifices for a cause comes from research by Swann, Gomez, Dovidio, Hart, and Jetten (2010). In several studies by these authors, individuals who were more "fused"[2] with their group

---

2. *Fused* here is defined as viewing oneself as one with the group.

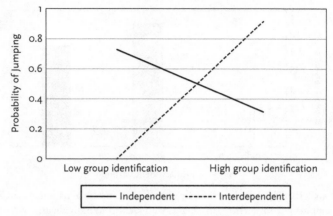

FIGURE 5.4. Predicted probability of jumping by self-construal, interdependent versus independent, and group identification (Study 4).

(as assessed through an unconscious measure of fusion) were more willing to sacrifice themselves for the group in a hypothetical trolley scenario in which participants are presented with a choice to throw oneself in front of a trolley, hence, surely dying to save other individuals (e.g., members of one's group); such "fused" individuals also endorsed more strongly the idea of fighting for the group, donated more money for a group's cause, and put more effort in performance on the group's behalf.

The readiness to fight and make sacrifices on the group's behalf reveals a pronounced support for such a fight by collectivistically minded individuals. In Internet surveys and face-to-face interviews conducted by Maryland's START center in 12 Arab countries (e.g., Egypt, Morocco), we found that individuals who self-identified as members of their religion or their nation, rather than as individuals, tended more to support the killing of American civilians (Kruglanski, Gelfand, & Gunaratna, 2012; see Figure 5.5).

This support for violence, and a willingness to sacrifice one's self, is directly tied to the connection between the LoS and a collectivistic mindset.

Significance Loss and Support for Violence

If LoS due to a personal failure or to the disparagement of one's group by its detractors invites a collectivistic shift, it may encourage individuals to fight against the group's enemies (Zartman & Anstey, 2012). Fighting and violence are primordial means of asserting dominance and superiority over

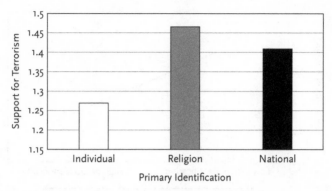

FIGURE 5.5. Participants who primarily identify as members of nation or religion more likely to support terrorism than participants who identify as individuals.

rivals; hence, the quest for significance may induce one's combativeness and the readiness to fight.

Several of our findings support the hypothesized link between significance loss and the proclivity toward fighting. For instance, in a recent survey that we conducted with detained former members of the Sri Lankan Liberation Tigers of Tamil Eelam (LTTE), mentioned in Chapter 3, we found that (a) the degree to which they felt anger in the last few weeks, (b) the degree to which they felt shame in last few weeks, and (c) the frequency of their recently feeling insignificant were all significantly correlated with support for violent actions and for aggressive struggle against the Singhalese majority (Webber et al., 2018). These findings suggest that a LoS may in the right circumstances prompt support for violence on one's group's behalf.

On Sin and Martyrdom

Loss of significance, and a subsequent willingness to support or engage in violence, may happen in diverse ways. One of those ways, particularly pertinent to young unmarried men in a religious culture, is by having "sinful" thoughts on forbidden matters. If our theory is correct, arousal of such thoughts may ultimately encourage support for sacrifice and martyrdom for one's group, designed to restore a sense of significance. Recently, we carried out an experimental study that tested this idea (Bélanger & Kruglanski, 2012).

Religious participants were exposed to neutral stimuli (toasters) or sexual images (scantily dressed women in a Victoria's Secret advertisement). The latter were assumed to arouse forbidden thoughts and, hence, induce sexual

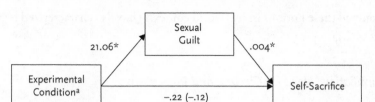

FIGURE 5.6. Indirect effect of the experimental manipulation on willingness to self-sacrifice through sexual-guilt. [a] 0 = neutral images, 1 = sexual images $*p < .05; **p < .01; ***p < .001$

guilt in our participants. We measured sexual guilt in this study through the Revised Mosher Sexual Guilt Inventory (Mosher, 1998), and we measured participants' willingness to self-sacrifice for an undefined social cause using Bélanger, Caouette, Sharvit, and Dugas's (2014) Self-Sacrifice Scale. For example, one sample item from this scale is "Under the right circumstances, I would sacrifice my life for an important cause." Consistent with our theory, religious participants who were exposed to sexual (vs. neutral) stimuli reported greater sexual guilt, which in turn was positively associated with their readiness to self-sacrifice for a cause (see Figure 5.6).

Significance Loss, Need for Closure, and Extremism

As described in Chapter 3, LoS tends to introduce a sense of self-uncertainty and confusion about one's worth. Because most persons desire to feel that they are worthy of respect, suggestions that they are not (e.g., in the form of disparagement by others) is upsetting and *inconsistent* with the self-image one would like to uphold; hence, it is confusing and induces uncertainty. This unpleasant psychological state introduces a motivation to remove it, arousing the need for certainty and closure (Kruglanski, 2004). In turn, the latter need motivates individuals to self-identify in terms of their group memberships and to embrace the group's narrative that offers desirable certainty and closure. In instances of intergroup conflict, where the outgroup is branded as the enemy, the group narrative typically includes anti-outgroup statements and encourages the ingroup members to oppose the outgroup by all means necessary.

Consistent with these notions, our work examined NFC effects on extremism and political violence. We assumed that LoS augments individuals' NFC and, hence, predisposes them to embrace a group-promoting narrative that offers closure and restores a sense of significance. Three sets of studies examined these notions in real world contexts (mostly) characterized by violent intergroup conflict.

Humiliation, Need for Closure, and Radicalism

Several studies addressed the entire chain of processes starting with the LoS, continuing with its impact on the NFC, and ending with the consequent support for extremism (Webber et al., 2017). These studies were carried out in diverse cultural contexts and addressed different geopolitical circumstances in which our research participants were embedded. Accordingly, our specific assessment of extremism differed somewhat due to the political context and nature of the violent extremism being studied. In some cases, the extremism pertained to religious fundamentalism; in other cases, it concerned ethnonationalist ideology and advocacy for violence against the perceived enemies of one's ethnic group. The questions we used to measure extremism thus varied appropriately from study to study to acknowledge and reflect those differences.

We also assessed the LoS in a number of ways, corresponding to its individual and collective sources. In some of the studies, our measures tapped personal feelings of shame and humiliation, whereas in others the measures inquired into the perceived humiliation of one's group and its mistreatment by detractors. Based on our theoretical analysis, we assumed that these different sources of significance loss would have similar impact on participants' NFC that would then manifest the same relation to extremism.

Study 1: Muslim Terrorism Suspects in the Philippines

Study 1 examined suspected Islamic militants from the Abu Sayyaf Group (ASG) imprisoned in the Manila Bicutan prison in the Philippines. According to the National Counterterrorism Center, the ASG is the most violent Islamic separatist group in the southern Philippines, whose aims are to create an independent Islamic state in western Mindanao and the Sulu Archipelago. The ASG, which in 2015 pledged allegiance to the Islamic State, has used terrorist means to advance its ends, including the kidnapping of foreign nationals, rape, child sexual assault, drug trafficking, and numerous bombings (Banlaoi, 2006). Given this background, it is not surprising that the US Department of State has labeled the ASG as a "foreign terrorist organization." Study 1 thus provided a unique opportunity to examine our variables of interest with an actual group of extremists.

For obvious logistical reasons, this particular sample limited us to a correlational design that utilized survey instruments. Furthermore, we focused in this study on LoS of the personal variety: Our reasoning for this decision was twofold. First, previous terrorism experts have specifically identified various personal circumstances as potential motivators toward extremism (e.g., Pedahzur, 2005). Second, unlike other theories that explain extreme behavior exclusively in terms of group level deprivation (see Chapter 4), our theory assumes that personal LoS would motivate individuals to seek NFC and consequently be attuned to closure providing collective narratives. This idea suggests that a confluence of personal motivation and collective narratives about group grievances combine to inspire extremism. To examine these possibilities in this study, we operationally defined LoS as individuals' personal feelings of humiliation.

Indeed, our Philippine study yielded the expected results: detainees' personal feelings of insignificance—measured by their feelings of humiliation and having been laughed at in their daily lives—was positively related to their NFC. In turn, their NFC was positively related to an Islamist Extremism Scale constructed with the assistance of Muslim clerics (see Figure 5.7) and containing items like "Jihad is the only remedy for jahliliyah (ignorance)," "Armed jihad is a personal obligation of all Muslims today," and "True Muslims should adhere strictly to the literal meaning of the Qu'ran." Specifically, the significant positive correlation between feelings of insignificance and Islamist extremism (represented by the appropriate line) was rendered nonsignificant when the relation between feelings of insignificance and NFC were controlled for statistically. This means that the relation between feelings of insignificance and Islamist extremism was *mediated* by the NFC.

Although these findings are encouraging, Study 1 only examined a religious form of extremism. Violent extremism, however, is not solely tied to

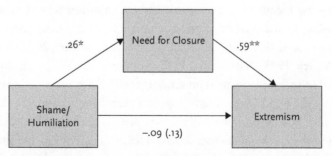

FIGURE 5.7. Indirect effect of loss of significance (shame/humiliation) on extremism through increased need for closure (Study 1). *p < .05; **p < .01, ***p < .001

a religious narrative it may also be guided by secular ideologies. Indeed, one of the most "effective" terrorist organizations to date, the LTTE, was widely regarded as secular. In Study 2, we administered surveys to a large sample of detained LTTE members to examine the hypothesized relations between these individuals' LoS, NFC, and their tendency to espouse extremist attitudes.

Study 2: Liberation Tigers of Tamil Eelam

The LTTE was officially recognized as a terrorist organization by more than 32 nations. Under the autocratic leadership of Velupillai Prabhakaran, this organization carried out a 30-year struggle, starting in 1979, against the Sinhalese majority in Sri Lanka, during which thousands of civilians lost their lives, including heads of state, politicians, journalists, and academics. In 2009, the Sri Lankan military defeated the LTTE and detained the roughly 12,000 surrendered LTTE members in rehabilitation facilities. Comprehensive efforts were made to deradicalize these individuals to reintegrate them into society.

The LTTEs cadres were assigned to rehabilitation centers according to the severity of their crimes, which was determined on the basis of, among other factors, their position and status in the LTTE organization and the number of killings they committed. Moderate- and low-risk individuals were housed in residential facilities, and high-risk individuals were imprisoned. Our study examined only high-risk individuals detained in the Boosa detention facility in Galle, Sri Lanka. This category of risk included, for instance, the LTTE Black Tigers, an elite cadre trained and responsible for more than 330 suicide missions.

As in Study 1, participants completed a series of questionnaires that tapped personal LoS, NFC, and extremism. LoS was operationalized by items that tapped personal feelings of shame. Shame and humiliation—also assessed in Study 1—are members of the same cluster of emotions related to *perceived devaluation*, and they are believed to comprise an evolutionary adaptation to the loss of social standing (Elison, 2005; Elison & Harter, 2007; Kaufman, 1992; Miller, 1993; Nathanson, 1992; Tomkins, 1963). Extremism measures used in this study focused on support for violence against the Sinhalese, tapped by the items "Armed fight[ing] is a personal obligation of all Tamils today" and "Suicide bombers will be rewarded for their deed in the afterlife." We found that as shame increased, so did levels of extremism and that NFC mediated this relationship (see Figure 5.8). As in our previous studies, the

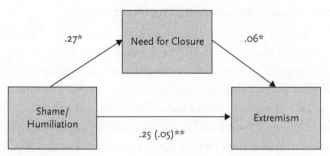

FIGURE 5.8. Indirect effect of loss of significance (shame/humiliation) on extremism through increased need for closure (Study 2). $^*p < .05; ^{**}p < .01, ^{***}p < .001$

significant correlation between shame and extremism (indicated by the appropriate line) becomes insignificant once the relation between shame and the NFC is statistically controlled for.

Study 3: General Muslim Populations

The goal of Study 3 was to move beyond incarcerated populations of extremists and extend the findings to general, representative samples. To that end, we tested our hypothesis with a large sample of participants living in three Asian and Middle Eastern countries: Egypt, Indonesia, and Pakistan. We asked participants to report the extent to which they thought they had been successful in accomplishing their important life goals. Researchers have suggested that perceptions of the self as valuable are inherently linked to people's views of personal success or failure (Carver & Scheier, 1998; Crocker, Brook, Niya, & Villacorta, 2006). Moreover, instead of just focusing on one form of extremism, our survey included items assessing both Islamist extremism and the support for violence as a general means to achieving political goals. As we had predicted, perceptions of personal failure were associated with increased NFC, which, in turn, was associated with increased support for both Islamist and general extremism (represented by support for violence against one's enemies).

While the results of Studies 1 through 3 are supportive of our hypothesis, they are limited in their ability to suggest that humiliation and loss of personal significance *cause* the observed changes in NFC and extremism. Statistical modeling suggests that the pathway occurs as predicted, but it is impossible with survey methodology to demonstrate causality without manipulating the relevant constructs in an experimental design. To address this issue, we carried out Study 4.

Study 4: Experimental Manipulation of Significance Loss

Instead of having participants recount their experiences of personal LoS, we manipulated this variable in the laboratory. Individuals were either randomly assigned to a condition designed to prime feelings of personal insignificance or to a control condition where no such manipulation was attempted. Participants in the LoS condition were asked to think back to a time when they were humiliated and to describe the details of this situation. Participants who professed to have never experienced such a situation were further instructed to describe a similar situation that someone they cared deeply about, like a child or a spouse, may have experienced. In the *control* condition, participants thought back to the last time they watched television and provided a detailed description of what they had watched and how this made them feel.

We expected that thinking back to a situation that threatened people's sense of personal significance would lead to increased agreement with, and endorsement of, politically extreme attitudes compatible with one's political orientation. Thus, whatever a person's attitude on an issue might have been, we expected that in the condition of significance loss it would become even more pronounced (i.e., her or his positions on relevant issues would be more polarized). We also expected that this tendency toward extremism would be mediated by increases in NFC. We created a measure of extremism that assessed unwillingness to compromise on core tenets of one's political ideology.

Participants were presented with materials related to their previously identified political orientation: Democrats read about liberal issues, and Republicans read about conservative issues. Next, they were presented with statements taking extreme positions on issues where conservatism and liberalism conflicted such as pro-choice versus pro-life or the definition of marriage. These statements professed that there is no room for ambiguity in the values at stake and that those values should never be compromised, no matter the circumstances. We found, consistent with our theory, that manipulated LoS increased individuals' political extremism and that this relation was statistically mediated by individuals' NFC. In other words, LoS elevated individuals' NFC, which, in turn, augmented their political extremism.

Studies 1 through 4 found consistent support for the proposed model as it pertains to personal instances of lost significance: In four unique samples, we found correlational and experimental evidence that feelings of insignificance boost extremism through increasing the need to restore certainty and closure. According to significance quest theory (Kruglanski et al., 2014), however, this relationship should not be limited to personal circumstances of LoS but should also be socially related LoS occasioned by affronts to one's social identity. Accordingly, subsequent studies examined our model in reference to a social-identity type of LoS.

Study 5: Moroccan Immigrants in Spain

As we did with our examination of personal LoS (Studies 1 and 2), we first tested our proposed model in the field with a group of at-risk individuals. To that end, we conducted a survey with young Muslim immigrants in the El Puche neighborhood of East Almeria, Spain. The majority of El Puche residents are first-generation immigrants from Morocco (Checa, Arjona, & Checa y Olmos, 2010). This group generally perceives itself as stigmatized and discriminated against by the local Spanish population (Dietz & El-Shohoumi, 2007; Martin-Munoz, 2003; Murshed & Pavan, 2011). This perception has a basis in reality; indeed, a substantial number of native Spaniards view immigrants as a serious national problem (Zapata-Barrero, 2009), as abusers of the welfare system, and as responsible for the rise in crime (Enesco, Guerrero, Callejas, & Solbes, 2008).

Muslim immigrants in Spain also face various concrete manifestations of discrimination, including exclusion at the workplace and outright expressions of hostility on part of native Spaniards (Murshed & Pavan, 2011). The El Puche neighborhood in particular is one of the most stigmatized and reviled areas of Almeria (e.g., Fernández & Asenjo, 1998). From the present perspective, living under these dire circumstances and suffering discrimination related to one's social identity marks the population we studied as at-risk for extremism. We treated the perceived maltreatment of Muslims by the Christian majority in Spain as an index of a group-based LoS.

As a measure of extremism, we examined support for the implementation of Sharia, the Islamic law, as the leading legal system in Spain. Meaning "path" in Arabic, Sharia guides all aspects of Muslim life including daily routines, familial and religious obligations, and financial dealings. It is derived primarily from the Qur'an and the Sunna—the sayings, practices, and teachings of the Prophet Mohammed. In the present context, wishing for Islamic law to govern all aspects of life in a predominantly Catholic Western country clearly deviates from the normative attitudes of the Spanish population as a whole and, therefore, qualifies as extremism.

The results of this study's results showed, as hypothesized, that perceived ingroup maltreatment was positively correlated with extremism and that

NFC fully mediated this relationship. Thus, our Study 5 found support for the notion that perceived humiliation of one's group may induce extreme attitudes via increasing the appeal of certainty and closure, just as was the case with personally based LoS.

Need for Closure, Group Glorification/Victimization, and Extremism

The series of studies just described corroborate the hypothesized relation between LoS, whether personal or group-based, and extremism and highlight the mediating role in this relationship of the need for certainty and closure. Recently, Dugas et al. (2016) carried out five additional studies looking more specifically at the process whereby NFC may mediate extremism. Specifically, these authors assumed that NFC may enhance people's orientation toward, and dependence on, their group (Kruglanski et al., 2006); in the case of intergroup conflict, this should then lead to intergroup violence mediated by ingroup glorification and the perception of the in-group as being unjustly victimized by the outgroup.

In the first two studies, conducted in Palestine's West Bank (Study 1) and in the United States (Study 2), NFC was shown to lead to a greater sense of moral license to engage in violence against a deliberately unspecified *outgroup*, mediated by an increase in the ingroup's perceived victimhood. The next two studies replicated the identical mediation pattern among Catholic students in Northern Ireland (Study 3) and Jewish Israelis (Study 4), showing greater moral licensing to engage in violence against the respective outgroups, Irish Protestants and Palestinians, respectively. Finally, Study 5, with Israeli Jews, found that experimentally heightened NFC promoted greater moral license and more extreme moral decisions against members of the outgroup. These effects were again mediated by ingroup glorification and the group's perceived victimhood.

In summary, there is mounting empirical evidence that LoS introduces a disquieting self-uncertainty among individuals that evokes (and/or enhances) their NFC. In turn, this need augments the tendency to turn to one's group, glorify it, and support an extreme version of its shared reality, including the readiness to defend it by all means necessary. If LoS represents the motivational force behind violent extremism, then there is the possibility that enhancement of personal significance through nonviolent means may *reduce* extremism. We therefore examined this possibility empirically as well.

The Deradicalization Context

Recently, we performed an empirical study of a deradicalization program for former members of the LTTE in Sri Lanka (Webber et al., 2018). The Sri Lankan program was intended to enhance individuals' sense of personal significance through educational, vocational, spiritual, recreational, psychosocial, and cultural activities that may convey to them a sense of respect and caring on part of the Sri Lankan authorities. Additionally, these activities aim at equipping individuals with new capabilities (e.g., in educational and vocational realms) and embedding them within supportive social networks, thus building their self-confidence and increasing their chances of a successful reintegration into the Sri Lankan society upon release.

We found that beneficiaries of the program's full-fledged scope—as compared to a control group that received only a minimal version of the program (see Webber et al., 2018 for details)—exhibited a decline of their support for violent extremism against the Sinhalese over time (see Figure 5.9). Of particular interest, these differences were mediated by our measures of LoS (see Figure 5.10). In other words, the significant relation between exposure to the full-fledged Sri Lankan deradicalization program and reduced support for violence against the Sinhalese became nonsignificant once we statistically controlled for the beneficiaries LoS measure.

What is even more interesting, the beneficiaries' positive attitude toward the Sinhalese and their negative attitudes toward violence exceeded those expressed by a matched (demographically) sample of community Tamils who never belonged to the LTTE. Finally, the postrelease attitudes of the beneficiaries were once again mediated by their feeling of significance or

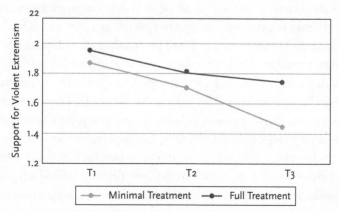

FIGURE 5.9. LTTE extremism across three time points.

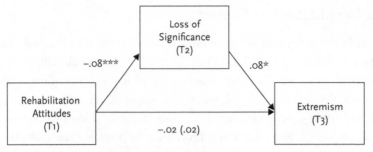

FIGURE 5.10. Indirect effect of rehabilitation attitudes on extremism through loss of significance. *$p < .05$; **$p < .01$, ***$p < .001$

insignificance. In other words, feeling positive and conciliatory toward the Sinhalese and eschewing violence as a means to political attainment were positively correlated with the beneficiaries' sense of personal significance.

Social Networks, Significance Loss, and Support for Violence

Our significance quest theory of radicalization (described in Chapter 3) assigns an important role to social networks in promoting violent extremism. According to this theory, social networks in which individuals are embedded may validate the perception of group grievance and legitimate violence aimed at redressing it and redeeming the group's lost significance. Our team explored these notions in three different geopolitical contexts and with three different populations: Moroccans, Sri Lankans, and Indonesians (for details, see Jasko, Webber, Kruglanski, & Gelfand, 2018).

In all three contexts, we compared individuals belonging to social networks known to differ in their commitment to violence as a means of defending the group cause. In Morocco, we compared the inhabitants of Tetuan, known for their relatively radical fundamentalist views, with the dwellers of Casablanca, representing a less-radicalized social milieu. Our (relatively) radicalized network in Sri Lanka consisted of former members of the LTTE with members of the Tamil community who never belonged to the group. Finally, in Indonesia, we compared groups that, according to area experts, are Jihadist in orientation with those identified as Islamist and yet others identified as moderate.

In all three samples, we replicated the same finding: Individuals perceived loss of collective significance was more related to their support for violence in groups classified as more versus less radical. Consistent with our theory, the social network matters, and the extent to which the network's ideological narrative condones violence as a means to the group's defense moderates their members' tendency to support violence to address the group's perceived humiliation (i.e., significance loss). Of interest also, a finding that emerged in all our samples was that the relation between individual LoS and support for violence was weaker in the more radical versus the less radical groups. This finding suggests that belonging to a radical network can actively suppress the effect of personal insignificance on violent extremism. Possibly, membership in a radical network facilitates the transformation of individual upsets and humiliations into feelings of collective indignity. Further research is needed to probe this possibility.

Summary

There is by now substantial evidence concerning the psychological process of radicalization and the role the quest for personal significance plays in it. The empirical data supportive of our model were obtained through a variety of methods, including correlational and experimental designs, and were carried out in different world locations varying in culture, population demographics, and sociopolitical circumstances (including prison or detention centers, conflict zones or conflict-free regions, immigrant minorities, and majority samples). Though our various studies addressed different pieces of the radicalization "puzzle," collectively they converge in consistent support for our present theory. Thus, there is evidence that significance loss promotes identification with the group to which one belongs and motivates securing one's standing in that collective, presumably to compensate for one's individual failures and humiliations. Of course, noblesse oblige, the attainment of status in a group requires embracement of the group narrative and the readiness to do what seems to be needed on the group's behalf.

Our evidence attests, furthermore, that the collectivistic identification prompted by significance loss reduces an individual's fear of death and increases the approval of violence in the group's defense. We also have evidence that the relation between LoS and extreme commitment to a progroup narrative is mediated by the NFC occasioned by a self-uncertainty produced by significance loss. Significance restoration also seems to be involved in the deradicalization process: Tamil beneficiaries of the rehabilitation program in Sri Lanka were more conciliatory and less supportive of violence upon their release into the community to the extent that they had a strong sense of personal significance.

Finally, we now have evidence concerning the role of social networks in legitimizing violence in response to perceived group humiliation. Across different cultural samples and in diverse geopolitical circumstances, we find that the more radical the social network, the more its members support violence if they perceive that their group has suffered a LoS at the hands of an outgroup nemesis.

Whereas the present body of empirical data offers substantial support for significance quest theory, further research is needed to explore the theory's additional implications that haven't yet been empirically investigated. In particular, such work may profitably study the relations hypothesized to obtain between the 3Ns of radicalization in terms of the influence that each of them receives in driving the process for different individuals and under different circumstances.

References

Allport, G. W., & Ross, J. M. (1967). Personal religious orientation and prejudice. *Journal of Personality and Social Psychology, 5*, 432–443.

Arndt, J., Greenberg, J., Solomon, S., Pyszczynski, T., & Simon, L. (1997). Suppression, accessibility of death-related thoughts, and cultural worldview defense: Exploring the psychodynamics of terror management. *Journal of Personality and Social Psychology, 73*, 5–18.

Atran, S., Sheikh, H., & Gomez, A. (2014). Devoted actors sacrifice for close comrades and sacred cause. *Proceedings of the National Academy of Sciences, 111*, 17702–17703.

Banlaoi, R. C. (2006). The Abu Sayyaf group: From mere banditry to genuine terrorism. In D. Singh & L. Salazar (Eds.), *Southeast Asian affairs 2006* (pp. 247–262). Singapore: Institute of Southeast Asian Studies.

Becker, E. (1962). *The birth and death of meaning: A perspective in psychiatry and anthropology.* New York, NY: Free Press of Glencoe.

Bélanger, J. J., Caouette, J., Sharvit, K., & Dugas, M. (2014). The psychology of martyrdom: Making the ultimate sacrifice in the name of a cause. *Journal of Personality and Social Psychology, 107*, 494–515.

Bélanger, J. J., & Kruglanski, A. W. (2012). *On sin and sacrifice: How intrinsic religiosity and sexual-guilt create support for martyrdom.* Unpublished manuscript. University of Maryland.

Brewer, M. B., & Gardner, W. (1996). Who is this "we"? Levels of collective identity and self representations. *Journal of Personality and Social Psychology, 71*, 83–93.

Carver, C. S., & Scheier, M. F. (1998). *On the self-regulation of behavior.* New York, NY: Cambridge University Press.

Checa, J. C., Arjona, Á., & Checa y Olmos, F. (2010). *Actitudes recientes hacia los inmigrantes en El Ejido* (España) [Recent attitudes toward immigrants in El Ejido (Spain)]. *Convergencia, 17*, 125–154.

Crocker, J., Brook, A. T., Niya, Y., & Villacorta, M. (2006). The pursuit of self-esteem: Contingencies of self-worth and self-regulation. *Journal of Personality, 74*, 1749–1771.

Dietz, G., & El-Shohoumi, N. (2007). Muslim women in southern Spain between discrimination and empowerment. *Arab Diaspora Women, 24*, 116–117.

Dugas, M., Schori-Eyal, N., Kruglanski, A. W., Gelfand, M. J., Klar, Y., Touchton-Leonard, K., & Roccas, S. (2016). *The hurt justifies the means: Need for cognitive closure, group centrism, and intergroup hostility.* Unpublished manuscript. University of Maryland, College Park.

Elison, J. (2005). Shame and guilt: A hundred years of apples and oranges. *New Ideas in Psychology, 23*, 5–32.

Elison, J., & Harter, S. (2007). Humiliation: Causes, correlates, and consequences. In J. L. Tracy, R. W. Robins, & J. Tangney (Eds.), *The self-conscious emotions: Theory and research* (pp. 310–329). New York, NY: Guilford Press.

Enesco, I., Guerrero, S., Callejas, C., & Solbes, I. (2008). Intergroup attitudes and reasoning about social exclusion in majority and minority children in Spain. In S. R. Levy & M. Killen (Eds.), *Intergroup attitudes and relations in childhood through adulthood* (pp. 105–125). Oxford, England: Oxford University Press.

Fernández, F., & Asenjo, R. (1998). Almería y los almerienses. *La visión subjetiva del espacio urbano almeriense* [Almeria and Almerians. The subjective view of Almeria urban space]. Almería: Instituto de Estudios.

Fishbach, A., & Shah, J. Y. (2006). Self-control in action: implicit dispositions toward goals and away from temptations. *Journal of Personality and Social Psychology, 90*, 820–832.

Greenberg, J., Pyszczynski, T., Solomon, S., Simon, L., & Breus, M. (1994). Role of consciousness and accessibility of death-related thoughts in mortality salience effects. *Journal of Personality and Social Psychology, 67*, 627–637.

Jasko, K., Webber, D., Kruglanski, A. W., Gelfand, M., & Muh, T. (2018). *Social networks moderate the effects of quest for significance on violent extremism.* Unpublished manuscript. Jagiellonian University, Kraków, Poland.

Kaufman, R. (1992). *Strategic planning plus: An organizational guide* (Rev. ed.). Newbury Park, CA: SAGE.

Kay, A. C., Shepherd, S., Blatz, C. W., Chua, S. N., & Galinsky, A. D. (2010). For God (or) country: The hydraulic relation between government instability and belief in religious sources of control. *Journal of Personality and Social Psychology, 99*, 725–739.

Kruglanski, A. W. (2004). *The psychology of closed mindedness.* New York, NY: Psychology Press.

Kruglanski, A. W., Gelfand, M. J., Bélanger, J. J., Sheveland, A., Hetiarachchi, M., & Gunaratna, R. (2014). The psychology of radicalization and deradicalization: How significance quest impacts violent extremism. *Political Psychology, 35*, 69–93.

Kruglanski, A. W., Gelfand, M. J., & Gunaratna, R. (2012). Terrorism as means to an end: How political violence bestows significance. In P. R. Shaver & M. Mikulincer

(Eds.), *Meaning, mortality, and choice: The social psychology of existential concerns* (pp. 203–212). Washington, DC: American Psychological Association.

Kruglanski, A. W., Pierro, A., Mannetti, L., & De Grada, E. (2006). Groups as epistemic providers: Need for closure and the unfolding of group-centrism. *Psychological Review, 113*, 84–100.

Martin-Munoz, G. (2003). *Marroquies en Espana, Estudio sobre su integracion* [Moroccans in Spain, Study on Integration]. Madrid, Spain: Fundacion Respol.

Miller, G. F. (1993). *Evolution of the human brain through runaway sexual selection: The mind as a protean courtship device.* Unpublished doctoral dissertation. Stanford University, Stanford.

Mosher, D. L. (1998). Revised Mosher Guilt Inventory. In C. M. Davis (Ed.), *Handbook of sexuality related measures* (pp. 290–293). Thousand Oaks, CA: SAGE.

Murshed, S. M., & Pavan, S. (2011). Identity and Islamic radicalization in Western Europe. *Civil Wars, 13*, 259–279.

Nathanson, D. L. (1992). *Shame and pride: Affect, sex, and the birth of the self.* New York, NY: W. W. Norton.

Orehek, E., & Kruglanski, A. W. (2018). Personal failure makes society seem fonder: An inquiry into the roots of social interdependence. *PloS one, 13*(8), e0201361.

Orehek, E., Sasota, J. A., Kruglanski, A. W., Dechesne, M., & Ridgeway, L. (2014). Interdependent self-construals mitigate the fear of death and augment the willingness to become a martyr. *Journal of Personality and Social Psychology, 107*, 265–275.

Orehek, E., Vazeou-Nieuwenhuis, A., & Kruglanski, A. W. (2017). *Failure makes society seem fonder: An inquiry into the roots of social interdependence.* Unpublished manuscript. Department of Psychology, University of Pittsburgh.

Oyserman, D., & Lee, S. W. (2008). Does culture influence what and how we think? Effects of priming individualism and collectivism. *Psychological Bulletin, 134*, 311–342.

Pedahzur, A. (2005). *Suicide terrorism.* Cambridge, England: Polity.

Rousseau, J. J. (1968). *The social contract.* London, England: Penguin. (Original work published 1762)

Schachter, S. (1959). The psychology of affiliation: Experimental studies of the sources of gregariousness.

Singelis, T. M. (1994). The measurement of independent and interdependent self-construals. *Personality and Social Psychology Bulletin, 20*, 580–591.

Swann, W. B., Jr., Gómez, Á., Dovidio, J. F., Hart, S., & Jetten, J. (2010). Dying and killing for one's group identity fusion moderates responses to intergroup versions of the trolley problem. *Psychological Science, 21*, 1176–1183.

Swann, W. B., Jr., Gómez, A., Seyle, D. C., Morales, J., & Huici, C. (2009). Identity fusion: the interplay of personal and social identities in extreme group behavior. *Journal of Personality and Social Psychology, 96*, 995–1011.

Templer, D. I. (1970). The construction and validation of a death anxiety scale. *Journal of General Psychology, 82*, 165–177.

Tomkins, S. S. (1963). *Affect, imagery, consciousness. Vol. 2. The negative affects.* New York, NY: Springer.

Trafimow, D., Triandis, H. C., & Goto, S. G. (1991). Some tests of the distinction between the private self and the collective self. *Journal of Personality and Social Psychology, 60,* 649–655.

Webber, D., Babush, M., Schori-Eyal, N., Moyano, M., Hettiarachchi, M., Belanger, J. J., . . . Gelfand, M. J. (2017). The road to extremism: Field and experimental evidence that significance loss-induced need for closure fosters radicalization. *Journal of Personality and Social Psychology, 114,* 270–285.

Webber, D., Chernikova, M., Kruglanski, A. W., Gelfand, M. J., Hettiarachchi, M., Gunaratna, R., . . . Bélanger, J. J. (2018). Deradicalizing detained terrorists. *Political Psychology, 39,* 539–556.

Williams, L. M. (2006). An integrative neuroscience model of "significance" processing. *Journal of Integrative Neuroscience, 5,* 1–47.

Zapata-Barrero, R. (2009). Policies and public opinion towards immigrants: The Spanish case. *Ethnic and Racial Studies, 32,* 1101–1120.

Zartman, W. I., & Anstey, M. (2012). The problem: Preventing identity conflicts and genocide. In I. W. Zartman, M. Ansteys, & P. Meerts (Eds.), *The slippery slope to genocide: Reducing identity conflicts and preventing mass murder,* (pp. 3–34). New York, NY: Oxford University Press.

6 PROFILES IN VIOLENT EXTREMISM

A striking feature of radicalization is its diverse manifestations. The thousands of individuals who end up as violent extremists seem to have preciously little in common. They come from different cultures, are of different genders, vary in educational level, and differ in how happy or satisfying their personal life has been. At a deeper level, however, these seemingly disparate cases share essential features in common. The psychological process of radicalization (discussed in Chapter 3) underlies the trajectories of diverse individuals en route to violent extremism. The following are some of their stories.

Tatiana Menake

One September morning in 2006, Tatiana Menake, 27, went shopping for a sequined top at a store in Colombo, the Sri Lankan capital. Such a garment is often worn at weddings and other ceremonial festivities in Sri Lanka—not this time, though. Menake was buying the garment to conceal the denim vest she would wear the following day, one which would be filled with 3 mm steel balls and loads of a C-4 plastic explosive connected to two detonators, one on each side of her body. The next day, Menake set out on her assigned mission—a suicide bombing intended to blow up the Sri Lankan prime minister, Ratnasiri Wickremanayake. Menake failed, though she tried her best.

Her preparations were thorough. She scouted the prime minister's mansion and monitored his comings and goings for three days in an attempt to choose the best time and place for the attack. But ultimately, it was her diligence that brought about her downfall. Because of her extended presence near the prime minister's residence, the police guarding the premises noticed her and became suspicious.

Several things about her appearance and demeanor raised questions. Her traditional shalwar—a long tunic over baggy pants—was out of place in the neighborhood, in which women tended to dress in jeans and miniskirts. She could have been a servant, but her erratic pattern of movement belied that possibility. On her third day of reconnaissance, the guards stopped Menake at the mansion gate. She claimed that she was visiting a sick aunt, but her story didn't seem to add up, and she was questioned further. What finally gave her away was a distinctive cyanide necklace that the police discovered on her, the type worn by all members of the LTTE organization to which she belonged. To prevent her from using it, the police beat Menake unconscious. Subsequently she was transported to a detention center where attempts were made to get her to cooperate and provide information about her handler, the LTTE operative responsible for preparing and launching her on her mission. But how did she get to that point?

Menake's life story is a sad one. Her father was an alcoholic who used to beat her mother, finally killing her when Menake was three years old. When Menake turned seven years old, her father repeatedly raped her during a drunken binge that lasted for four days. She was rescued by her grandfather, who took her to his home and cared for her over the next eight years, until he and his wife died. Menake was 15 at the time. Her aunt and uncle took her in but regarded her as a burden. Two years later, they got rid of her by offering her to the LTTE as a human tax, one that the organization levied from Tamil families in the area.

At the outset, Menake, just 17, didn't want to go and didn't want to fight. "I do not want to die," she told the woman officer who interrogated her after her arrest, yet her wishes didn't count for much. She was quickly dispatched to the LTTE training grounds with 150 other women where she spent the next seven months in grueling physical exercise, intense indoctrination, and combat and weapons training. On completion, she was assigned to the intelligence-gathering division of the organization where her job was to clip newspaper articles, a job that she found boring. In 2002, Menake volunteered to join the Black Tigers, the prestigious suicide squad of the LTTE. Why did she choose to do so? By her own account, she was depressed and in pain. She had suffered nerve damage to her spine after falling from an LTTE tractor, and the doctor told her she might become paralyzed when she became older—she felt she had no reason to continue living. Other girls were volunteering to become suicide bombers, and she decided to do so as well. Joining the ranks of the suicidal unit would be an honor, she wrote in her application letter. Relevant to the present perspective, in a 2006 interview Menake told journalist Jan

Goodwin that she believed joining the Black Tigers would give *purpose to her life*, and she had been quite prepared to make the *thatkodai*, the "gift of self."

The story of Menake's "last meal" with Pottu Amman, LTTE second-in-command and head of the Black Tigers unit, is instructive. Perhaps for the first time in her life, Menake felt like a *celebrity*. Her dinner companion was strikingly handsome and basking in an air of worldly importance, pursued as he was by the Interpol and the Sri Lankan government. They took a photograph together, the "last picture," to be displayed on the clock tower in the northern city of Jaffna in homage to her extraordinary deed. The honor did not end there. It was explained to her that following her death she will be considered a mahaveera, a "great warrior," and paid incomparable respect. Posthumously, she would also be accorded an official *military rank* in the LTTE, which exact degree of prestige would be determined by the importance of her target (Goodwin, 2008).

The road to the suicidal bombers' unit, the famed Black Tigers outfit, was fraught with tense anticipation. Menake waited for over a year before she was finally admitted. The LTTE selects its members carefully. Those accepted must first prove their mettle—they have to demonstrate their commitment, idealism, and competence—only then can they be trusted to carry out their mission reliably. Menake apparently qualified. Her training was tough and meticulous. She was taught how to use the explosive vest and how to jump into a vehicle carrying her designated target. As mentioned, despite all the training, ultimately she failed to hit her target—others in her unit, however, did not.

Before the wars in Iraq and Syria completely tipped the scales, the Tamil Tigers held the world record in suicidal attacks. From 1987 until the time of their demise in 2009, they carried out close to 300 such attempts that, among others, resulted in the death of former Indian Prime Minister Rajiv Gandhi (d. 1991), commander of the Sri Lankan navy (d. 1992), Sri Lankan President Premadasa (d. 1993), and countless other officials and innocent bystanders. In fact, the LTTE is known to have pioneered the use of suicide belts years before they became a staple in suicide bombers' standard operating equipment (Neary, 2009).

Note that all elements of our 3N model were prominently present in Tatiana Menake's case. Her volunteering to the Black Tigers unit was motivated by her quest for significance, to have purpose in life and to matter, as she herself attested. The narrative in the LTTE advocated suicide attacks as a praiseworthy testimony of commitment to a sacred cause, of Tamil independence, and she was immersed in a network of girls who were volunteering to become suicide bombers, socially validating the notion that this deed is prestigious and significance affording.

Marwan Abu Ubeida

In contrast to Tatiana Menake, whose life was tragic and ridden by humiliation, Marwan Abu Ubeida, a young Iraqi militant, was a child of privilege. His father was a successful businessman who provided well for Marwan and his six brothers. Yet by 2005, the 20-year-old Marwan was a suicide terrorist-in-training at Abu Mussab al Zarqawi's insurgent group (the Attawhid). On orders of his commander, he agreed to be interviewed by a *Time* magazine correspondent, Bobby Gosh (2005). The interview provided invaluable insights into the young insurgent's state of mind and motivations.

His *nom de guerre* consisted of two elements: the first name "Marwan" is a common Iraqi name (hence, it is at once symbolic of the nation and conveniently inconspicuous), and the second name "Abu Ubeida" was the name of a seventh-century general (Abu Ubeida al Jarrah), the admired Islamic hero and the conqueror of Syria at the time. In high school, Marwan was drawn to, and excelled in, Islamic studies, much surpassing his brothers in this domain. He also acquired the reputation of a ferocious fighter, distinguished by extraordinary courage and determination. His first involvement with violent militancy occurred when American forces—in their attempts to quell an Iraqi protest in Fallujah—fired at a crowd of demonstrators of which Marwan was a part. Twelve people were killed, many more were wounded, and Marwan swore to avenge them. Shortly after the incident, his friends and he got hold of weapons abandoned by the Iraqi army and opened fire at US soldiers who occupied a building in Fallujah—this was Marwan's initiation into a career of anti-American insurgency.

His resentment of the American occupation soon combined with his religiosity. The Zarqawi group, impressed by Marwan's fighting capability, had him meet Abu Anas al Shami, Attawhid's spiritual guide. The fight against the Americans and their supporters was now couched in jihadist terms, imbuing Marwan's life with a new sense of mission. After months of fighting as a foot soldier, he volunteered to become a suicide bomber, and finally, after a long wait, he heard that he made the list. By his account, this day was the happiest of his life. In the *Time* interview, he claimed to be ready to die, to be looking forward to it, and praying for a large number of American casualties.

Along with other recognized volunteers, he underwent a special program designed to discipline the mind and to cleanse the soul. He studied the lives of jihadists and listened to taped speeches about the rewards that had awaited them in heaven. His thoughts were occupied by the "final stage," after a mission would be assigned to him. He hoped for an important one, directed perhaps by al Zarqawi himself. To Marwan, this would be a time of utmost exhilaration. He expected to be spending it in prayer and purification, preparing to meet Allah and receive a divine blessing for his deeds. "It doesn't matter whether people know what I did," he told Gosh. "The only person who matters is Allah—and the only question he will ask me is 'How many infidels did you kill?'"

As in the case of the Sri Lankan terrorist Menake, the radicalization of Abu Ubeida attests to the presence of the 3N factors identified in our theory. He was clearly ambitious and eager to make a contribution that would earn him significance and recognition. He was clearly immersed in an ideological narrative in which killing numerous infidels constituted the route to significance. And he was clearly under the spell of Attawhid's al Shami and other members of the Zarqawi network, all of whom supported the narrative of jihad against the American invaders and their supporters.

Hanadi Jaradat

A particularly deadly act of suicidal terrorism was perpetrated by Hanadi Jaradat, a 29-year-old lawyer from Jenin, a town in the West Bank of the Jordan River. On October 4, 2003, she blew herself up in the Maxim restaurant in Haifa—co-owned by Arabs and Jews—killing 21 people (Jews and Arabs) and wounding 51 others. What pushed an educated woman, charged with the responsibility of providing for her family, to perpetrate a massacre in which men, women, and children—all innocent civilians, some of her own ethnicity—were killed?

Her story is one of suffering and religiosity, wrapped together with nationalist devotion and revenge. When Jaradat was 21, her fiancé, Abed al-Rahim Jaradat (a distant cousin) was killed by the Israel Defense Forces. Her family's oldest son, Fadi, paid for her to go to law school, and she attended the Philadelphia University in Amman, Jordan. After she graduated, she clerked for a year and then found employment in a law firm in Jenin. Her economic prospects and earning power were good. Things were looking up for Jaradat when in 2003, her cousin Saleh (aged 34) and her beloved brother Fadi (aged 24) were killed in front of her own eyes by the Israeli security forces. In an interview with the Jordanian daily *Al Arab al-Yaum*, she swore revenge: "Your blood will not have been shed in vain," she is reported to have said. She continued, "The murderer will yet pay the price and we will not be the only ones who are crying... If our nation cannot realize its dream and the goals of the victims, and live in *freedom and dignity*, then let the whole world be erased."

The Israeli journalist Vered Levy-Barzilai (2003) gleaned information from diverse sources to depict Jaradat's background and personality. Like Marwan, the Iraqi insurgent, Jaradat was also deeply religious, always modestly dressed and spending hours on end in prayer and Qu'ranic study. Her piety and religious devotion only intensified after the death of her brother and cousin. Throughout the day, she was glued to the Qu'ran, which she kept reading incessantly. She was also deeply idealistic and concerned about the fate of the Palestinians. "The goal of liberating Palestine is bigger and more important than my private pain," she stated in her interview (Levy-Barzilai, 2003), "And I have to be happy that I received my beloved brother as a shaheed (the Arabic term for 'martyr')."

Jaradat's other family members shared her idealism—200 of them were in Israeli detention and 12 were named as shaheeds. Her father, Taisir, said in an interview with Al-Jazeera television: "My daughter's action reflected the anger that every Palestinian feels at the occupation." He expressed great pride in her daughter's deed and asked family and friends to pay no condolences. "I will accept only congratulations for what she did," he stated in the interview. "This was a gift she gave me, the homeland, and the Palestinian people. Therefore, I am not crying for her."

Following the death of her brother and cousin, Jaradat was inconsolable. She fasted as one does during the Ramadan months, eating no food throughout the day, well before the Ramadan commenced. She constantly referred to her aim of revenge. During the mourning period over her brother, members of the Islamic Jihad's women's movement visited Jaradat. It has been speculated that this meeting is where the idea of her suicide attack germinated. She appeared ripe for the action and, as a mature and responsible person, was very capable to bring it off. The horrific facts in consequence of her deed sadly vindicate that assessment.

Once again, our 3N ingredients of radicalization seem to be present in Jaradat's road to violence. She felt deeply humiliated and deprived by the loss of her loved ones to the Israeli enemy; she was immersed in a family network of militants committed to violent resistance to the Israelis; and she was deeply idealistic and devoted to the narrative that violent terrorism serves the cause of liberation from the Israeli occupation.

Luiza Gazujeva

As in the case of Hanadi Jaradat, revenge and, hence, reaffirmation of one's downtrodden significance played an important role in a November 29, 2001 attack on the Russian commandant Geidar Gadzhiev in the Urus Martan district of Chechnya. The attacker in this case was Luiza Gazujeva, 23, whose husband, two brothers, and cousin were killed by the Russian military, specifically at the hands of Gadzhiev. It was alleged that Gazujeva was summoned to watch Gadzhiev torture her husband and brothers and that Gadzhiev murdered Gazujeva's husband in cold blood. The account of Gazujeva's final encounter with Gadzhiev is striking. Apparently she approached him and asked whether he recognized her. When he brushed her off and refused to engage with her, she detonated an explosive device that was strapped to her body. Two Russian soldiers were killed in the explosion, and two were wounded. Gadzhiev was taken to a hospital where he died several days later.

No one knows for certain what transpired in Gazujeva's mind before the assault or what was the tipping point that pushed her to the ultimate sacrifice. One can only speculate. Rage at the torturer of her husband and brothers likely played a role. It is also clear that she lived in a social context where suicide attacks constituted an honorable way of striking against one's detractors. Khava Barayeva—who committed the first Chechen suicide bombing on June 6, 2000—became a famous "superstar" among members of the Chechen resistance and was even immortalized in a song by a famous Chechen songwriter Timur Mutsaraeva.

There is also little knowledge about Gazujeva's religious beliefs and her devotion to the ideal of an Islamic state in Chechnya. John Reuter, in a report sponsored by the American Committee for Peace in Chechnya, remarks that terrorist recruiters use religious fundamentalists as one means of attracting potential members to the movement. Reuter (2004) comments that many of Russia's documented suicide bombers have turned to Islamic fundamentalism before embarking on their missions. Yet, the overall nationalist context may also have provided a sufficient ideological background to the "Black Widows"[1] acts, including Gazujeva's suicide.

---

1. *Black Widow* is the term used to refer to Chechnyan women suicide bombers many of whom volunteered for the mission in response to their husbands or fiancés being killed by the Russian occupiers.

Hayashi Ichizo

As the saying goes, the more things change, the more they remain the same. Consider the following story of Hayashi Ichizo, a kamikaze pilot in World War II. Also known as *tokkotai* in Japanese, an abbreviation of *tokubetsu kogeki-tai*, meaning "Special Force Units," kamikaze pilots committed aerial suicide missions throughout the war. Ichizo died at the age of 23 at a Battle of Okinawa when he crashed his plane into an American destroyer. Though Ichizo's story unfolded at a vastly different time and place and in circumstances that seemingly have little in common with those of Gazujeva, Jaradat, Abu Ubeida, or Menake, a close look reveals some fundamental psychological similarities in the dynamics that brought them to their extreme acts.

Ichizo's family was Christian and well-educated. His father was appointed as an assistant professor at the Department of Agriculture at the University of Tokyo but died a sudden death soon thereafter, when Ichizo was but two years old. His mother, Hayashi Matsue, faced severe economic difficulties, struggling to support herself and her four children as a teacher in the local elementary school. Despite these hardships, Ichizo's childhood was a happy one. Raised by his uncle and aunt in a secure and loving environment, he enjoyed special attention and privileges as the male heir to the Hayashi family. Ichizo was a successful student at the Fukuoka High School and later at the Imperial University in Kyoto, where he majored in economics. When the time arrived to enlist in the military, Ichizo volunteered for the Japanese navy, primarily to avoid the bullying for which the army was known. Entries in Ichizo's diary months before his suicidal death reveal how torn he was about the prospects that awaited him. On February 23, 1945, the entries reflect noticeable resentment about his assignment. In his words "To be honest, I cannot say that the wish to die for the emperor is genuine, coming from my heart. However, it is decided for me that I die for the emperor."

Yet, a short time later, on March 2, 1945, the entry reflects a growing enthusiasm for the mission "My only wish is to die for the emperor. How consoling it is to know that you would be honored upon death. At least, people would remember me. When I think how I would live in their mind, I feel pleased." And subsequently on March 19, 1945, less than a month before his death, he wrote:

> I have a wish to make a difference in the world [The idiomatic Japanese expression is "to throw a stone"]. I cannot deny that one element of that is my wish that people recognize my existence . . . If my death is

a glorious battlefield death, then I will welcome my fighting . . . Our ancestors' wish was to die beside the emperor. Loyal individuals wished to do so. (cited in Ohnuki-Tierney, 2006, pp. 170–173)

In an undated letter to his mother, Ichizo writes,

Mother, I am a man. All men born in Japan are destined to die fighting for their country. You have done a splendid job raising me to become an honorable man (rippana otoko) . . . I will do a splendid job sinking an enemy aircraft carrier. Do brag about me . . . be pleased that someone like me [using a phrase expressing humbleness] was chosen to be a tokkotai pilot. I will die with dignity as a soldier. (cited in Ohnuki-Tierney, 2006, pp. 173–174)

Philosophically minded Ichizo sought solace in the Danish existential philosopher Kierkegaard, in whose works *The Concept of Dread* and *The Sickness unto Death* despair is a major theme. As Ohnuki-Tierney (2006) summarizes it, "Hayashi found this meaningful because he was torn between his deep attachment to life, and his equally deep sense of obligation to fight in defense of his homeland" (p. 182).

Indeed, Hayashi's testimony reflects a deep commitment to the nationalistic narrative, generally shared in the Japanese social milieus of the time, whereby dying for country and the emperor bestows an untold honor and significance, whereas shirking that duty for the sake of survival is ignominious and shameful.

Major Nidal Malik Hasan

According to Wikipedia ("Nidal Hasan," n.d.), "on November 5, 2009, a gunman shouting 'Allahu Akbar' (God is Great) opened fire in the Soldier Readiness Center of Fort Hood, killing 13 people and wounding 30 others." That morning, Major Nidal Malik Hasan gave away furniture from his home, as well as copies of the Qu'ran. All the evidence suggested that the shooter in this case was Nidal Hasan. Indeed, he was tried and convicted for the crime.

Nidal Malik Hasan is a US citizen whose parents came from a small Palestinian town, al-Bireh. He was born and educated in Virginia and was a lifelong devout Muslim who attended prayers regularly. Hasan graduated from Virginia Tech University in 1997. He received his medical degree from the Uniformed Services University of the Health Sciences in Bethesda,

Maryland, in 2001 and interned at the Walter Reed Hospital. Dr. Val Finnel, Hasan's classmate at the Uniformed Services University, reported that Hasan viewed the "war against terror" launched by the United States and its allies as a war against Islam. At the end of a class on environmental health, in a final presentation Hasan chose to talk about the war against terror. This was a highly unusual topic for the occasion in which others made presentations about completely apolitical environmental topics like dry cleaning chemicals and mold in homes. In the final year of his residency in Walter Reed, Hasan made another presentation under the title "The Qu'ranic World View as It Relates to Muslims in the US Military" in which he proposed that Muslim soldiers be given the option to be released from service and be treated as "conscientious objectors." According to a report by his aunt, in the years after 9/11, Hasan had been harassed about being a Muslim. According to other relatives, Hasan hired an attorney to pay the military back for the college and education he received to gain his release from the service. He was about to be shipped for a tour of duty in Afghanistan on November 28, 2009, fairly close in time to his fateful decision to carry out the shooting at Fort Hood. Several sources attest that Hasan was quite upset about his impending deployment because he feared that he would have to fight or kill fellow Muslims. During his internship at Walter Reed Hospital, Hasan counseled victims of posttraumatic stress disorder returning from Iraq and Afghanistan. He became well aware of the horrors of war and the harrowing experiences that returning soldiers were recounting to him.

It is generally agreed now that Hasan was exposed to a radical brand of Islamist ideology. He is known to have attended the Dar Al-Hijra mosque in Falls Church, Virginia, which had also been attended by Nawaf al-Hazmi and Hani Hanjour, who both participated in the 9/11 attack, as well as by Ahmed Omar Abu Ali, who apparently provided material support to Al Qaeda and to a conspiracy to assassinate President George W. Bush. It is also of interest that the mosque's imam at the time was Anwar al-Awlaki, later on known not only as an advisor to the 9/11 hijackers but also a senior Al Qaeda member and regional commander. It appears that Hasan sent al-Awlaki numerous email messages from December 2008 onward.

According to the journalist Brian Ross, in one of the emails from Hasan to al- Awlaki, Hasan wrote: "I can't wait to join you [in the afterlife]" (Martosko, 2014). In turn, after the Fort Hood shooting, al-Awlaki praised Hasan and encouraged other Muslims to follow in his footsteps. In a subsequent interview, al-Awlaki attested that Hasan decided on his own whether violence is acceptable in Islam. Al-Awlaki himself regarded shooting Westerners and other "infidels" as acceptable and as a form of jihad. Accordingly, he considered Hasan's shooting of the soldiers as blessed because "the soldiers who were killed were not normal soldiers, but (rather) those who were trained and prepared to go to Iraq and Afghanistan" to fight Muslims and wage war against Islam, as Hasan perceived it (Martosko, 2014).

There is no question that Hasan viewed his shooting of US soldiers as an honorable action blessed by God and deserving of the highest praise, which likely had given him a sense of great significance. It also seems likely that he suffered a prior loss of significance from being personally harassed about being a Muslim and that he was exposed to a violence justifying narrative through his networking and communications with Anwar al Awlaki.

Tsarnaev Brothers

Consider now the story of the Tsarnaev brothers, Dzokhar and Tamerlan— the confirmed perpetrators of the Boston Marathon bombing in April 2013. Tamerlan, the older brother, appears to have been poorly assimilated to US culture and society, with no American friends by his own account. Tamerlan's family was on welfare, his parents on the verge of divorce, and he was unemployed and supported by his wife, a college dropout. Ostensibly, Tamerlan was pursuing a boxing career that apparently ended in a disappointment as he was disqualified from participating in the US Olympic team on bureaucratic grounds. In addition, he was feuding with his successful Maryland-based uncles, Alvi and Ruslan, who viewed the Boston Tsarnaevs as "losers."

It seems likely that Tamerlan was quite humiliated by all those sorrowful circumstances and that, in response, he entertained dreams of glory (e.g., as an Olympic boxer, a hope that crashed) whose realization appeared possible by becoming a hero or a martyr according to the extremist narrative he adopted. A note captured in the location where Dzokhar was finally apprehended indicates that he perceived his brother as a martyr and a hero and that he too craved a similar recognition (Koplowitz, 2014). It was also reported that on a visit to Dagestan—a largely Muslim area in southern Russia that borders Azerbaijan, Georgia, and the troubled Russian region of Chechnya—Tamerlan had contacts with a network of Islamic militants who probably influenced his views and attitudes. The case of the brothers Tsarnaev contains the 3N elements of our significance quest theory. There is evidence that Tamerlan experienced a pronounced desire to matter and stand out amplified by the failures of his personal life (the need component of the 3N factors), that he was exposed to Islamist rhetoric (the narrative component), and that he was in contact with individuals (including his own mother) who supported such rhetoric and his admiring younger brother who echoed his views and adopted his objectives (representing the network component). Whereas Dzokhar seemed better adjusted to the American realities than Tamerlan, the latter apparently had considerable influence over him and was able to convince him in the heroic importance of the attack they were planning.

Diana Ramazanova

On January 6, 2015, Diana Ramazanova tried to detonate two hand grenades in a police station in the main tourist area of Istanbul, Turkey. The first grenade failed to go off. As she took out the second grenade, she was shot by a police officer, but the resulting explosion still rattled the police station, killing her and an officer and injuring another one. January 10, 2015—four days after the suicide bombing occurred—would have been her 19th birthday.

Ramazanova was a teenager originally from the region of Dagestan. She moved back and forth from Dagestan to Moscow, and many reports suggest that she had strained relations with her family, her stepfather in particular. Members of her family described her as "not deeply religious" and remarked that she "wore bright makeup, dressed fashionably, and attracted attention" (Stewart & Tomlinson, 2015). Her step-father described her as "depraved" and recalled how "in Moscow, Diana worked in the restaurant at the Kursk station" and how he "always scolded her for wearing short skirts." Yet, from this seemingly mundane existence, she rose in the span of six months to become a foreign fighter on behalf of the Islamic State. One wonders, what precipitated this seemingly unlikely transition?

In May 2014, Ramazanova crossed into Turkey legally using a tourist visa to meet her future husband, Abu Aluevitsj Edelbijev, a Norwegian citizen of Chechen origin. The two met on social media and are believed to have met for the first time in person during that visit. In July 2014, the couple was married and crossed the border illegally into Syria to join up with Islamic State militants. Ramazanova's husband was killed in a battle in December 2014, an event that left her deeply distressed and traumatized. Eleven days before she carried out the suicide bombing, Ramazanova crossed the border illegally back into Turkey and traveled over 1,000 kilometers to Istanbul.

As is typically the case with foreign fighters and suicide bombers, Ramazanova's friends and families could not even imagine how someone who seemingly shared their values and aspirations could possibly find terrorism appealing and were taken completely by surprise on learning about Ramazanova's act. Ramazanova's mother-in-law spoke to members of the Norwegian media, trying to explain her daughter-in-law's aberrant behavior: "I don't think she could take it anymore. She said that [her husband] Abu was in peace and that she wanted peace too. . . . We had regular contacts through instant messaging online. Everything seemed normal. We had contacts no later than . . . the evening of January 5. She spoke about her family and sent pictures" (Stewart & Tomlinson, 2015). The mother-in-law added: "There was nothing that suggested that this could happen. It was as much of a shock for us when she blew herself up as when my son decided to go to Syria." In light of the present analysis, however, Ramazanova's actions seem less mysterious. Like Luiza Gazujeva, she was probably deeply upset and belittled by the death of her husband and viewed it a matter of honor to avenge it. Her immersion among Islamic militants in Syria exposed her to the violence-justifying narrative and lent her the network support for her act. Once again then, her seemingly unique and incomprehensible case seems to fit the general radicalization process depicted in the 3N model.

Hayat Boumeddiene

The change from a secular, life-loving young woman to a committed Islamic fanatic repeats itself in the case of Hayat Boumeddiene who gained notoriety as a member of the network that carried out the January 2014 attack on the *Charlie Hebdo* magazine in Paris, in which 12 people lost their lives. Boumeddiene was married to Amedy Coulibaly who, in parallel to the attack on the Charlie Hebdo offices, fatally shot a police woman on a Paris street and killed four people at a kosher grocery before he was killed by the police.

Reports indicate that Boumeddiene had a troubled past. She was only eight when her mother died of a heart ailment. She didn't get along with her stepmother and was therefore placed in a group home with an Algerian family, a "house of nonbelievers" as her father Mohamed Boumeddiene described it. Indeed, Boumeddiene appeared completely westernized and nonreligious, sporting a black bikini in a photo with her husband during a vacation in the Dominican Republic. Yet, in time, the couple gravitated toward the Islamic religion and explored it in depth, with the help of Djamel Beghal,[2] who happened to be one of Al Qaeda's top European recruiters. "I

---

2. Coulibaly met Beghal through his friend Cherif Kouachi, who knew Beghal from prison.

had a difficult past, and religion answered all my questions and brought me peace" Boumeddiene told the police during an early interrogation in 2010 (Birnbaum & Mekhennet, 2015). The kind of religion the couple found was in all likelihood a fundamentalist, violence-justifying brand of Islam, the same professed by Beghal.

An essential core belief in Beghal's, Boumeddiene's, and Coulibaly's ideology was the utter justifiability of violence against the West. In a 2010 interview, Boumeddiene asserted "When I see innocent people massacred in Palestine, Iraq, Chechnya, Afghanistan where Americans send bombs and all that—and they're not terrorists? . . . When Americans kill innocent people . . . it is of course justifiable that men should take arms to defend their wives and children" (Birnbaum & Mekhennet, 2015). The couple's friends appeared to share these views. Beyond their relations with Beghal, Boumeddiene and Coulibaly were in close contact with Cherif Kouachi, the younger of the two brothers who perpetrated the *Charlie Hebdo* massacre. Boumeddiene fled France a day before the *Charlie Hebdo* attack and, as of this writing, is considered one of the most wanted fugitives in Europe.

The Waffle House Terrorists

On a Tuesday morning in November 2011, four men met inside a white van in the parking lot of a Walmart in Cornelia, Georgia. Moments later, a SWAT team burst out of a nearby truck, opened the doors of the van, and tossed several flash-bang grenades into the back of the van. The four men were pulled out of the van at gunpoint and pinned down on the ground, still in shock from the grenade burst. They were no typical teenage terrorists or radicalized jihadists: They were four elderly men in their 60s and 70s.

The so-called Waffle House Terrorists often met at a local Waffle House or Shoney's; they were planning to blow up federal buildings in Atlanta, Georgia, in an attempt to kill employees of the Bureau of Alcohol, Tobacco, and Firearms and the Internal Revenue Service. What could have prompted these four men of advanced age to contemplate murder and mayhem of their fellow Americans?

The story of the group's most vocal member and leader, Fred Thomas, is telling. Thomas lived most of his life near Washington, DC, had served in the US navy, and had worked subsequently for several government contractors. Upon his retirement, Thomas and his wife moved to a small, mountain town in Georgia to be closer to a son who resided there. Old age didn't agree much with Thomas. He was suffering from several ailments, including a kidney mal-function and a chronic obstructive pulmonary disease, causing him to have to drag around a tank of oxygen. He had torn rotator cuffs and couldn't lift his arms over his head. As *Esquire* magazine reports it, "he had always been a man of action, and now he was enduring the irrelevancy of old age in a place where he was unknown" (Junod, 2012).

In a post to an online forum, he regretfully wrote of having been young and "seeing older people through the years and thinking that those older people were years away from me and that winter was so far off that I could not fathom it or imagine fully what it would be like.... But, here it is ... I have regrets. There are things I wish I hadn't done ... things I should have done" (Junod, 2012).

As an outlet for his pent-up feelings of frustration and regret, Thomas turned to the Internet. He blogged, posted messages, and engaged in conversations with like-minded disgruntled individuals who held strong pro-gun and antigovernment sentiments. Among others, he became an active con-tributor to the Liberty Forum, the message board of the Militia of Georgia. It is there that he found an opportunity to once again initiate action and a place to spin the fantasy of overthrowing the US government by "patriotic assassinations" of objectionable politicians. These comments elicited consid-erable praise from other contributors to the board. Encouraged, he joined the Militia of Georgia for a time, but when its leader's Jimmy Wynn's positions on immigration appeared too mild to Thomas, he quit. He began leading the group that ultimately spun the plots to attack government targets. Along with co-conspirator Dan Roberts, 68, Thomas was convicted and sentenced to five years in prison.

Discussion

The foregoing stories of radicalized individuals seem quite different from each other, and the backgrounds of their protagonists have little in common. The Tamil, Tatiana Menake, was an abused woman, raped in her childhood by her father, betrayed by her relatives, submitted to a cruelly repressive regime in the organization she was forced to join, and ultimately assigned a boring and an insignificant job to perform. Her life story reads like a tragic yarn, her chances for a rewarding life minimal to begin with and her future largely hopeless. Now that her final mission too has failed, the life that awaits her is even worse than before. In her interview with Goodwin (2008), Menake re-flected on the hopelessness of her existence and its sad fate—to never marry, have a family, or embrace one's own child, to never lead a normal life like most other people.

How different her circumstances have been from those of Marwan Abu Ubeida, whose life has been anything but a failure. Born to a wealthy family, well-educated, and brimming with confidence and assertiveness, he was recruited to the Zarqawi organization because of his demonstrated competence and courage in battle. Whereas Menake encountered disdain and disrespect for most of her life, Abu Ubeida enjoyed the admiration of friends and colleagues. Whereas Menake was pushed into terrorism against her will, Abu Ubeida actively sought out participating and enthusiastically embraced life in an extremist group against the advice and expressed wishes of his family. Though fated to commit suicide, Abu Ubeida sounded exuberant and enthusiastic when interviewed—full of life and optimism, ironically, in the shadow of his contemplated death. Menake's story is one of a lost soul, whereas Abu Ubeida's is one of a found destiny that he confronted with devotional exuberance, marveling at the grandeur of his contemplated act.

Hanadi Jaradat's circumstances are different from both Menake's and Abu Ubeida's. She was older and more mature and accomplished than both. Her life centered on her family, while Menake had no family to speak of and Abu Ubeida willfully distanced himself from his. Indeed, Jaradat's whole life was about her family and so was her death to a large extent. As the oldest daughter of an ailing father, she bore the responsibility for the family's welfare and supported it materially, however she could. And so at the age of 29, Jaradat was a shining example of personal fortitude, pulling herself up by her bootstraps, overcoming major obstacles, and attaining her objectives against overwhelming odds. A woman in a traditional society, the daughter of an impoverished family, she was determined nonetheless to obtain university education, which she did with determination and tenacity. Whereas Menake and Abu Ubeida seem youthfully extreme and unbalanced, Jaradat appeared to be the paragon of harmony and balance, with her religious devotion complementing her professional competence and dedication to her family.

Even Jaradat's extreme act of suicide appears to derive quite rationally from her values and obligations: Prompted by the killing of her beloved brother and cousin and the earlier death of her fiancé at the hands of the Israelis, her action appears to have been one of revenge, a payback for blows to her family, yet also an act embedded in her deep religiosity, exploited by the launchers of the suicide attackers who took advantage of her pain and misery.

Luiza Gazujeva's circumstances were yet different. Though also impassioned by a desire for revenge, the target of her attack was much more personal than Jaradat's. Jaradat struck against innocent civilians (including several Arabs), who either worked or happened to be present at a public restaurant; in contrast, Gazujeva's target, the commandant Gadzhiev, was personally responsible for the torture and ultimately the murder of her husband.

From the psychological perspective, the *retribution motive* that seemingly played a key role in motivating Jaradat, Gazujeva, Abu Ubeida, and Hasan (though less so in motivating Menake) to embark on their violent missions is linked to humiliation and the desire to erase it. Watching loved ones suffer or lose their lives to a powerful adversary or seeing members of one's nation or religion defeated and abused makes a person feel weak and helpless, unworthy to be taken seriously and treated with respect. Defeat at the hands of another is insulting and demeaning; hence, a natural way of restoring honor is by striking directly back at one's detractor. Such an act disproves the notion of one's impotence and removes the insulting power differential that the original defeating circumstance created. The medieval practice of dueling represents the psychological basis of revenge as well as anything: It expresses the duelers' supreme commitment to the value of honor, attested by the *willingness to die* in the attempt to avenge one's insult, and, should the revenge be successful, it demeans one's enemy in return for the harm that he or she perpetrated.

Over six decades ago, revenge played a role in prompting Hayashi Ichizo to become a suicide attacker. Essentially a gentle soul, born into a well-educated family and philosophically minded to boot, Ichizo was in part motivated by revenge, as shown in his diary entry from February 23, 1945, two months before his death. The passage allows a close glimpse into his emotional state of mind and the presence of revenge motivation in his contemplations: "I can't bear the thought of our nation being stampeded by the dirty enemy (he wrote) I must avenge [it] with my own life" (cited in Ohnuki-Tierney, 2006, p. 170).

Revenge played an important role in Major Nidal Hasan's murderous outbreak as well, but the circumstances of his act seem very different from those of the attackers we have described so far. For one, he was an American citizen—born, raised, and educated in the United States—and an officer in the US military; in a certain sense then, the violence he unleashed was against members of his own group. Yet, according to testimonials, Hasan came to identify himself primarily as a Muslim rather than as an American. In that sense, even though objectively this instance represents an American attacking other Americans, subjectively Hasan may have experienced alienation from his compatriots and may have felt that the people he was trying to kill in Fort Hood were enemies of his primary group and its faith.

The humiliation and harassment Hasan suffered at the hands of his military colleagues might have contributed to his heightened identification with
the suffering of Muslims more generally. Perceived grievances by Muslims as a
group may have then become his personal concerns and may have added to his
sense of powerlessness and frustration. Above all, these concerns might have
increased his readiness to embrace the extremist ideology preached by Anwar
al-Awlaki, whom Hasan admired, and to carry out the acts of violence that
al-Awlaki incited. As mentioned earlier, according to sources, four days after
Hasan's November 5 attack, Al-Awlaki posted an entry on his blog praising
Hasan as a hero who did the right thing and encouraging other Muslims in
the US military to follow suit. It is likely that Hasan himself held a similar
view of his actions and believed himself a hero and a martyr for the cause
of Allah.

The Tsarnaev brothers were poorly integrated immigrants from Chechnya
whose anger and bitterness likely pushed them to extremism against America,
especially the older brother Tamerlan. As noted earlier, it seems plausible that
Tamerlan's disappointment with the United States had to do with his and his
family's failure to do well in the "promised land" to which they immigrated.
Despite promising beginnings and the encouraging examples of their more
successful relatives, the Tsarnaev brothers' own life circumstances in America
obviously generated a negative state of mind that likely pushed Tamerlan to
violence, with his younger brother Dzhokhar in tow.

The same idea applies to Tatiana Menake whose life of misery and humiliation may have induced in her the desire to do something of value and, hence,
gain through death the recognition that eluded her in life. Thus, although her
actions weren't motivated by revenge as such—and her personal misery and
humiliation had little to do with the suffering of the Tamil people—her decision to sacrifice her life had as much to do with regaining her sense of personal
significance as that of all the other suicide attackers we have described.

Finally, the aged Fred Thomas, suffering from a bitter sense of frustration and disappointment, found a mission—striking at a government that he
considered unjust and despicable—that in his eyes and those of his associates
would imbue his life with utmost significance. He most likely believes that,
should he have succeeded, he would have erased all his past failures and life
debacles. In his own mind, he would have ended up a hero, a role model of
what an individual can do for his society, remembered forever and revered
by those who shared his perspective on the evil nature of the American
government.

Summary

Despite the considerable surface differences between Menake, Ichizo, Jaradat, Gazujeva, Abu Ubeida, Hasan, Thomas, and the Tsarnaevs—revenge, the eradication of dishonor, or failure, or the hope for great personal achievement seemed to have been part and parcel of the motivation that prompted these completely different human beings to end their lives on the altar of a collective cause of some sort. These sundry stories of suicidal attackers strongly hint that the issue of honor and either personal or collective significance constitute a common theme and a major underlying factor inducing their motivation to commit the act.

In addition, to the quest for significance that seems to have motivated, unexceptionally, the extremists described in this chapter, it is clear as well that they were all exposed to violence-justifying narratives that portrayed aggression against an alleged enemy as a sacred duty whose fulfillment would bring one honor and glory. Finally, all the presently portrayed extremists were supported in their radical views by networks of friends, similarly minded colleagues, or family members. Thus, the three *N*s of our model—the need, the narrative and the network—seem invariably present in the life circumstances of individuals who ultimately turned to violent extremism.

References

Birnbaum, M., & Mekhennet, S. (2015, February 2). Hayat Boumeddiene, wife of Paris attacker, becomes France's most-wanted woman. *Washington Post*. Retrieved from https://www.washingtonpost.com/world/europe/wife-of-paris-attacker-now-frances-most-wanted-woman/2015/02/02/b03c6950-a7da-11e4-a162-121d06ca77f1_story.html?utm_term=.00a728d8e4c6

Goodwin, J. (2008, January 16). When the suicide bomber is a woman. *Marie Claire*. Retrieved from http://www.marieclaire.com/politics/news/a717/female-suicide-bomber/

Gosh, B. (2005, July 4). Inside the mind of a suicide bomber. *Time Magazine*. Retrieved from http://www.time.com/time/magazine/article/0,9171,1077288,00.html

Junod, T. (2012, January 18). Counter-terrorism is getting complicated. *Esquire*. Retrieved from http://www.esquire.com/news-politics/a12404/waffle-house-terrorists-0212/

Koplowitz. H. (2014, May 22). What did Dzhokhar Tsarnaev write on the boat? Read Boston bombing suspect's note here. *International Business Times*. Retrieved from http://www.ibtimes.com/what-did-dzhokhar-tsarnaev-write-boat-read-boston-bombing-suspects-note-here-1588472

Levy-Barzilai, V. (2003, October 16). Ticking bomb. *Haaretz*. Retrieved from http://www.haaretz.com/ticking-bomb-1-of-2-1.102722

Martosko, D. (2014, May 21). FBI chief: Fort Hood shooting was inspired by al-Qaeda despite the government terming it "workplace violence." *Daily Mail*. Retrieved from http://www.dailymail.co.uk/news/article-2635598/FBI-chief-Fort-Hood-shooting-WAS-inspired-al-Qaeda-despite-government-terming-workplace-violence.html

Nadal Hasan. (n.d.). *Wikipedia*. Retrieved from https://en.wikipedia.org/wiki/Nidal_Hasan

Neary, L. (2009, May 21). Tamil tigers: Suicide bombing innovators [Transcript]. *NPR Talk of the Nation*. Retrieved from http://www.npr.org/templates/story/story.php?storyId=104391493

Ohnuki-Tierney, E. (2006). *Kamikaze diaries: Reflections of Japanese student soldiers*. Chicago, IL: University of Chicago Press.

Reuter, J. (2004). Chechnya's suicide bombers: Desperate, devout, or deceived? Retrieved from https://jamestown.org/wp-content/uploads/2011/01/Chechen_Report_FULL_01.pdf?x87069

Stewart, W., Tomlinson, S. (2015, January 16). Pregnant teen suicide bomber who blew herself up at Turkish police station was called 'depraved' by relatives for wearing short-skirts before marrying ISIS jihadist. *The Daily Mail*. Retrieved from https://www.dailymail.co.uk/news/article-2913638/The-PREGNANT-teenage-suicide-bomber-blew-throwing-grenades-police-jihadist-husband-killed-fighting-ISIS.html

7 THE DERADICALIZATION PROCESS

Deradicalization, the road back from violent extremism, can happen under the appropriate circumstances, and, given the correct approach, violent extremists are capable of reforming and relinquishing terrorism. This process may occur at *three* different levels: at the level of the individual who may leave the organization on her or his own accord; at the level of the organization that may "spontaneously" decide to deradicalize; and at the level of a specifically engineered deradicalization program. In this chapter, we consider these three levels from the perspective of our significance quest theory and examine the successes and shortcomings of specific deradicalization programs in addressing the factors that cause, or contribute to, radicalization.

Individual Deradicalization

Deradicalization may be possible when an individual feels dissatisfied and disenchanted with the extremist organization of which he or she is a member. In terms of our theory, this individual may come to feel that participating in the group's activities no longer lends significance to her or his life, and, to the contrary, it confers upon her or him shame and ignominy. The specific reasons for these feelings may vary across cases. Some individuals might feel that their leaders are hypocritical, disappointing, and not really dedicated to the sacred cause that they had pretended to care for. Others might feel that the specific activities of the organization—for example, kidnapping individuals for ransom or engaging in narco-trafficking to fund the organization's activities—are inconsistent with the lofty ideals that prompted them to join the organization to begin with. Yet, others might feel that the way they are treated in the organization is disrespectful and humiliating, hence lowering their sense of personal significance rather than elevating it as had been hoped.

Dissatisfaction with the organization, its leadership, and its activities may not be independent from the cumulative hardships that come with leading the life of an extremist. From the psychological perspective, people's cognitive judgments are typically biased by their motivations. The latter, in turn, may be strongly influenced by the hardships of being "on the run" and unable to enjoy the everyday comforts that most people take for granted. Consider the statement of Adriana Faranda, a member of the Italian Brigade Rosse, on the mundane difficulties of extremist existence:

> Choosing to enter the Red Brigades . . . is a choice so total that it involves your entire life, your daily existence. It means choosing to occupy yourself from morning till night with problems of politics, or organization, and fighting . . . and no longer with normal life—culture, cinema, babies, the education of your children, with all the things that fill other people's lives. . . . And when you remove yourself from society, even from the most ordinary things, ordinary ways of relaxing, you no longer share even the most basic emotions. You become abstracted, removed. . . . You become closed off, become sad, because a whole area of life is missing. (Jamieson, 1989, pp. 267–268)

In terms of the analysis of extremism offered in Chapter 3, the motivational imbalance prompted by a disproportionately aroused quest for significance seems to be reduced here by a resurgence of previously suppressed needs for safety, comfort, etc.

Individuals may spontaneously deradicalize because they are extricated, voluntarily or forcibly, from the group dynamics (i.e., the network) of the violent organization. In some cases, this removal may happen if the individual member enlists in the military (Robert Oreil, personal communication, January, 2009); in other cases, the separation occurs when the detainee is incarcerated (as illustrated by the accounts of former Euskadi ta Askatasuna [ETA] members recorded by Reinares, 2011). Outside the sphere of influence of the group norms, individuals may be able to listen to other voices and reflect on their life course in a less constraining manner that a distance from one's ingroup may afford.

Group Deradicalization

Often, an entire group may decide to abandon violent extremism as means to their goals. Typically, this occurs in a top–down fashion and is instigated by the organization's leaders. The Egyptian journalist Makram Mohammed Ahmed, who personally witnessed the deradicalization of leaders of the Egyptian Islamic Group (Gemmah Islamiyah),[1] remarked (personal communication, Cairo, May 2010) that the deradicalization of that group occurred in the aftermath of a near complete failure of their violent activities against Copts (i.e., Egyptian Christian ethno-religious group) and tourists. The Egyptian population, which sees tourism as a main source of revenue on which many Egyptians depend for livelihood, strongly disapproved of the attacks on tourists in particular. As a consequence, the Egyptian people turned against the extremists, who soon found themselves in prison, their weapons' caches confiscated, and their safe houses compromised.

When their violent ways appeared not to have worked—and brought Gemmah Islamiyah members fear and suffering rather than glory—the organization leaders began to see the error of their ways and accept that Islam forbade violence and instead preached tolerance toward others, even if they were nonbelievers. They then carried out a tour of prisons to dissuade their followers from violence and published books advocating their newly discovered moderation. This process exemplifies a motivationally biased judgment in which the leaders' wishes and desires, in this case to end their and their followers' fear and suffering, affected their religious opinions.

A successful deradicalization based on a top–down approach also occurred in Algeria where the Islamic Salvation Army (Armée Islamique du Salut; AIS) successfully deradicalized in the period between 1997 and 2000. The Algerian Armed Islamic Group (Groupe Islamique Armé; GIA), however, did not deradicalize as successfully (Ashour, 2009). Ashour (2008) noted:

> The AIS had a consolidated, charismatic leadership that was willing to deradicalize. That leadership was influential enough to disarm the 7,000 militants that made up the organization, without causing any splits, as well as influencing several hundred militants from other smaller militias and factions. The GIA did not have this type of leadership . . . Additionally, the AIS was able to interact with other armed organizations, FIS factions, moderate Islamist individuals and political parties to support de-radicalization and reconciliation. The GIA had very limited interactions with the "other." (p. 2)

---

1. Gemmah Islamiyah is distinct from the Indonesian group, Jemmah Islamiyah, with a similar sounding name.

According to Ashour (2008), the deradicalization of the AIS also occurred in the context of their inability to succeed when confronted with a great pressure from the government and the military, on the one hand, and from other Islamist organizations (like the GIA) on the other hand. The latter groups in particular carried out massacres that mainly targeted civilians in electoral districts that supported the AIS. Indeed, "the massacres became a regular phenomenon in 1997 when there was a massacre occurring almost every day—the total number in 1997 exceed 300 massacres" (Ashour, 2008, p. 7).

Known cases of top–down deradicalization underscore the importance of the social network element in producing this phenomenon. Those groups that successfully deradicalized—namely, the Egyptian Islamic Group and the Algerian AIS—had a strong and unified leadership that wielded considerable influence over their followers. In contrast, groups whose spontaneous deradicalization was partial and not as successful—like the Egyptian Al Jihad group or the Algerian GIA—had leadership that was split about the desirability of deradicalization (in case of the Al Jihad organization) or had weaker control over the rank and file members (as in the case of the GIA; Ashour, 2008).

Engineering Deradicalization

Radicalization in Prisons

Deradicalization, or rehabilitation programs as they are sometimes called, are carried out with militants in detention centers or jails. The incarcerated terrorism suspects are either awaiting trial or, if convicted, are serving out their prison terms. The objective of deradicalization programs is to convince these inmates that upon their release, they should abstain from engaging in violent activities or from supporting them in any shape or form. Prisons contain conditions for deradicalization and therefore constitute a critical venue where violent extremism can be confronted and possibly turned around. It is important to note, however, that prisons can also be conducive to radicalization for several reasons.

First, imprisonment is typically a degrading situation in which people are deprived of their freedom and ordered around by prison guards, whose attitude toward inmates can be humiliating and demeaning. Second, at least initially, for many individuals imprisonment is a novel situation shrouded in considerable confusion and uncertainty. Entering inmates are likely to be disoriented and confused about the norms of conduct in their new environment and about the risks and dangers to themselves that may lurk there. Third, prisons are often populated with individuals for whom violence is a stock in trade. The prison culture thus is infused with the potential for violence that renders it accessible, and largely acceptable, in the prison environment.

Under these circumstances, individuals may be particularly attracted to clear-cut ideological narratives that dispel their confusion—especially narratives that promise them empowerment and significance. In terms of our present theoretical model then, prisons contain all the basic ingredients that may foster radicalization. The motivational element of significance loss is there, and if the radical, violence justifying ideology is present as well and reinforced by the penitentiary's social networks (e.g., led by articulate and charismatic radicalized inmates), the likelihood of prison radicalization should be high indeed.

It is not surprising, therefore, that prisons have been increasingly named as potential breeding grounds for Islamic radicalization—at times, in the form of grassroots radicalization that springs up independently of a systematic recruitment effort. Islam is the fastest-growing religion in US prisons (Ammar, Weaver, & Saxon, 2004; *Terrorist Recruitment*, 2003) as well as in jails in other Western countries (Beckford, Joly, & Khosrokhavar, 2005; Guessous, Hooper, & Moorthy, 2001; Spalek & Wilson 2002). Although not all prison conversions to Islam are of a radical, jihadist nature and the potential threat (of violent extremism) from high conversion rates to Islam is not always clear, recent studies and the personal histories of a number of high-profile terrorists do suggest that prisons can be incubators for radical Islam. Individuals like Robert Reid, the notorious "shoe bomber"; Jose Padilla, suspected of plotting to build and detonate a "dirty bomb"; Christian Ganczarski, accused and sentenced for directing a 2002 truck bombing near the El Ghriba synagogue on the Djerba Island of the coast of Tunisia; and Robert Richard Pierre, sentenced for the 2003 Casablanca bombing were all radicalized in prisons. So apparently were Abu Musab al Zarqawi, the founder of Al Qaeda in Iraq and later the Islamic State (IS), while in Jordan's Suwaqah prison, and Ayman al Zawahiri, the current leader of Al Qaeda who also served time in Cairo's prison following the assassination of Egypt's President Anwar Sadat in 1981.

A prominent homegrown example of prison radicalization is the case of the American Kevin James. While serving time at California State Prison–Sacramento for a robbery conviction, James not only converted to radical Islam but founded his own terrorist group, Jami'yyat Ul-Islam Is-Saheeh. In 2009, James was convicted of conspiring to bomb synagogues, military bases, and an Israeli consulate in California, in a plot described by the then-Assistant Director of Public Affairs for the Federal Bureau of Investigations as "the one that operationally was closest to actually occurring" since the events of September 11, 2001.

A Study of Prison Radicalization

Although specific case studies as those previously mentioned can be vivid and striking, their scientific value hinges on the degree to which they reflect a broader epidemic of Islamic radicalization in prisons. The uncertainty over *why* radicalization occurs in prisons—and to a lesser extent, whether it actually occurs—could be attributed to a lack of quantitative data and the presence of mostly anecdotal accounts. Exceptional in that regard is an empirical study by Trujillo, Jordán, Gutiérrez, and González-Cabrera (2009) who investigated the spread of Islamist ideology in 25 Spanish jails.

The study was conducted via questionnaires administered to prison officials. According to those interviewed, the spread of Islamist radicalism did occur to varying degrees, and radicalization within a given prison was facilitated by factors such as levels of group identity, indoctrination, and vertical cohesion within the prison (i.e., the extent to which the radicalization was driven by strong Islamist leaders and the extent to which a radical organization was hierarchically structured).

To our knowledge, the work of Trujillo et al. (2009) constitutes the only *quantitative* study examining Islamic radicalization in prisons. The dearth of such research is unsurprising, given that access to the populations of interest—prisoners and terrorists—is difficult, and even when access is actually given to human subjects, ethical concerns about their freedom to participate in the research are formidable. Nonetheless, a reliable body of empirical work on the subject is crucial if future policy is to be adequately informed. With this aim in mind, we recently conducted research in the Bicutan prison in Manila, the Philippines, to investigate whether a systematic trend of inmate radicalization over time can be discerned in that particular setting (Kruglanski et al., 2016).

Importantly, our research differed from Trujillo et al.'s (2009) work in that it examines radicalization at the individual level, rather than at the prison level, and among individuals arrested on charges of terrorism rather than among prison officials. In that sense, our study constitutes a rare direct examination of possible radicalization, whereas Trujillo et al.'s work tapped *opinions about radicalization* held by prison staff. Furthermore, our present study examined radicalization longitudinally, which addresses the process of radicalization as a tendency that unfolds over time. Our study was also distinct from prior inquiries of prison radicalization because we investigated psychological and demographic variables that may potentially *moderate* prison radicalization and predispose some individuals rather than others to radicalize.

To provide a quantitative assessment of prison radicalization, our study directly measured extremist attitudes among terrorism suspects detained in Bicutan prison at two points in time, two years apart. The conditions in which inmates are held at the facility include all the necessary ingredients for radicalization. The overcrowding, prolonged wait for a trial, forced separation from loved ones, and the inmates' perception that the system is unfair to them—that we have amply witnessed on our visits to Bicutan—may produce a profound motivation to regain their lost significance. In addition, all political detainees—suspected members of the Abu Sayaaf Group, a group recognized as a terrorist organization by the US Department of State and affiliated with the Indonesian Jemaah Islamiyah,[2] as well as to Al Qaeda and IS—are held together in a compound. The situation creates a powerful group dynamic led by charismatic radical clerics who propound radical attitudes and violence justifying ideologies as a means of significance restoration. Given these circumstances, we hypothesized that we would find a systematic increase over time in the inmates' support for radical attitudes and opinions.

In our research, we used an instrument designed to tap radicalization, comprising of three components: radical Islamism, anti-Western attitudes, and support for violence. The radical Islamism measure consisted of a set of statements we developed in consultation with Islamic clerics at the Hadija Mosque in Singapore to which interviewees would indicate their degree of agreement on a seven-point scale. These statements included items like, "The Qu'ran should only be understood according to its literal meaning," "Political leaders in our country should be selected solely by Islamic clerics," "Under no circumstances does Islam support the killing of civilians" (reverse scored),[3] "I think it is important for Muslims to revive the Caliphate," and "The goal of Jihad is to restore justice for Muslims worldwide."

The anti-Western component included statements such as "The aggression of Western countries must be stopped by any means possible," "Exposure to the culture of Western countries has a harmful effect on our country," "Western countries often violate other people's human rights around the

---

2. Islamiyah was responsible for the horrific bombing in Bali in 2002 in which 202 people lost their lives.

3. This item is reverse scored such that high degree of agreement with the statement (e.g., marking six on a seven-point scale) is scored as a low agreement with the opposite statement (i.e., two on the corresponding scale).

world," and "Western nations are forcing their values on Muslims throughout the world," among others.

The third component of our instrument pertained to attitudes supportive of violence as a means of advancing one's political agenda. Items in this subscale of our measure were: "If violence does not solve problems, it is because there was not enough of it"; "The only way to teach a lesson to our enemies is to threaten their lives and make them suffer"; "Killing is justified when it is an act of revenge"; and "Armed Jihad is a personal obligation of all Muslims today," among others.

We administered these measures to a sample of inmates at the Bicutan facility consisting of two waves of survey-based data collection, carried out in October 2010 and November 2012. Participants were all men and alleged members of the Abu Sayaaf Group. Their participation was entirely voluntary. Our results strongly confirmed the hypothesis of radicalization: We found that, over time, our respondents tended significantly more to endorse radical Islamism, became more anti-Western in their attitudes, and tended to endorse violence more as a way of dealing with perceived enemies.

Furthermore, our study discovered some significant variables that moderated our participants' radicalization. Specifically, increased support for violence between Waves 1 and 2 was more drastic among single participants, as well as participants who were married yet without children. This finding may be because a spouse and/or children already provide a source of significance, which in turn may diminish the drive to seek out other, potentially radical means of significance restoration, such as terrorism. In addition, age and education attenuated the change that occurred over time in participants' negative attitudes toward the West, with younger and less educated participants developing more negative attitudes, while no appreciable change in attitudes was observed among older and more educated participants.

Reversal of the same prison-related factors that promote the embracement of a radical ideology, may also enable the deradicalization of previously radicalized individuals. Specifically, violent extremists who find themselves incarcerated might come to feel that their radical attitudes didn't bring them significance and, to the contrary, resulted in their imprisonment and humiliation. Their suffered disgrace and disorientation in the novel prison environment may incline them to be open-minded to options that were previously denied or suppressed, including the possibility of changing direction and relinquishing one's radicalized ways. For instance, the ETA militants interviewed in prison by Reinares (2011) often reflected about their life course and decided to abandon their violent activities as a consequence of their reconsideration. The big question, therefore, is: How can conditions that would motivate detained extremists to undertake such a decision be created in a detention center or prison?

Deradicalization Programs

In recent decades, several countries that have imprisoned violent extremists have experimented with specific programs aimed at deradicalizing these inmates and releasing them back into society. Much has been written about these programs already (e.g., Rubin, Gunaratna, & Gerard, 2011; El-Said & Harrigan, 2013), and they have been both praised and criticized on various grounds. Because the governments involved typically do not allow any independent empirical assessment of their efficacy, most of the commentary about the various programs is largely speculative. In what follows, we offer a novel analysis of these deradicalization efforts from our present theoretical perspective. Specifically, our aim is to review the contents of the various programs with an eye to discerning whether they appropriately address the need, narrative, and network factors that, according to our model, determine the processes of radicalization and deradicalization.

The Saudi Program

It is generally agreed that the Saudi deradicalization program initiated in early 2004 is the best endowed and most sophisticated enterprise of its kind. The program has also served as a model to other nations. The Saudis have had extensive experience with violent extremism, and the involvement of Saudi citizens in Al Qaeda has been considerable. Of the 19 hijackers who attacked the United States on September 11, 2001, 15 were Saudi citizens. Saudis have also provided much of the Al Qaeda leadership and supplied volunteers for the Islamist militants fighting in Iraq and Syria.

There are several possible reasons for the disproportionate presence of extremism in Saudi Arabia. First, *Wahabism*, the puritanical, fundamentalist form of Islam, is the state religion in Saudi Arabia, and in its exported form, it is thought to have radicalized many young Muslims in various world locations. Second, Islam's most holy sites—the mosques in Mecca and Medina—are located in Saudi Arabia, making it a central place to Muslim's worldwide. Further, US forces were stationed there after the US-led Gulf War, upsetting many Muslims and motivating Osama bin Laden to call for jihad against the United States and the Saudi regime, the US's major ally in the region.

The danger that Al Qaeda and its affiliates have posed to the Saudi kingdom has led to the establishment of the Saudi deradicalization program and the investment of considerable resources in its development. The Saudi program is indeed impressive in its thoroughness and the thoughtfulness of its conception. The Saudis are considered to have a "soft" approach to counterterrorism built on three components: prevention, rehabilitation, and aftercare. Their deradicalization program is part and parcel of this approach, focusing on the second component: rehabilitation.

Essentially, the Saudi program is premised on the idea that extremists are misinformed about the true tenets of Islam; therefore, the program is designed to alter detainees' religious beliefs through dialogue and lectures while also providing them with psychological counseling and social support. It is of interest to consider how elements of the Saudi program relate to the present model of deradicalization that emphasizes the motivational, ideological, and social aspects of the process.

The Need

The Saudi program incorporates several features that bear on detainees' sense of significance and self-worth. First, the very fact of incarceration carries with it a humiliation—and hence significance loss—in part produced by the fact that prisoners may no longer provide for their families. In response, the Saudi program provides extensive care to a detainee's family, including an alternative salary paid to the family in place of the detainee's salary, children's schooling, and family healthcare. Such attention to family needs conveys to the detainees that they matter and that their needs are important, which should contribute to their sense of significance. In this vein too, detainees are given leaves to attend important family events such as weddings, funerals, or visiting the sick. El-Said and Barrett (2013) explain:

> When beneficiaries start their home leave from the Care Center, each is given around 2000 Saudi Riyals to buy gifts so as not to go home empty-handed, which would be humiliating for the beneficiary and to help them pay their way during their visit. All this dovetails well with the tribal culture of the country, where gifts (are customary). (p. 215)

Upon release, those detainees who are no longer seen as prone to extremism are provided with jobs, apartments, cars, and government grants. The Advisory Committee of the program, in conjunction with the local chambers of commerce, enrolls the released detainees in courses to help them start their own businesses; in short, they are given all the means necessary to feel significant and appreciated.

There are some psychological elements in this process that are worthy of note. First, the various perks received by the "graduating" detainees could be considered as bribes or extrinsic inducements that might lower their "intrinsic" motivation and undermine their acceptance of the deradicalization message. In other words, there could be a danger that the detainees would accept the gifts while maintaining their commitment to the extremist ideology. To guard against that possibility, the Saudi program ensures that participants are not promised release from prison or the rehabilitation facility. In addition, in many cases released detainees are induced to take government jobs that commit them to an action that is dissonant with the extremist ideology that views the government as illegitimate (Boucek, 2009; Rabasa, Pettyjohn, Ghez, & Boucek, 2010).

Last but not least important, the program's originators and implementers refer to detainees as "beneficiaries" rather than as extremists, terrorists, or detainees. This language is emblematic of a respectful, benevolent attitude toward the inmates whom the program aims to help. Such a positive epithet is also future focused, namely, on the future benefits to follow from reeducation. This language helps detainees part way with their extremist past, letting "bygones be bygones" and looking toward a positive new tomorrow. From the psychological perspective, this usage should induce psychological processes aiming to align the detainees' attitudes with their actions and hence solidifying their support for their new ideological moderation.

The Narrative

Though of immense psychological importance, concern about the detainees' sense of significance is generally seen as a mere sideshow of the Saudi deradicalization program. Instead, the center stage is accorded to the renowned counseling program carried out under the auspices of the Saudi Ministry of the Interior. The counseling program consists of four subcommittees of the overarching Advisory Committee that governs the program: the religious subcommittee, the psychological and social subcommittee, the security subcommittee, and the media subcommittee (Rabasa et al., 2010). Of these, the religious subcommittee is charged with the brunt of the ideological conversion task to alter the detainees' "hearts and minds."

The subcommittee's composition of religious clerics (*ulama*), university professors, and counselors are selected with great care for their communication style and their ability to strike up a personal relationship with the detainees. Its activities consist of two major elements: individual counseling meetings with the detainees, in which their views are heard and their extremist interpretation of Islam is challenged and counterargued, and religious lectures. Whether in the short sessions lecture program, lasting up to six two-hour sessions, or the long sessions lecture program, lasting six weeks of intensive study, up to 20 students meet with two clerics and a social scientist for discussions concerning such central Islamic concepts as *jihad, takfir* (excommunication), *al wala wal bara* (loyalty to Muslims and enmity to others), and other relevant topics.

The ideological education of the Saudi program is based on the Qur'anic notion of *Munasah* (advice) whereby rulers need to consult and discuss issues with their flock. Accordingly, in individual or group sessions, the detainees are never forced to make a decision but rather are given options to choose from (El-Said & Harrigan, 2013). Citing the Saudi Ministry of Interior, El-Said (2012) reports that this approach is designed to deal:

> With wrong conviction of the detained person in order to change and substitute them with correct convictions that agree with the middle way of Islam and tolerance. This is realized by using the method of dialogue, wisdom and gentle preaching by competent people, specialized in religious, psychological and social sciences with a follow-up by security experts. (p. 37)

The fact that the Saudi state religion is the Wahabi version of Islam constitutes both a strength and a weakness of the Saudi program. The strength stems from the fact that the puritanical and fundamentalist Wahabi ideology is not too remote in its tenets from the extremists' belief system (Rabasa et al., 2010). In particular, Wahabism justifies violence and aggression against nonbelievers if they are seen to occupy a Muslim land, like in Iraq or Afghanistan, for example. Because the ideological distance between the detainees' beliefs and that of the program officials isn't considerable, the task of converting them to the state version of the religion is relatively easier. But this aspect leaves the program open to the criticism that it does not deradicalize the detainees in any fundamental sense and that it opens to them the possibility to seek glory, and significance, in violence and terrorism, albeit outside Saudi Arabia.

Indeed, there seems to exist a disconnect between the language of moderation and tolerance adopted in the Saudi deradicalization program, on the one hand, and the encouragement of youngsters to join jihad against "infidels" and "apostates," as long as they are found outside the borders of the kingdom, on the other hand. This perplexity wasn't lost on the mujahidin upon their return home. According to Abu Jandal, Osama bin Laden's former bodyguard in Afghanistan:

> Yesterday we were told to go to Afghanistan for jihad against non-believers who occupied a Muslim country. Suddenly after returning from Afghanistan we were arrested and harassed to prevent us from fighting the Americans who now attacked another Muslim country, Iraq. We got very confused. We lost the ability to distinguish right from wrong. Who is a Muslim and who is not these days? (cited in El-Said & Barrett, 2013, p. 203).

In that sense, when graduates of the Saudi programs rejoin the fight outside of the country's borders, this does not unequivocally qualify as recidivism, because the program's essential narrative permits it. This concept is not well understood by outsiders. According to Porges (2011), for instance, "confidence in Saudi Arabia's program was shaken when Ali al-Shihri, an ex-Guantánamo detainee who graduated from the Saudi rehabilitation program in 2008, appeared in Yemen as the deputy commander of al-Qaeda in the Arabian Peninsula." (El-Said & Harrington, 2013, p. 203).

The Network

A notable strength of the Saudi deradicalization process is its adroit utilization of the social process in promoting detainees' conversion to the state-supported version of Islam. A major issue confronting any deradicalization program is the problem of "communicator credibility"—whether or not detainees will trust the people attempting to deradicalize them. Progenitors of the Saudi program were acutely sensitive to this issue and highlighted the credibility of its committee members from the very get-go. Indeed, "when members of the Advisory Committee initially meet with a prisoner, one of the first things that they stress is that they are not employees of the Interior Ministry or associated with the security forces" (Rabasa et al., 2010, p. 71). Furthermore, clerics and scholars who implement the program typically share considerable background with the detained militants; not only do they come from the same community, but often "they have remained autonomous and critical of the regime and they become messengers of the King because they understood the dangers of terrorism . . . for the Islamic Umma, and were determined to mediate between the state and society, including militants" (El-Said & Barrett, 2013, p. 211).

Particularly impressive is the Saudis work with families of detainees and the utilization of family dynamics to promote and maintain deradicalization. According to Boucek (2008), "one of the keys to the [Saudi] programme's success is the extensive social support given to a detainee and his family" (p. 60). This policy includes creating a positive relationship between the Care Program and the families, as well as involving the families in the deradicalization process to which their member is subjected. According to Abdulrahman Al-Hadlaq (2011), former General Director of the Ideological Security Directorate at the Ministry of the Interior of Saudi Arabia, "the families of the detainees also require rehabilitation to prevent them from following the same deviant paths. In the rehabilitation process, these families are usually given generous financial and social support a concerted effort on part of the Saudi government to win their hearts and minds." (p. 66).

When the detainees are released, their families' support is recruited by the state to help oversee their activities and report on any tendencies to revert to their former, extremist modes of attitudes and behavior. To ensure the families' support for the program, they need to be assured that it is for the benefit of their loved one, to "prevent him from straying from the right path" (Al-Hadlaq, 2011, p. 66). Furthermore, while in custody, the detainees are held at facilities in close proximity to their families to afford continual family connection and reimmersion of the detainee in the family network presumed to be supportive of rehabilitation. Finally, when detainees are released, they and the heads of their family "publicly renounce violence and the family is held responsible for keeping their children under control" (p. 66).

Attention to the social process involved in deradicalization is also reflected in the Advisory Committee's policy of segregating the detainees by separating the hard core of committed individuals from the more peripheral members. This action is wise from the group dynamics perspective in that it prevents the extremist leaders from holding sway over their followers. Segregation also creates a psychological space for the leaders as well, in which, free from the obligation to serve as models for their followers, they may reflect on their life course in the terrorist organization and hopefully find it wanting.

Among the more important socially relevant elements of the Saudi deradicalization program is its anchorage in long-standing Saudi customs and traditions and, hence, in the shared reality of the group from which the militants themselves originate (Hardin & Higgins, 1996). Importantly, these include the Saudi traditions of prisoner rehabilitation programs and the use of religious leaders in the correctional system. Rabasa et al. (2010) stated:

There is precedent for a sheikh to visit a prisoner in Saudi Arabia (as) asking a religious figure to intercede after the arrest of a loved one is not an uncommon practice. In rural Saudi Arabia, if one's son or nephew were arrested, the village imam was often asked to visit the prison and discuss the situation with the detainee. (p. 65)

The Yemeni Program

In 2002, the Yemeni President Ali Abdullah Saleh convened a meeting of ulama with the aim of establishing a Committee for Religious Dialogue with militants held in Yemeni prisons, in the hope to convince them to see the true meaning of Islam and, hence, to deradicalize. Supreme Court Justice Hamoud Al-Hitar was entrusted with heading up that program. The central concept of the Yemeni program was that of dialogue. This notion had to do as much with the process whereby deradicalization was accomplished as with the contents of beliefs that were targeted for change. According to Judge Al-Hitar (2011):

Holding a dialogue means reciprocating logic and words during a conversation . . . it means the revision and discussion between two equal parties, a process that is not controlled by any one of them, done quietly and far from quarreling and prejudices. It is a kind of refined intellectual civility. (p. 111)

Furthermore, "the Qu'ran . . . establishes the role of dialogue and clarifies rules pertaining to the art of dialogue. . . . It establishes the art of influence and persuasion in calling others to do good and return to God" (Al-Hitar, 2011 p. 113).

Need

The rules of dialogue, according to Al-Hitar, implicitly address the motivation for significance that, on our present view, underlies militants' extremism; these rules do so by placing a major emphasis on treating the detained militants with respect, specifically by

- acknowledging the other party;
- giving the opportunity for both parties (to the dialogue) to discuss a given subject;
- agreeing at the outset to accept the outcome of the dialogue, whatever it might be;

- providing consideration for the feeling of the other and the avoidance of sarcasm and irony; and
- practicing equality in speech, avoiding boring long lectures and interruption.

As Al-Hitar (2011) put it, "the detainees are treated well throughout their detention . . . [and] the mutual respect between the detainees and their dialogue counterparts plays a big role in the success of the initiative" (p. 119).

Nonetheless, a possible major lapse of the Yemeni Dialogue Program, as far as the motivational element is concerned, pertains to the failure to provide the released detainees with alternative means to significance. According to testimony, inability of released detainees to find employment and provide for their families constitutes a major source of humiliation and frustration. This inability may have pushed some former extremists to gravitate right back to Al Qaeda, a group that promised them a reasonable salary and, hence, a path to respect as the responsible heads of families. According to El-Said (2013), the Huthi rebellion in Yemen in 2004 put considerable pressure on the resources of the state: "This meant terminating resources originally planned for the Dialogue Committee, particularly for released detainees (p. 252). A former detainee described the consequences clearly:

> Marriage became a liability; we were no longer able to support our own family. Worse, we became a burden on our own parents and family members. Instead of supporting them, we began relying on them, but they are poor and had little to give. We started to feel that we lost our dignity as men. Al Qaeda became an attractive option because it continues to give $300 for each member, much more than the State could give. Hence, several detainees rejoined Al Qaeda after their release. (El-Said, 2013, p. 252)

As Rabasa et al. (2010) summarized it, "the inability of the Yemeni government to provide adequate post-release care was central to the program's collapse" (p. 21). The Yemeni program was discontinued in 2005.

Narrative

The main thrust of Al-Hitar's (2011) concept of dialogue, however, was directed at extremists' ideology and aimed at persuading them in the falsity of their interpretation of the Qu'ran, particularly as it concerns the use of violence and the true meaning of jihad:

Dialogue is an effective means to deal with distorted beliefs that lead to extremist behavior, and counter the religious exaggerations which run against the essence of Islamic teachings . . . The danger of these distorted beliefs lies in two things. First, Islam is portrayed as a religion that is anti-moderation. This runs counter to the Qu'ran where Islam is presented as a religion of freedom, justice, equality, safety and forgiveness. Secondly, these distorted beliefs and behaviors have provided additional fuel for others, consciously or unconsciously, to attack Islam and Muslims, and to escalate hatred against Islam and Muslims by further escalating these distorted beliefs. (p. 114)

Despite these claims, there is at present little clarity as to what was actually said to detainees in the Religious Dialogue Program and what was the ultimate essence of their commitment to nonviolence. According to Rabasa et al. (2010), "the Yemeni program did not address the issues of participating in violence abroad. It focused solely on activity within Yemen. For instance, Al-Hitar told a reporter, 'Resistance in Iraq is legitimate, but we cannot differentiate between terrorism and resistance in Iraq's situation because things are not clear in this case'" (p. 53).

Network

The Yemeni Dialogue Program may also be faulted for not paying sufficient attention to the social process whereby persuasion is accomplished. First, credibility of the communicators tasked with the deradicalization enterprise may have been questionable. Thus, at the initial session Judge Al-Hitar introduced the ulama about to address the detainees as representatives of the government, the very entity that the militants aimed to oppose, possibly undermining their credibility in the militants' eyes.

Second, it appears that detainees were released on the basis of a rather limited number of sessions—two, according to some sources (El-Said & Harrigan, 2013)—and over a relatively brief period, ranging from 10 days to 4 months for different groups of detainees. It is doubtful that a thorough persuasion could have taken place within a restricted number of sessions over such a short time span.

Third, it appears that the evaluation of the detainees' ideological change was rather cursory and superficial. According to Al-Hitar (2011), detainees "benefited from pardon as they had submitted themselves voluntarily and were committed to the results of the dialogue" (p. 118). Specifically, each detainee needed to sign a statement of commitment prior to release and "to swear in the name of God . . . that they will commit to the results" (p. 119). Again, the extent of ideological change that such commitment represents is difficult to assess; it could mean anything from a temporary suspension of engagement to a thorough ideological change. Without systematic data on this topic, this judgment is anyone's guess.

In summary, though it contained important ingredients, the Yemeni program is generally viewed as rather "unsuccessful, if success is defined as changing militants' worldview" (Rabasa et al., 2010, p. 52). Indeed, many have underscored that the Yemeni program's main preoccupation was to ensure that militants would not connive against the government and, instead, would recognize its legitimacy (Boucek, Beg, & Horgan, 2008). Specifically, "the Yemeni program did not address the issues of participating in violence abroad. It focused solely on activity within Yemen" (Rabasa et al., 2010, p. 53). To that extent, however, if dissuading the militants from violence within Yemen was the program's main objective, one can claim a measure of success, as indexed by the low rate of militants' recidivism according to judge Al-Hitar (2011).

Singapore

After September 11, 2001, Singapore's Internal Security Department (ISD) thwarted a joint operation of Al Qaeda and Jemmah Islamiyah (an Indonesian terror organization) to blow up the embassies of the United States, the United Kingdom, Australia, and Israel, as well as to attack other targets (Gunaratna & Bin Mohamed Hassan, 2011). This plot was quite ambitious in nature, and, had it materialized, the casualties would have been on the order of the infamous 9/11 Al Qaeda attacks in New York and Washington, DC. Approximately 60 individuals suspected of involvement in this plot were arrested and detained.

Concerned about the possible widespread radicalization of Singaporean Muslims, the Singaporean government approached two senior clerics, Ustaz H. Ali H. Mohammed and Ustaz H. Mohammed Hasbi Hassan, with the request to examine the ideological thinking exhibited by the detained militants. On the basis of initial interviews with the detainees, the two clerics realized that the detainees' religious beliefs were seriously out of step with mainstream Islam. To rectify their deviant views of major Islamic concepts, the two ustaz founded the Religious Rehabilitation Group (RRG). The RRG has become the mainstay of the Singaporean deradicalization program—without doubt one of the most comprehensive and carefully administered programs of this kind on record thus far.

A distinctive, and essential, feature of the Singaporean program is that it is rooted in Singapore's Muslim community. The RRG is a voluntary coalition of religious teachers and scholars that since 2002 has evolved into an effective multifaceted organization that offers religious council to both the detainees and their families, publishes pamphlets and manuals for religious counseling, and organizes international meetings of religious and secular scholars engaged in the study of radicalization and deradicalization (Gunaratna & Bin Mohamed Hassan, 2011).

Whereas the RRG's work with the detainees has focused primarily on religious teaching and dialogue, other community organizations have joined together to supplement these activities by providing extensive support to the detainees' families. This organization, the Interagency Aftercare Group (IAG) consists of the Yayasan Mendaki, Association of Muslim Professionals, and the Taman Bacaan, in partnership with the Islamic Religious Council of Singapore, the Community Development Council, the National Council of State Services, the Singapore Malay Journalist Association, the Family Service Center, and others.

The IAG's support includes financial assistance and skill training for the wives of detainees, tuition fee subsidies, pocket money for detainees' children at school, fee waivers for their participation in schools' activity programs, counseling to detainee spouses and children, help in crisis management for detainees' families, and other forms of help detainees' release intended to facilitate their reinsertion into society (Jerard, 2009; Rabasa et al., 2010). Finally, while in detention, the inmates are offered vocational training designed to develop their vocational skills to improve their chances of finding suitable employment upon their release.

Need

The extensive care provided to the detainees' families—who potentially face a humiliating destitution after the major bread winner is placed under arrest— likely prevents a considerable sense of significance loss on the detainees' part. Weekly family visits are also allowed and encouraged by the government, attesting to the respect and concern for the detainees' welfare. The palpable evidence that the families are suffering—economically, emotionally, and socially—as a consequence of the detainees' involvement with extremism may evoke guilt and motivate them to seek alternative routes to meaningful existence, possibly afforded by the vocational education opportunities offered.

Narrative

A particularly strong suit of the Singaporean program is the ideological counternarrative addressed at the detainees. First, this narrative is offered by clerics of impeccable authority, graduates of the foremost Islamic universities such as the Al Azhar University of Cairo, the Madinah University of Saudi Arabia, and the International Islamic University of Malaysia. Second, unlike the Wahabi ideological discourse in the Saudi deradicalization program that justified violence (*jihad musallah,* or armed jihad) against infidels under some circumstances (i.e., against occupiers of a Muslim state), the Singaporean theological discourse highlights the peaceful and tolerant essence of Islam. Such discourse disavows violence and suicide and interprets foundational Islamic concepts like *jihad* and *al wala wal bara* (loyalty and enmity) from a moderate perspective.

From this perspective, therefore, it is more likely that the Singaporean program would eventuate in a full deradicalization, including abandoning the idea of overthrowing the secular state and replacing it with a caliphate or IS (Daulah Islamiyah), as well as relinquishing the concept of violence against infidels and intolerance toward other religions or points of view. In contrast, the Saudi and the Yemeni programs that allowed militant jihad in some circumstances might have effected a less comprehensive disengagement and a readiness to re-engage in violence.

Network

An important aspect of the social dynamic of the Singaporean deradicalization program resides in the fact that the RRG and the IAG organizations are nongovernmental entities acting largely on their own accord. These organizations thus represent the detainees' own communities that likely carry substantial weight and have considerable credibility with detainees. The extensive aftercare program also likely contributes to preventing the families from radicalizing and enlists their help in influencing the detainee to keep to the way of moderation.

In summary, the Singaporean program contains several important psychological elements that should contribute to its effectiveness: It is sensitive to the detainees' sense of self-respect and personal significance; it provides an unequivocal ideological counter narrative that stresses moderation and tolerance and prohibits violence; and it engages a social process based on credibility of the deradicalization message, enlisting a family group dynamic that supports the detainees newly found moderation. Indeed, the Singaporean program is generally viewed as an example of an effective deradicalization enterprise, and it claims a particularly low rate of recidivism. Of the over 50 released detainees, there is by now only one example of a rearrest (Rubin et al., 2011).

The American Program in Iraq

The US military made a concerted effort to rehabilitate tens of thousands of suspected militants in Iraq who were incarcerated in various detention facilities, including Camp Bucca in Umm Qasr in southern Iraq, as well as Camps Taji, Remembrance II, and Cropper in the center of the country. In the spring of 2007, all detainees in Iraq, regardless of the circumstances of their detention, were treated as enemy combatants. Yet in many cases, the arrests were arbitrary and based on questionable intelligence. The glaring unfairness of this situation created a considerable pool of resentment among the detainees, breeding a sense of disenfranchisement and humiliation that was likely to be exploited by the few extremists in their midst.

Task Force 134 (TF-134), drawn from the coalition's military, was charged with detainee command and control, including the rehabilitation program. It was led by Major General Douglas Stone and was coordinated through General David Petraeus (for detailed discussion, see Angell & Gunaratna, 2012). The program included around 100 military attorneys and paralegals, mostly from the navy and the air force. The TF-134 was charged with determining whether detainees were an "imperative security risk" or an "enduring security risk." Detainees in the former category were encouraged to participate in an extensive deradicalization program, whereas those in the latter category were assumed to be too extreme to be deradicalized and, in addition, to pose the risk of radicalizing others.

Was the approach to detainee rehabilitation taken by TF-134 psychologically sound? From the present theoretical perspective, the answer is affirmative. Modeled closely after the Saudi and the Singaporean programs, it contained the motivational, ideological, and social elements that are essential to effective deradicalization.

Need

According to Major General Douglas Stone, the intent of the deradicalization program in Iraq was that "detainees gain a sense of dignity, self-worth, a life purpose and commitment to nonviolent tolerance" (Angell & Gunaratna, 2012, p. 233). An important way in which this objective was pursued involved several educational programs designed to provide the detainees with various capabilities and skills. Attendance at these programs was voluntary;

they included educational courses in Arabic, math, and computer training, all taught by civilian contractors with pertinent expertise, as well as art activities and civic courses.

It appears that these programs were, by and large, successful. There have even been cases where detainees have pleaded to stay longer in the detention center to complete the educational classes they were taking. Occasionally, family members have implored the center's authorities to keep their loved ones in detention until their educational training has been completed. One detainee remarked:

> When I was detained, I was surprised to hear that there is a school where I can enroll myself. It was an honor to participate. It was run by the American Army who supplied us with textbooks and stationary. I attended an 8-week course where I learned reading and writing and Qu'ran reading. . . . My thanks to the education program and my thanks to Allah. (Angell & Gunaratna, 2012, p. 205)

Narrative

As with the Yemeni, the Saudi, and the Singaporean programs, the ideological part of the Iraqi program was carried out by clerics and was fitted specifically to the circumstances of the Iraqi population. The Islamic Discussion Programs (IDPs) aimed at promoting a moderate interpretation of Islam, one incompatible with violence and characterized by humanity and tolerance. A Socratic method was employed in which extreme interpretations of the Qur'an were challenged, and moderate interpretations were offered.

> Besides the Qur'an, which was the principal book used in each class, the Taqrib was also used. The Taqrib was written by the jurist Abu Shuja Isfahani from the Shafti school of Islamic Jurisprudence (d. 1197 C.E.). In addition, Hadiths were regularly used in classes. Hadiths are narrations originating from the words and deeds of . . . prophet Muhammad, and are regarded by traditional schools of jurisprudence as important tools for understanding the Qur'an. (Angell & Gunaratna, 2012, p. 232)

The detainees learned that according to Islam, the greatest crime of all is *qatl*, the killing of another human being. The Qur'an commands explicitly:

And do not take any human being's life—which God has willed to be, sacred—otherwise than in [the pursuit of] justice. Hence, if anyone has been slain wrongfully, we have empowered the defender of his rights [to exact a just retribution]; but even so, let him not exceed the bounds of equity in retributive killing. [and as for him who has been slain wrongfully], behold, he is indeed succored by God. (Qur'an 17:33)

In these terms, the greatest sin according to Islam is the killing of innocent people, and this "debt" will not be forgiven by God even to legitimate martyrs. Unlike the Yemeni and the Saudi programs that justified militant jihad against occupying forces, the clerical program in Iraq had the objective to convince the detainee that jihad against the coalition forces or against other Muslims accused of heresy (*Takfir*) is not sanctioned by Islam. Whereas initially the detainee participation in a four-day IDP was voluntary, in 2009 it became mandatory and a precondition for release, by order of Major General Quantock.

Network

Following the Saudi and the Singaporean programs on which it was modeled, the Iraqi program contained several elements intended to create a social process conducive to authentic deradicalization. Consider the policy of separating the extremist detainees from the general population of incarcerated individuals. Because of the arrestees' anger and humiliation on being deprived of their freedom, detainees should be particularly vulnerable to persuasion by ideologies that promise a significance-restoring revenge. According to Angell and Gunaratna (2012), "what was realized that while [the initial] focus was . . . on rehabilitating the more radical detainees, moderate detainees were being recruited into extremist networks while in detention" (p. 236). In this sense, the separation policy reflects an appreciation of the detainees' psychological state and the process of social influence that may affect them.

Appreciation of the social process and the anchorage of detainees' attitudes in the social networks in which they are embedded is reflected in how *detainees' families* were involved in rehabilitation, modeled after the Saudi and the Singaporean programs.[4] A major element of family involvement was

---

4. As noted earlier, cultivating good relations with the detainees' families, by extending them financial and moral support, has been the staple of the Saudi deradicalization program (Al-Hadlaq, 2011), and, similarly, in Singapore the IAG has provided assistance to families of detainee, in the form of financial aid, professional training for wives of detainees, and educational subsidies for the children of detainees (Angell & Gunaratna, 2012).

the visitation policy implemented by the TF-134 early in 2004. Families were able to conduct weekly visitations in which they were permitted brief physical contact with their incarcerated relatives, primarily hugs and kisses with children and wives. During these visits, detainees could share with their family members whatever money they had earned through paid works in the detention facility.

Importantly, too, during the more extended 60-minute communication periods, the detainees and their adult relatives (e.g., wives) were afforded time for "grown-up" discussion while their children spent time at a special playground in which they played with unarmed American soldiers. Angell and Gunaratna (2012) describe it:

> It was incredible to witness the interaction and see how excited the children were to play with the American soldiers. At the conclusion of the 60-minute... part of the visitation, every visiting child was offered something to take with him/her. There was always an abundant supply of stuffed animals in addition to clothing, school supplies and toys from which to choose. (p. 197)

In summary, the American-led deradicalization program in Iraq has resulted in the release of tens of thousands of detainees into the Iraqi society. Of those, only a small percentage were rearrested—approximately six percent, according to General Stone (US Department of Defense, 2008). Does the low recidivism rate attest to success of the program? According to Angell and Gunaratna (2012), the answer is yes:

> We have plenty of actions to support the hypothesis that the rehabilitation programs work in the successful transformation of destructive ideologies. Beside the significant reduction in violence and increase in intelligence that markedly took place after the initiation of the rehabilitation programs in 2007, we have countless examples of the impact the programs have made on Iraqi detainees. . . . Detainees have asked to have combined compounds where both Sunni and Shiite, who are tired of the senseless violence, can live together without fear and in peace. (p. 377).

This conclusion notwithstanding, it should be noted that numerous former detainees in Camp Bucca, proceeded to join IS and lent it considerable military expertise and professionalism (cf. Jasko, Kruglanski, Hassan,

& Gunaratna, 2018). This may be more reflective of the political struggle between the Sunnis and the Shia in post-2003 Iraq rather than of the failure of the Iraqi deradicalization program as such (Kaltenthaler, Dagher, McCulloh, Kruglanski, & Gelfand, 2018).

The Sri Lankan Program

As noted earlier, the Tamil Tigers organization—more specifically known as the Liberation Tamil Tigers of Eelam (LTTE)—has been one of the most vicious terrorist organizations in history. It still holds the world record in suicide attacks launched by a single organization, and its victims were major politicians, such as the prime minister of India, Rajiv Ghandi; the president of Sri Lanka, Ranasinghe Premadasa; and numerous ministers, generals, academics, and journalists.

In 2009, in a decisive push to defeat the LTTE, about 20,000 of militants were killed by Sri Lankan forces. The remaining 11,500 LTTE cadres were detained in camps and exposed to various deradicalization programs. Unlike the programs in Muslim states that highlighted the moral inadmissibility of violence against civilians and utilized theological narratives to make the point, the Sri Lankan program centered on refocusing the detainees (referred to as "beneficiaries," as in the Saudi program) to their personal lives and away from collectivistic concerns, such as LTTE's quest for an independent state.

To be sure, the Sri Lankan program was launched in circumstances where violence and fighting were pretty much removed as a viable option. Given their total defeat by the Sri Lankan forces—violence and fighting could hardly qualify as a means to significance and, in fact, could be perceived as a road to a vast humiliation. Thus, the Sri Lankan program was designed to help beneficiaries come to term with their violent past, adopt a peaceful lifestyle, and become equipped with the necessary skills to reconnect with mainstream civil society.

Need

The Sri Lankan program emphasized the importance of giving respect to the detained "beneficiaries" and treating them well. Within the deradicalization centers, the beneficiaries had freedom of movement and of religious practice. The military personnel with whom they were in contact were unarmed, though armed cadres guarded the peripheries of the Protective Accommodation and Rehabilitation Centers (PARCS), as the detention centers were called. Furthermore, the detainees were offered a variety of courses for self-expression and reflection, such as art and yoga classes. They were also encouraged to engage daily in various sports such as cricket, volleyball, and traditional Sri Lankan sports, along with other athletic activities (Hettiarachchi, 2014).

Narrative

In a context where the defeat of the LTTE was indisputable and years of armed struggle had failed to advance the group's ethnonationalist agenda, the main objective of the Sri Lankan program was to help "beneficiary thinking away from violence and separatism" (Hettiarachchi, 2014, p. 26) so they "champion peace building initiatives with values of moderation, tolerance, and co-existence" (p. 18). To achieve these goals, the Sri Lankan program took a holistic approach, implementing a wide range of courses to facilitate the acquisition of interpersonal skills deemed pivotal to beneficiaries' adherence to peace and future reinsertion into mainstream society. In that regard, beneficiaries' participation in emotional intelligence and counseling training courses appears to have been important vectors of change. In these sessions, beneficiaries were taught different techniques to manage and express their emotions, cope with adversity, help others in need, and resolve conflicts in a peaceful way (Hettiarachchi, 2014).

In the same vein, the Sri Lankan program facilitated a series of formal and informal interactional initiatives that allowed beneficiaries and staff members to engage in stimulating discussion related to "family, future, and peace building . . . society, social responsibility and contributing towards the economy . . . to cultivate a sense of citizenship" (Hettiarachchi, 2014, p. 25). Key to enabling these discussions was establishing good rapport between beneficiaries and the various professionals on the premises.

Among these formal initiatives, beneficiaries took part in a mentorship program. Hettiarachchi (2014) reports:

> Successful and well-respected persons in the Tamil community engaged as mentors and role models, reflecting a sense of responsibility and a shared future that is achievable through unity rather than divisions. They motivated the beneficiaries to work hard and to build a successful future. These business people, film stars, and athletes were testimony to the ability of people from the region to make a successful life with the opportunities available in Sri Lanka. (p. 26)

As can be gleaned from all these efforts, attempts were made to convince beneficiaries of a better, more secure, and sustainable future, while proposing alternative ways of reaching personal significance without resorting to violence.

Network

The Sri Lankan program placed considerable emphasis on the social element of deradicalization. First, the hard-core, fully committed LTTEs were separated from the other, more peripheral members. This separation was meant to weaken the social ties and the group dynamic that tied the beneficiaries to the organization. Also, a special effort was invested in reconstructing the ties between the detainees and their families that had been deliberately and systematically weakened by the LTTE organization. Specifically, the LTTE claimed that joining its ranks is tantamount to joining a new family whose members are completely devoted to each other and, hence, the ties with the "old" families had to be severed. As a consequence, many detained LTTE members had sparse relations with their natural families, and the families' needs were superseded by needs of the organization. Rebuilding family relations was thus defined as a foremost priority for the Sri Lankan deradicalization program.

No visits except those with the immediate family were allowed, and conditions were set to allow the families to spend time with the beneficiaries, thus strengthening the family ties and keeping them going. The rehab coordinators made special calls to arrange family visits one to three times per week. The families' transportation was fully paid for, and they were given meals at the center. Places inside the facilities were specifically set aside for families to visit and bond with the beneficiaries. The staff at the detention centers was also charged with promoting the reconstruction of family ties by having the beneficiaries think back to their *past family life*, prior to joining the organization, and also to their future life with their family. The staff was also tasked with helping the family members reestablish their relationships with the beneficiaries, including extending them care and encouraging the creation mutual bonds of loyalty between the beneficiaries and their families (Hettiarachchi, 2014).

Another specific way the Sri Lankan program used the social process in deradicalizing LTTE members was by arranging multiple marriages between couples who had been together while in the LTTE, but who were previously prevented by the organization's strict rules from actually marrying. The marriage ceremonies were also geared to cement the new future for the erstwhile LTTE cadres. The families participated in the ceremonies—lavish entertainment programs with dancing and singing by beneficiary troupes—as did high-ranking Sri Lankan dignitaries, whose presence lent special air of significance to the occasion. Post wedding, the couples were moved to a special camp facility called the "Peace Village" where they could commence their married life. These marriage ceremonies were a time when beneficiaries and their families interacted with Sinhalese and Tamils from other parts of the country, as well, promoting a different shared reality from that forged in the LTTE. The idea was to create a sense of how Sri Lanka people from various backgrounds can live together in mutual respect and cooperation.

Unlike other deradicalization programs discussed earlier, the Sri Lankan program has been systematically evaluated by our team, as described in detail in Chapter 5. The results suggest that over a period of one year the militancy of the LTTEs placed in the PARC camps substantially decreased, and thousands of former members were released into the community. The recidivism rate attributed with the reintegration of Tamil Tigers in the community is zero percent (Dharmawardhane, 2013). At least in part, this outcome seems attributable to the Sri Lankan deradicalization program and the treatment of the beneficiaries while in custody. It is important to bear in mind, however, that the beneficiaries' return to moderation occurred in the context where the violent option seemed pretty much off the table following the LTTEs conclusive defeat by the Sri Lankan military. This aspect of their situation may have impelled the beneficiaries to be more open to alternative ways of attaining their self-regard and a sense of significance, such as through the opportunities for personal development and education afforded by the deradicalization program. It is unclear whether the same outcome would have been achieved if the militant option was still viable and whether the Sri Lankan program would have had a similar effect if that were the case.

Other Deradicalization/Counterradicalization Programs

The deradicalization programs described above were certainly the most extensive and thoughtful efforts to win back the hearts and minds of incarcerated militants. Yet there were other attempts to counter the trends of radicalization and/or immunize audiences against the appeal of extremist rhetoric.

Bangladesh

In 2005, Bangladesh established a covert and hybrid deradicalization/ counterradicalization program (El-Said & Harrigan, 2013), fronted by several nongovernmental organizations created for that purpose. The program targets individuals (e.g., madrasa students) identified as vulnerable to radicalization. The main de/counterradicalization vehicle is lectures by scholars and clerics about various Islamic issues such as Islam and peace, Islam and modernity, Islam and human rights, Islam and tolerance, and other similar concepts. In addition to those lectures, seminars and workshops on related topics are offered, as is financial assistance and help in finding a job or setting up a business. Again, it appears that the Bangladeshi program, though not as specific and focused as some of the major programs described earlier, recognizes the importance of the ideological element and also of providing radicals or potential radicals with alternative means of leading a meaningful life. In this way, the program addresses the significance motive and reduces the appeal of violence as a means to that end.

Malaysia

Malaysia's approach to coping with Islamist insurgency and terrorism is based on frameworks developed in response to waves of Communist insurgency in 1948–1960 and 1968–1989. That framework was guided by the notion of KESBAN—"Keselamatan dan Pembangunan" or security/defense and development—encompassing the totality of measures undertaken by the government to protect and strengthen the society against subversion, lawlessness, and insurgency. To immunize the population against the appeal of militant Communist ideology that promised a betterment of the citizens' existence, the Malaysian government and its military undertook a variety of economic development projects. These initiatives included "infrastructure development, the upgrading of cultural productivity, the construction of the East-West Highway, educational development, construction of houses for the very poor, and the construction of dams and hydroelectric plants" (Harrigan, p. 143).

In addition, the armed forces provided the population with medical and dental services and participated in a variety of community projects such as sporting activities, art exhibitions and displays, and minor engineering projects (e.g., help in highway and bridge construction; El-Said & Harrigan, 2013). These activities apparently succeeded in isolating the Communist insurgency from the rest of the population and creating the feeling that the government cared about its people and attended to their needs. In addition, the government carried out an ideological counternarrative by disseminating leaflets to the insurgents and their supporters. It also recruited surrendered militants to carry the anticommunist message to village audiences in remote areas that were particularly susceptible to radicalization.

The Malaysian government's 20th-century approach to win the population's hearts and minds and thus reduce the people's readiness to embrace the extremist antigovernmental narrative, also guided the effort to deradicalize Islamic extremists in the early 2000s. According to El-Said and Harrigan (2013), 154 religious extremists were arrested between 2001 and 2010 and held in a detention facility in Kamunting. There, a deradicalization program was implemented that was modeled to a large extent after the Saudi program. The program included religious teachings that stressed Islam's moderation and tolerance toward non-Muslims, exploring basic Qur'anic concepts like jihad, takfir, and al Wala wal Bara. The program also included vocational courses in agriculture and management, intended to prepare the detainees for reintegration in society post release.

Family cooperation was also sought in convincing the detainees to renounce violence, akin to the Saudi program. Thus, the Malaysian program is based on awareness that deradicalization requires winning the hearts and minds of extremists by giving them respect, equipping them with alternatives to violence as a way to gain significance, providing them with a compelling counternarrative denouncing violence as a means to an end, and utilizing the social process toward enhancing the persuasive impact of the moderation message. A critique sometimes leveled against the Malaysian program is that it makes release contingent on participation in the program, thus raising the question whether the detainees' avowed attitude change in the course of the program and if their pledges of moderation are in fact authentic. Nonetheless, it is remarkable that of the 154 detained Islamic militants only 6 remain in custody and none of those released have been rearrested.

Summary

In this chapter, we have considered the phenomenon of deradicalization in its various manifestations. As we have seen, deradicalization can occur spontaneously on both the individual and the group level. The process may be facilitated by specific programs engineered to persuade participants to disengage from supporting and participating in violence. In our discussion, we found it is useful to distinguish between degrees of deradicalization representing the extent to which personal engagement in violence, or support for violence, has been reduced or delimited. An individual who continues to support violence attitudinally—and perhaps materially without, however, giving up on her or his other concerns, such as career, family, and recreation—is less radicalized than one who volunteers to risk her or his life for the cause. One who denies the very legitimacy of violence is yet less radicalized—or more deradicalized—than one that justifies it under some circumstances.

Similarly, an individual who delimits engagement in violence to a certain place and time, or to a certain type of targets—say, Western occupiers of a given country—is less radicalized than one who supports violence more broadly, such as against Westerners in general. We have argued, moreover, that attitudinal and behavioral change involved in both radicalization and deradicalization is governed by a process in which individuals' needs, the narratives to which they are exposed, and the social networks of which they are members play a significant part.

To greater or lesser extent, this set of factors has been addressed into all known programs of deradicalization and likely determined their effectiveness. Thus, for instance, the need element (quest for significance) has been represented by the respect accorded detainees in rehabilitation centers and by programs that augment their capability to obtain honorable work upon release, designed to boost their self-esteem (e.g., educational courses of various sorts). Theological dialogues and discussions about the true nature of Islam and its rejection of wanton violence represent the narrative element of deradicalization. And the recruitment of detainees' families or ex-militants as agents of deradicalization mobilize the network process, without which authentic change of attitudes and behaviors may be difficult to attain.

It is of interest to speculate about the relative weight of needs, narratives, and networks in different instances of deradicalization. For instance, it is plausible that where the detainees' group is cohesive and intact—with leaders and followers held in the same quarters—it is probably more effective to first break this network's dynamic before addressing the ideological narrative and the detainees' needs through appropriate programs and activities. It is also important to determine whether a given detainee is particularly motivated by the significance gain aspects represented by the glory of martyrdom rather than by the significance loss aspect and the felt desire to regain one's significance by acts of revenge. Detainees from collectivistic cultures might be more sensitive to the network processes rather than to theological narrative presented for their consideration—as may people who are relatively low on the quest for significance dimension and are rather susceptible to persuasion and acceptability to one's ingroup. These issues could be a worthy topic of the next generation of research on radicalization and deradicalization. The findings of such research could enhance our ability to design more efficient deradicalization programs and to identify the best practices in this domain that fit specific circumstances.

References

Al-Hadlaq, A. (2011). Terrorist rehabilitation: The Saudi experience. In R. Gunaratna, J. Jerard, & L. Rubin (Eds.), *Terrorist rehabilitation and counter-radicalisation: New approaches to counter-terrorism* (pp. 59–69). New York, NY: Routledge.

Al-Hitar, H. A. (2011). Dialogue and its effects on countering terrorism: The Yemeni experience. In R. Gunaratna, J. Jerard, & L. Rubin (Eds.), *Terrorist rehabilitation and counter-radicalisation: New approaches to counter-terrorism* (pp. 109–121). New York, NY: Routledge.

Ammar, N. H., Weaver, R. R., & Saxon, S. (2004). Muslims in prison: A case study from Ohio state prisons. *International Journal of Offender Therapy and Comparative Criminology, 48,* 414–428.

Angell, A., & Gunaratna, R. (2012). *Terrorist rehabilitation: The U.S. experience in Iraq.* Boca Raton, FL: Taylor and Francis.

Ashour, O. (2008). *Islamist de-radicalization in Algeria: Successes and failures* (Policy brief no. 21). Washington, DC: Middle East Institute.

Ashour, O. (2009). *The De-radicalization of Jihadists: Transforming armed Islamist movements.* London, England: Routledge.

Beckford, J. A., Joly, D., & Khosrokhavar, F. (2005). *Muslims in prison: Challenge and change in Britain and France.* Basingstoke, England: Palgrave Macmillan.

Boucek, C. (2008). Counter-terrorism from within: Assessing Saudi Arabia's religious rehabilitation and disengagement programme. *RUSI Journal, 153,* 60–65.

Boucek, C. (2009). Extremist re-education and rehabilitation in Saudi Arabia. In T. Bjorgo & J. Horgan (Eds.), *Leaving terrorism behind: Individual and collective disengagement* (pp. 212–223). New York, NY: Routledge.

Boucek, C., Beg, S., & Horgan, J. (2008). Opening up the jihadi debate: Yemen's Committee for Dialogue, In T. Bjorgo & J. Horgan (Eds.), *Leaving terrorism behind: Individual and collective disengagement* (pp. 181–192). New York, NY: Routledge.

Dharmawardane, I. (2013). Sri Lanka's post-conflict strategy: Restorative justice for rebels and rebuilding of conflict-affected communities. *Perspectives on Terrorism, 7,* 1–10.

El-Said, H. (2012). *De-radicalising Islamists: Programmes and their impact in Muslim majority states.* London, England: International Centre for the Study of Radicalisation and Political Violence.

El-Said, H. (2013). Yemen's passive approach to countering terrorism. In H. El-Said and J. Harrigan (Eds.), *Deradicalising violent extremists: Counter-radicalisation and deradicalisation programmes and their impact in Muslim majority states* (pp. 227–260). New York, NY: Routledge.

El-Said, H., Barrett, R. (2013). Saudi Arabia: the master of deradicalization. In H. El-Said and J. Harrigan (Eds.), *Deradicalising violent extremists: Counter-radicalisation and deradicalisation programmes and their impact in Muslim majority states* (pp. 194–226). New York, NY: Routledge.

El-Said, H. & Harrigan, J. (2013). *Deradicalising violent extremists: Counter-radicalisation and deradicalisation programmes and their impact in Muslim majority states.* New York, NY: Routledge.

Guessous, F., Hooper, N., & Moorthy, U. (2001). *Religion in prisons 1999 and 2000.* London, England: Great Britain Home Office Research Development and Statistics.

Gunaratna, R., & Bin Mohamed Hassan, M. F. (2011). Terrorist rehabilitation: the Singapore experience. In R. Gunaratna, J. Jerard, & L. Rubin (Eds.), *Terrorist rehabilitation and counter-radicalisation: New approaches to counter-terrorism* (pp. 36–58). New York, NY: Routledge.

Hardin, C. D., & Higgins, E. T. (1996). Shared reality: How social verification makes the subjective objective. In R. M. Sorrentino & T. E. Higgins (Eds.), *Handbook of motivation and cognition* (Vol. 2, pp. 28–84). New York, NY: Guilford.

Harrigan, J. (2013). Malaysia: A history of dealing with insurgency and extremism. In H. El-Said and J. Harrigan (Eds.), *Deradicalising violent extremists: Counter-radicalisation and deradicalisation programmes and their impact in Muslim majority states* (pp. 140–160). New York, NY: Routledge.

Hettiarachchi, M. (2014, February). *Sri Lanka's rehabilitation program: The humanitarian mission two.* Colombo, Sri Lanka: Research & Monitoring Division, Department of Government Information. Retrieved from http://www.sinhalanet.net/wp-content/uploads/2014/08/Sri-Lankas-Rehabilitation-Program.pdf

Jamieson, A. (1989). *The heart attacked: Terrorism and conflict in the Italian state.* London, England: Marion Boyars.

Jerard, J. (2009). Report on a conference organized by the International Centre of Political Violence and Terrorism Research (ICPVTR). *S. Rajaratnam School of International Studies.* Retrieved from https://www.rsis.edu.sg/wp-content/uploads/2015/04/Report-International-Conference-On-Terrorist-Rehabilitation.pdf.

Kaltenthaler, K., Dagher, M., McCulloh, I., Kruglanski, A.W., & Gelfand, M.J. (2018). *ISIS in Iraq: Understanding the Social Foundations of Terror.* Unpublished manuscript.

Kruglanski, A. W., Gelfand, M. J., Sheveland, A., Babush, M., Hetiarachchi, M., Ng Bonto, M., & Gunaratna, R. (2016). What a difference two years make: Patterns of radicalization in a Philippine jail. *Dynamics of Asymmetric Conflict, 9,* 13–36.

Porges, M. L. (2011, July 1). Reform school for radicals. *The American Interest.* Retrieved from http://www.the-american-interest.com/articles/2011/07/01/reform-school-for-radicals/

Rabasa, A., Pettyjohn, S. L., Ghez, J. J., & Boucek, C. (2010). *Deradicalizing Islamist extremists.* Santa Monica, CA: Rand.

Reinares, F. (2011). Exit from terrorism: A qualitative empirical study on disengagement and deradicalization among members of ETA. *Terrorism and Political Violence, 23,* 780–803.

Rubin, L., Gunaratna, R., & Gerard, J. A. (2011). *Terrorist rehabilitation and counter-radicalization.* London, England: Routledge.

Spalek, B., & Wilson, D. (2002). Racism and religious discrimination in prison: The marginalization of imams in their work with prisoners. In B. Spalek (Eds.), *Islam, crime and criminal justice* (pp. 96–112). Portland, OR: Willan.

Terrorist recruitment and infiltration in the United States: Prisons and military as an operational base. Hearing before the US Senate Subcommittee on Terrorism, Technology and Homeland Security. 108th Congr. 1st sess. (2003) (testimony of Michael Waller).

Trujillo, H. M., Jordán, J., Gutiérrez, J. A., & González, J. (2009). Radicalization in prisons? Field research in 25 Spanish prisons. *Terrorism and Political Violence, 21,* 558–579.

US Department of Defense. (2008, June 9). Department of Defense news briefing with Major General Stone from the Pentagon. *GlobalSecurity.org.* Retrieved from http://www.globalsecurity.org/military/library/news/2008/06/mil-080609-dod02.htm

8 CAN REHABILITATION LAST?

ON PREVENTING RERADICALIZATION

According to the National Institute of Justice (2014), "recidivism refers to a person's relapse into criminal behavior; it is measured by criminal acts that resulted in re-arrest, reconviction or return to prison." In the present context, former violent extremists released into society are said to recidivate if they are found to plot, materially support, or consort with others known to be actively involved in terrorism and/or to belong to a terrorist organization. We are assuming that the same conditions that led individuals to *radicalize* in the first place, and which reversal promoted *deradicalization*, also contribute to a *reradicalization* and, hence, to recidivism. From the present perspective, these conditions belong to the familiar 3N categories of needs, narratives, and networks. Specifically, if individuals find themselves humiliated, discriminated against, and disparaged upon release from prison or other rehabilitation facility, they will be likely motivated to reaffirm their significance. The same may happen if they are re-exposed to a narrative that incites such quest and offers violence as the road to its fulfillment. Contacts with networks of relatives or friends that subscribe to that narrative would further magnify this option and, hence, increase the likelihood of re-radicalization.

In a sense, the process here is similar to factors that foster the recidivism of criminals: inability to find a respectable and sufficiently lucrative occupation upon release (the need component), exposure to cultural scripts and social norms (the narrative component) that prescribe given criteria for significance (e.g., material wealth and power) and condone criminal behavior (e.g., drug trafficking) as an acceptable way of achieving significance, and participation in a criminality-supporting social network. In what follows, we therefore discuss the problem of reradicalization of violent extremists in terms of our 3N model. We specifically consider macro-, meso-, and micro-level factors assumed to bear on the recidivism of deradicalized extremists.

The Macro Level

A country's political, social, and economic factors play an important role in determining the enduring success of deradicalization by influencing the likelihood that a former extremist will be able to find a satisfactory, significance-bestowing way of living that does not involve violence. One factor often mentioned in this regard is the degree to which the state is well organized and, hence, able to offer its citizens effective means to rewarding living, thus limiting the appeal of counternormative behavior. The well-known political science concept of *state failure* pertains to this issue.

State Failure

According to Messner (2013), from the Fund for Peace, a nongovernmental organization based in Washington, DC, state failure occurs upon

> the state's loss of control of its territory, or [where] the state no longer has a monopoly on the legitimate use of physical force within its borders; [upon] erosion of the state's legitimate authority to make collective decisions; the inability of the state to provide adequate public services; and the state's inability to interact with other states as a full member of the international community.

Releasing a deradicalized individual into a failed state may increase the likelihood of recidivism for two reasons. First, the former extremist may find it more difficult to find a respectable, significance-affording way of earning a living in the chaotic and unstable environment that characterizes such a state. Second, violent extremism is unlikely to be curbed or severely punished in such an environment, thus remaining a viable, if not the exclusive, road to significance available to the individual.

The porous borders of failed states facilitate drug and weapon smuggling, turning them into safe havens and training grounds for criminal and terrorist organizations alike (e.g., Carter, 2012; Dailey, Davis, & Managuelod, 2013). These organizations benefit from a large pool of low-cost insurgents looking for better socio-economic prospects (Collier, 2000; Urdal, 2006) and encounter fewer operational constraints, given that the state is in no position to offer effective counterterrorism measures. Under such conditions, social networks may emerge whose world views and narratives condone violence on behalf of various causes and whose existence and apparent successes may appeal to significance seeking individuals in their social milieu.

Population Demographics

The demographics of a given state's population may contribute to recidivism by creating social networks whose shared reality is supportive of extremism. Age, particularly the proportion of young males in a population, is a significant demographic factor in this regard. Young males with high levels of energy and testosterone are especially prone to be attracted to extreme, violence-supporting narratives that promise glamour and glory (hence, significance) through violent combat. Urdal (2006) attests that the risk of conflict outbreaks in a given state is substantially amplified by the presence of *youth bulges*, large cohorts of young people, age 15 through 24 years old. As these cohorts exceed 35% of the adult population, the chances of civil strife augment by 150% in comparison to countries with demographic structures where youth cohorts do not exceed 17% of the population.

Although social movements and youth cohorts are not necessarily violent, they might become so in the light of ideological narratives that advocate violence as the only form of collective action that may achieve political gains. If released into such an environment, former extremists are at high risk of recidivism.

Poverty and Material Benefits

The relation between poverty and violent extremism is controversial and has been the topic of a long-standing academic debate. With relatively small positive correlations between the two concepts in some studies (e.g., 0.25 in Schmid, 2005) and even negative ones in others (e.g., with Hizballah fighters; Krueger & Malečková, 2002), scholars have been tempted to conclude that the relation between the two is, at best, indirect and tenuous (e.g., Krueger & Malečková, 2002). Other investigators argue, however, that economic disparities including poverty and income inequality heighten the risk of political conflicts (Chen, 2003; Gurr, 1970; Li & Schaub, 2004). Relatedly, increasing evidence points to unemployment as a risk factor associated with violent extremism.

In support of this perspective, Schmid (2005) reports that "almost a quarter of the recruits of insurgent groups in Kashmir cited 'joblessness' as a recruiting motive" (p. 228). In our own research, out of a sample of 2,028 Tamil Tigers of the Liberation Tigers of Tamil Eelam (LTTE), 24.4% reported being unemployed before joining the organization. Similarly, Sozer and Sever (2011) analyzed the biographies of 1,500 Turkish Hizballah members and observed that one of the most important factors predicting involvement in violent acts was unemployment, followed by the number of years in the organization and the age at which members joined the organization. El-Said (2015) observed that 60% of Australia's neo-jihadists "emerged from one community: the Australian Sunni Lebanese community, namely, Lebanese Muslims, who suffer considerable socio-economic disadvantages compared to the main population," (p. 18) including lower employment rates than the Australian average.

Lastly, in 2014 the relation between unemployment and terrorism was examined using labor force participation rates included in the World Bank's World Development Indicators Database to predict terrorist incidents contained in the Global Terrorism Database, developed by the START group at the University of Maryland. These databases comprise 1,235 observations compiled from 2000 to 2009 across 151 countries. Results indicated a negative relation between employment and terrorism (Flowers, 2014). As a whole, these results culled from various terrorist organizations strongly suggest the possibility that economic disparities, especially unemployment, either create or aggravate perceived group grievances and alleged unfairness. This proposition is consistent with work linking such perceptions to different forms of significance loss such as social exclusion, alienation, feeling of injustice, disempowerment, and lesser psychological well-being (Donovan & Oddy, 1982; Furnham, 1985). In other words, whereas poverty and economic malaise may constitute neither the necessary nor the sufficient condition for reradicalization, it may well constitute a *contributing factor* to this phenomenon (Kruglanski & Fishman, 2006). To the extent that poverty lowers individuals' sense of personal significance, it may predispose them to embrace extremist narratives, particularly if these are supported by the social networks in which the impoverished persons are embedded.

Relevant to the last point, Cragin and Chalk (2003) found that social and economic development policies—including education, health, housing, farming, community-based cooperatives, and infrastructure projects—can be effective to inhibiting violent extremism in countries where they are implemented. These authors' results—based on public opinion polls measuring support for terrorist activities, interviews with government officials and academics; and research of local activities in Northern Ireland, the Philippines, and the West Bank Gaza Strip—led them to the following conclusions:

While economic development policies do not eradicate terrorism, they do *weaken local support for terrorist activities*. This decline in support occurs primarily when the beneficiaries of economic development programs actively discourage activities by extremist groups that threaten the beneficiaries' economic vitality. In their RAND report, Cragin and Chalk (2003) discuss the case of Northern Ireland, where individuals who benefited from these development programs "formed important mediation networks to reduce violence between supporters of militant Protestant groups and those sympathetic to the cause of the Real Irish Republican Army (RIRA)" (p. 10). As noted in Chapter 7, the Egyptian Gammah Islamiyah's attacks on tourists threatened to undermine the population's major source of revenue, consequently undermining the population's support for its activity. This led to the major arrests of the movement's leaders, confiscations of their weapons caches, and, ultimately, to the group's decision to relinquish violence.

Social and economic development policies can discourage individuals from joining terrorist groups by curbing their grievances and the appeal of financial incentives provided by terrorist organizations to recruit them. The latter point is important because it highlights the fact that those who join radical organizations may not do so exclusively for ideological reasons but for material incentives as well. For instance, O'Connell and Benard (2006) observed that many Iraqi insurgents were, in fact, paid-for-hire recruits risking their lives for relatively small sums of money (US$20–US$100). In exchange, they had to place improvised explosive devices (IEDs) along roadsides to kill US soldiers.

Note that monetary incentives shouldn't be construed merely as pertaining to materialistic motives to acquire various objects of desire. Wealth has an important symbolic value highly relevant to the motive of personal significance. Poverty, after all, bestows shame and humiliation, and the inability to be financially independent and to provide for one's family can be a major occasion for significance loss. Payments offered by terrorist organizations may lure impoverished youths as a way to greater power, independency, and, hence, mattering and significance.

It is also important to remember that a significance increment that comes from monetary payments isn't mutually exclusive with deriving major significance additionally from other sources, such as defense of one's nation and religion and engagement in courageous combat against one's group's enemies. In short, monetary resources are an important source of felt significance; as such they can be appropriately utilized by moderates and extremists alike to encourage individuals' adherence to their ideological narratives and actions that these dictate.

Cragin and Chalk (2003) aptly emphasize that the moderating impact of states' economic promises depends on their fulfillment. If the economic promises turn out to be empty, they may backfire by building resentment and reducing support toward the state. The latter has been observed with the Fuerzas Armadas Revolucionarias de Columbia (FARC) in Columbia and the jihadists in Yemen, where disengaged militants did not have access to promised funds and either contemplated or actually rejoined radical groups in response (Arndt, Greene, & Maksimowicz, 2010). Even when the economic promises are fulfilled, however, other factors may mitigate the positive effects of economic measures implemented by the state. Despite the provision of job opportunities, housing, stipends, and free aftercare counseling to former extremists, community resistance to the acceptance of erstwhile extremists, their social stigmatization, and other social environment issues may come into play and reduce the likelihood that the deradicalized individuals will feel respected in their new milieu. We consider these issues next.

Meso-Level Factors

Community Resistance

An important obstacle that limits the efficacy of economic measures to promote effective reintegration of former extremists is *community resistance* to their reinclusion in mainstream society. Simply, community members might not be very keen on the idea of "rewarding" those that have perpetrated violence by accepting them into their midst as equal members. For instance, providing former members of the LTTE with access to grants, low-interest bank loans, livelihood start-up projects and applications for land, housing, and employment promoted feelings of unfairness on part of some members of the Tamil community at large (Hettiarachchi, 2014). After all, the Tamil civilians themselves suffered the most at the hands of the LTTE; hence, they were resentful about the advantages accorded their former detractors who terrorized the community in times past (Hettiarachchi, 2014).

Social Stigmatization

An important community challenge defined by the "Rome Memorandum"— a UN-sponsored document that elaborates the best practices for the rehabilitation of former terrorists—is developing "a positive, welcoming environment for the inmate—where the former inmate is accepted back into the community and where neighbors are helping ease their transition" (Global Counterterrorism Forum, 2012, p. 13). Unsurprisingly, creating a positive social atmosphere can be a thorny issue, especially in countries where terrorism has been rampant. The Sri Lankan government, for instance, finally defeated the LTTE after a 30-year military campaign that left an indelible mark on the whole community (Hettiarachchi, 2014). Similarly, the Columbian army has been battling the FARC since 1964, and even though the organization demobilized in early 2017, as of this writing, full reconciliation remains uncertain and appears to be fraying.

The scars of protracted conflict often run deep within society, and community members may have moral and emotional reasons against welcoming former militants. Consequently, individuals released from deradicalization programs are at risk of being stigmatized as "terrorists," "murderers," or "fanatics" and may face all manner of prejudice and discrimination including the denial of employment and housing.

Sociologists have long studied the relation between social stigma and recidivism. According to labeling theory (Lemert, 1951, 1967; Tannenbaum, 1938), *primary deviance* occurs when an individual engages in behaviors that violate cultural norms (e.g., political violence). As a response to repeated offenses, society stigmatizes the individual and labels her or him a "deviant," a "criminal," or a "terrorist," depending on the nature of the crime. Over time, these labels get internalized in the person's self-concept and the individual adopts behavior consistent with the labels, producing a self-fulfilling-prophecy-like phenomenon referred to as *secondary deviance*. Continued shaming and vilification eventually propel stigmatized individuals to join groups where they feel accepted as they are. Given that "like seeks like," stigmatized individuals are likely to join others also marked as deviants by society (Demant, Slootman, Buijs, & Tillie, 2008). Mounting evidence suggests that stigmatization is highly predictive of whether reformed criminals backslide into crime (Becker, 1966; Braithwaite, 1989; Lemert, 1972; Wakefield, 2006). Former militants too may recoil from social stigmatization and become motivated to reconnect to radical groups, increasing their risk of reoffending. In Ireland, for instance, former loyalists gravitated back to radical or criminal organizations after feeling marginalized and shunned by the Unionists (McAuley, Tonge, Shirlow, 2009; Mitchell, 2008).

As discussed in Chapter 7, many successful deradicalization programs (e.g., in Saudi Arabia and Sri Lanka) have incorporated measures to avoid stigmatization of former militants by referring to them as "beneficiaries" as opposed to "terrorists" or "detainees." This approach is consistent with the philosophy which conceives of "beneficiaries" as *victims* that have been misled by radical propaganda and exploited by charismatic leaders (Hettiarachchi, 2014; Parker, 2013). In Sri Lanka, these efforts were also complemented by a presidential amnesty offered to LTTE members joining the deradicalization program and a public declaration from the government "to treat them as your own children" (Hettiarachchi, 2014).

Social Vacuum

In his well-known poem, "No Man Is an Island," the English poet John Donne (1624/1990) captured with eloquence the gregarious nature of human beings and their need to belong. Extensive empirical research supports Donne's insight about the importance of *belongingness* as a fundamental human motive (e.g., Baumeister & Leary, 1995; Deci & Ryan, 2000). Time and time again, it has been found that connecting to others and having positive experiences in social networks are vital for physical as well as psychological well-being (e.g., DeLongis, Folkman, & Lazarus, 1988; Reis, Sheldon, Gable, Roscoe, & Ryan, 2000). Research also indicates that belonging to a supportive social network fosters a better ability to cope against stress (e.g., Cohen & Wills, 1985), whereas belongingness *deprivation* carries many deleterious consequences including greater risk of mental illness (Bloom, White, & Asher, 1979) and substantive reduction in immunocompetence, the body's ability to resist disease (Kiecolt-Glaser et al., 1984).

Given the importance of positive relationships, it appears crucial that, upon release from rehabilitation, former militants benefit from a decent social environment. Unfortunately, when released, former militants often enter a social vacuum, as Sim aptly (2012) noted; they are separated from their former comrades and feel alienated from the community to which they are attempting to return.

Such alienation may arise from several sources. In some cases, individuals may have joined a radical group against the will of their family or participated in gruesome acts of violence repudiated by their peers. Others may have been encouraged by the group to explicitly cut ties with their relatives; a stratagem intended to prevent individuals from leaving the extremist organization, while grooming them to accept it as their "surrogate family" (Decker & Van Winkel, 1996; Tobin, 2008). According to Hettiarachchi (2014) "a 'good LTTE cadre' was one that would refrain from visiting and maintaining family ties" (p. 29). In sum then, individuals leaving deradicalization programs risk the discomfort of experiencing fragmented social bonds. This may spell trouble for their return to civil society as they may be lured back into radical groups that would readily accept them as one of theirs (Horgan, 2009).

A burgeoning literature supports the foregoing perspective and indicates that stable social bonds are essential for desistance from violent extremism, social reinsertion (e.g., Garfinkel, 2007; Laub & Sampson, 2001), and the overall success of deradicalization programs (e.g., Bjorgo & Horgan, 2009; Fink & Haerne, 2008; Horgan, 2009). Relatedly, research with former criminal gang members has found that lacking strong social bonds upon reinsertion into society is a criminogenic factor associated with reoffending (Cottam, Huseby, & Lutze, 2008; Curry & Decker, 1998; Decker & Van Winkel, 1996; Tobin, 2008).

There are several reasons why social bonds with community members may protect individuals from sliding back into criminality or violent extremism. For one, feeling accepted and connected to others promotes a sense of personal significance, thus lessening the motivation to seek significance in an extremist organization or through commission of extremist acts. (Kruglanski, Chen, Dechesne, Fishman, & Orehek, 2009; 2013; Kruglanski, Gelfand, Bélanger, Gunaratna, & Hettiararchchi, 2014). Additionally, social responsibilities toward others may safeguard individuals from the temptation of rejoining a deviant group because of the costs associated with the severance of close personal relationships (Bjorgo & Horgan, 2009; Reinares, 2011).

Major deradicalization programs (see Chapter 7) are based on understanding the relevance of providing a supportive social environment to former militants. For instance, in the Saudi deradicalization program, family members participate in counseling sessions (Porges, 2010); furthermore, the program encourages the creation of social bonds by helping former militants to find a spouse (Boucek, 2008, 2009; Stern, 2004). In Singapore, families form part and parcel of the deradicalization program during and after the detention of their family member (Johnston, 2009). The Yemen program, on the other hand, provided little to no social support to released detainees and was considered a failure because of its high recidivism rates (Johnsen, 2006).

Recently, efforts have been made to develop comprehensive programs to support and empower families grappling with a radicalized relative. Family counseling programs such as those provided by Germany's EXIT and HAYAT initiatives (cf. Kruglanski, Webber, & Koehler, 2018) are intended to strengthen family bonds and encourage individuals from leaving the radical scene. The core principle of these interventions is to establish the necessary conditions so that families become a viable alternative group replacing the radical one. Family counseling thus focuses on creating a stable affective environment that facilitates coping with difficult life circumstances, such as grievances that could potentially further individuals' radicalization or recidivism. To that end, families receive professional assistance to learn "how to recognize provocation, how to deescalate conflicts, and how to create compromises that show respect to . . . a relative while maintaining clear boundaries" (Koehler, 2013, p. 187).

Concomitantly, "family members or friends that are opposing the (violence justifying) ideology are being empowered in their argumentation, their capacity to take action and alternative quotation. By teaching the relatives of radicalized individuals about arguments and ideological narratives used by radical groups, the family will be able to counter them" (Koehler, 2013, p. 188). Research on family counseling and deradicalization is still largely inchoate, and thus it is premature to judge its effectiveness in relation to recidivism rates. However, given the scientifically established importance of shared reality (Hardin & Higgins, 1996; Higgins, 2018) to guiding individuals' attitudes and actions, the emphasis on family support for moderation may constitute a significant component of policies intended to prevent radicalization and reradicalization.

In addition to macro factors, such as economics and state stability and the meso-level factors related to social environment issues, micro-level factors underlying recidivism also play a role in reradicalization. These factors are directly related to individuals' reinsertion into society and concern (a) education and aftercare opportunities for ex-militants, (b) the age of the recovering extremists, (c) wear-and-tear factors of continued extremism, and (d) aftercare services. We now consider them in turn.

Micro-Level Factors

Vocational Education

A potentially effective element of deradicalization programs is vocational training aimed at equipping released detainees ("beneficiaries") with means to productively reintegrate into their communities, thus providing them with tools for a respectable, significance affording, existence. Vocational training has been incorporated into several well-known deradicalization programs, including those of Saudi Arabia, Singapore, Iraq, and Sri Lanka (see Chapter 7). Vocational education allows former militants to acquire new job skills—for example, in electronics, carpentry, construction, cosmetics, or tailoring—that would increase their employability upon their release into the community (Parker, 2013). As already noted, vocational education has deeper ramifications than merely providing "beneficiaries" with a paycheck. Learning a trade is a formidable opportunity for former militants to provide for their family, acquire a sense of dignity, create financial stability, and become a fully functioning member of society (Arndt, Greene, & Maksimowicz, 2010). Ultimately, vocational training helps former militants to envision a future in which they feel significant and respected, replacing their prior "career" in violent extremism.

Scholars have proposed that educational programs "contribute to broaden intellectual horizons [of detainees], increase their self-esteem and self-efficacy, and to promote the individual's resilience to violent extremist messages" (Veldhuis, 2012, p. 9). In a recent article, Feddes Mann, and Doosje (2015) tested these propositions with young Muslims who were deemed "possibly vulnerable to radicalization" but that were not part of any radical groups. The authors implemented the Diamant Program, a three-month course composed of three modules. In the first module ("Turning Point"), young adults work on their social and professional skills to find a job or an internship. In the second ("Intercultural Moral Judgment") and third module ("Intercultural Conflict Management"), participants are guided through moral reflections and learn how to deal with social conflicts. Feddes et al. demonstrated that these modules had the combined effect of increasing self-esteem, self-efficacy, and empathy. The latter factor was negatively related to support for ideological violence (e.g., participants endorsed items like "If the prophet Muhammad is seriously insulted in a Dutch newspaper, I would understand it if Muslims react by using violence against others").

Another interesting piece of evidence for the effectiveness of vocational training in reducing recidivism comes from the US deradicalization program in Iraq, discussed in detail in Chapter 7. Prior to 2007, the recidivism rate in the US–Iraq program oscillated around 10%, but after initiating substantive re-education efforts, recidivism rates had declined to approximately 1% within a year (Angell & Gunaratna, 2012). Vocational education seems to have yielded good results in other deradicalization programs as well.

In Sri Lanka, Tamil Tigers who had access to vocational training—as part of a comprehensive deradicalization program—displayed a significant decline in support for armed struggle over a nine-month period, compared to a control group that did not have access to such opportunity (Kruglanski et al., 2014; Webber et al., 2018). The current recidivism rate of thousands of former members of the LTTE is currently zero percent after a four-year return to the community. Singapore also includes vocation training in its program, and the recidivism rates of detainees who completed the program was reported to be nil (Sim, 2012). Of course, the findings to date are incapable of illuminating what factors among the many that comprised the Sri Lankan program were specifically responsible for the low recidivism rates among its graduates and what role in it may be confidently attributed to vocational education.

Age

Among criminology's most robust empirical findings is an intriguing curvilinear relationship referred to as the age–crime curve. Time and time again, scholars have observed a "sharp increase in the rate of crime and other deviant behavior in mid-adolescence followed by an equally sharp decrease in these rates in early adulthood" (Blonigen, 2010, p. 90). This bell-shaped curve, which usually peaks around 18 years of age (Stolzenberg & D'Alessio, 2008), has been replicated across gender, countries, and most types of crime (Hirschi & Gottfredson, 1983, Nagin & Land, 1993). As discussed in the Population Demographics section earlier in the chapter, reported terrorists' demographics mirror relatively well the 15- to 24-year-old critical period of the age–crime curve.

Psychologists contributed to the explanation of the age–crime curve by investigating broader related themes such as *sensation-seeking*, namely, "the need for varied, novel, and complex sensations and experiences and the willingness to take physical and social risks for the sake of such experiences" (Zuckerman, 1979, p. 10). Akin to the age–crime curve, sensation-seeking, as well as the preference for immediate over delayed rewards, exhibit an inverted U-shaped function that peaks in mid-adolescence and declines into young adulthood (Harden & Tucker-Drob, 2011; Steinberg, Albert, Cauffman, Banich, Graham, and Woolard, 2008; Steinberg et al., 2009). Extensive research on sensation-seeking suggests that men are more likely to be categorized as sensation seekers than women (e.g., Zuckerman, Eysenck, & Eysenck, 1978). This lust for new experiences and adventure has also been found to predict a wide collection of risky behaviors, including substance abuse, reckless driving, unprotected sex, and crime (Arnett, 1996, 2000).

Explaining violent extremism in terms of sensation-seeking resonates with the story of thousands of foreign fighters—more than 25,000 according to the United Nations—who traveled to distant lands to join Islamist terrorist groups, waged war against their enemy, and indulged in sexual exploitation

(Younis, 2015). It is of interest to note that sensation-seeking typically involves engagement in rare and, in this sense, deviant behavior demonstrating individuals' uniqueness and independence. This deviance could be related to individuals' desire to assert their *autonomy* from social norms and conventions. In relation to the present analysis, sensation-seeking may represent persons' quest for significance and a demonstration to themselves, and others, that they individually matter and cannot be reduced to just blindly following the herd. In support of this hypothesis, longitudinal and experimental research has found that the lack of personal significance increases individuals' desire to engage in novel and exciting experiences (sensation-seeking), which, in turn, makes them more prone to supporting violence, wanting to self-sacrifice for a cause, and joining violent political groups (Schumpe, Bélanger, Moyano, & Nisa, 2018). Interestingly, the authors also demonstrated that support for political violence can be mitigated in two different ways. The first method involved having people describe their personal legacy (i.e., something they will pass on to make a meaningful, lasting and energizing contribution to humanity) which quelled their quest for significance and sensation seeking. The second method involved exposing sensation-seekers to an exciting—yet peaceful—political group to redirect their need for thrill and excitement in a prosocial direction. Taken together, these results attest to the importance of understanding individuals' psychological needs to develop effective strategies to prevent and counter violent extremism.

Wear and Tear

The foregoing discussion suggests that time can be a precious ally in decreasing the likelihood of reradicalization. Maturation that may reduce individuals succumbing to the motivational imbalance (discussed in Chapter 3) and the channeling of passion into violent extremism at the expense of other basic needs. Not to be underestimated, too, is the wear-and-tear factor, correlated with an enduring membership in a militant organization. Being continuously on the run, risking one's life, and losing comrades along the way can inflict a serious blow to a person's morale and, in that sense, be disempowering and significance reducing. In this vein, della Porta (2013) reports several interviews conducted with former members of the Brigate Rosse, introduced in Chapter 4. In the words of one apprehended extremist, "when they [the police] knocked on my door that morning, my first thought was 'I knew it'; the second was 'thank goodness, more sleep'" (Life History no. 1, pp. 75–76, cited in della Porta, 2013 p. 279).

One of the interviews conducted by Fernando Reinares with erstwhile members of the Basque ETA organization points to the same conclusion. This interviewee bluntly stated:

> You say to yourself shit, man. . . . I better get myself a life, because time is running out. . . . It's a matter of being that much older, and in my case, specifically of wanting to get married. . . . You are going on 40 years old, you're going to get married next year and you say to yourself well, shit, man I mean at this stage of the game to go packing a piece . . . that would be a bit . . . because you just got to . . . shit . . . well, we've all got to live a bit. (Reinares, 2011, p. 796)

These anecdotes in conjunction with the research previously described suggest that akin to employees in any organization, terrorists "working" under long stressful periods feel weighed down by the burden of their activism and eventually burn out. And, although active deradicalization can be made to occur, on occasion, the passage of time alone might suffice to curb individuals' enthusiasm for extremism and reduce the allure to them of reradicalizing.

Aftercare: Monitoring and Follow-Ups

To ensure that former militants do not regress to violent extremism, monitoring and follow-up programs are generally assumed to decrease the likelihood of recidivism. Monitoring is a traditional method of gathering intelligence about a former detainee that usually involves carefully watching and following this person's behavior, including his or her social interactions and communications. It has been argued that one of the reasons for Singapore's perfect scorecard on recidivism is their effective monitoring system: a massive network of hundreds of surveillance cameras, on closed-circuit television (CCTV), mounted across the city and recording every whereabouts of its citizens (Sim, 2012).

Aside from gathering intelligence, monitoring is also useful for *deterring* recidivism. For instance, Boucek (2009) indicates that graduates of the Saudi deradicalization program are explicitly told they will be monitored in the community "in very obvious ways and in a much more covert manner" (p. 219). And, indeed, it would not only be foolish but also extremely difficult to plot and put into action a terrorist attack while being under surveillance. Even if someone attempted to do so, authorities could intervene promptly and arrest those involved. Without a *proper* monitoring program, however, recidivism might go unnoticed, or worse, be discovered too late after bloodshed had occurred. Paradoxically, then, programs with an excellent monitoring program could display greater recidivism rates than those of weaker programs as a result of greater detection capabilities (Horgan & Braddock, 2010). On the upside, data accumulated through monitoring could eventually indicate behavioral patterns or precipitating factors linked to recidivism. Research has yet to examine what these might be.

Beside monitoring that enables the *detection* of possible recidivism, aftercare programs may contribute to its *prevention*. These programs allow frontline workers—such as psychologists, social workers, and clerics—to evaluate the needs of former militants and ensure that they can receive the necessary support for their full reinsertion into society and their community (Boucek, 2008; Boucek, Beg, & Horgan, 2008; Speckhard, 2011). A whole range of issues can be addressed through aftercare programs including psychological distress (e.g., stigmatization), marital disputes, or struggles with securing a bank loan, to name just a few. Alleviating the stresses associated with such problems could reduce the likelihood of recidivism in two ways: first, by reducing the significance loss that these problems may induce and, second, by strengthening the bond between the former militant and her or his counselor. This relationship increases the influence of the counselor over the militant. Lastly, follow-up meetings with former militants provide an opportunity to administer psychometric instruments and collect qualitative data that are important for understanding the individual's postrelease trajectory in reference to violent extremism.

Attitudes toward Deradicalization Programs

Beyond the plurality of components involved in a deradicalization program relevant to its success in forestalling reradicalization, an important aspect is militants' attitudes toward the program. Family counseling, psychological therapy, and dialogue are the cornerstones of deradicalization efforts; however, if the militants feel that these activities are pointless or objectionable, deradicalization efforts might fail, creating the potential for recidivism. Empirical evidence from our own assessment of the Sri Lankan deradicalization program supports this conclusion. As noted earlier, we found that the deradicalization program in this case was effective in reducing beneficiaries' support for terrorism over time as compared to a control group (Kruglanski et al., 2014; Webber et al., 2018). More important, however, beneficiaries' attitude change was moderated by their positive attitudes toward the program.

In other words, the deradicalization program was even more effective for those who positively appreciated it. This finding probably reflects the fact the detainees were treated well, felt supported throughout their stay, and were referred to as "beneficiaries" by the program's personnel. Interestingly, close observers of the program realized that something else had happened: Word spread out that the detainees were being well taken care of, and, as a consequence, some Tamil Tigers at large decided to surrender to join the deradicalization program. "We knew that the government will treat us well," revealed one individual in an interview (Hettiarachchi, 2014). From the Sri Lankan experience, it can be concluded that taking care of former militants is not only vital to deradicalizing militants currently in the program but a deradicalization program's positive reputation may also encourage active militants to leave terrorism behind.

The Sri Lankan experience stands in sharp contrast to detainees' mistreatment in incarceration facilities where use of torture and human rights violations were alleged to take place—the US-run Guantanamo Bay detention camp is an example that comes to mind. One fundamental question in this regard is whether there are grounds to transgress morality for the sake of security. In his provocative work on torture, Rejali (2009) adduced compelling arguments against the notion that torture is an effective method to collect intelligence. Specifically, false confessions are often fabricated under unbearable pain. Even when truth is told, torturers cannot tell facts from fiction. Similar conclusions were reached in the 2014 US Senate report on the Central Intelligence Agency's detention and interrogation program (Senate Select Committee on Intelligence, 2014).

Another vital question is whether tough treatment of terrorists facilitates deradicalization and reduces recidivism. On this point, the Saudi Minister of the Interior compared the recidivism rates of its deradicalization program to those associated with Guantanamo. This comparison is interesting given that individuals from similar or the same terrorist organizations were assigned to two different programs—the Saudi one and the one at Guantanmo—yet they reintegrated back into the same social environment, namely, Saudi Arabia. Specifically, the estimate was that the recidivism rate of former Guantanamo detainees was 20%, while those released from the Saudi program had a recidivism rate of 10% (US Department of State, 2011), that is, half the rate of Guantanamo former inmates. A possible explanation for this drastic difference is that repressive detention conditions in Guantanamo fueled resentment of the detainees toward their captors, leading them to seek revenge by joining or rejoining groups such as Al Qaeda or the Islamic State upon their release.

Although the present singular comparison does not warrant a strong inference, hundreds criminological studies support similar conclusions: Getting tough with criminals typically doesn't work. A meta-analysis conducted by Lipsey and Cullen (2007) indicates that punitive approaches do not reduce recidivism rates. If anything, data suggest that repressive methods increase these rates, while rehabilitation treatments significantly reduce them. In short, while it is likely to contribute to recidivism, torture and mistreatment of incarcerated militants is often unlikely to bring forth useful information. Thus, besides the moral argument against torture, its practice may be hardly worthwhile on pragmatic grounds.

Connecting the Dots

The present chapter offers a whistle-stop tour through the macro-, meso-, and micro-level factors that stymie or foster sustained deradicalization among former violent extremists. Although listing and describing these factors is necessary to move the discussion forward, one question is whether they can be subsumed under a smaller set of conceptually relevant variables. As the science of deradicalization matures, the organization and integration of its key concepts becomes increasingly important for two reasons. First, finding the common thread that connects these seemingly disparate elements might reveal a comprehensive set of core principles useful for theory building and the development of interventions. Second, contrary to laundry lists, finding commonalities is a scientific imperative that prevents the fragmentation of any ever-growing field of inquiry (Vallacher & Nowak, 1997). Based on our integrative 3N framework, we offer, therefore, three recommendations for preventing individuals from gravitating back to terrorist organizations.

Preventing the Arousal of Significance Quest

The role of grievance in regard to radicalization has been the focus of a long-standing debate in terrorism research. For the most part, this debate has revolved around the *nature* of the grievance—having to do with relative deprivation, humiliation, or foreign occupation—rather than questioning the generally accepted notion that grievances contribute to radicalization. In previous chapters, we discussed at length how these grievances relate to the significance quest. As can be gleaned from our present discussion, many factors related to recidivism inflict a loss of significance upon individuals and thus may well induce the motivation for significance restoration. For this reason, preventing the awakening of the significance quest among former militants appears of paramount relevance for their sustained deradicalization.

At the macro level, this prevention may come from an exposure to a stable political environment that does not exacerbate political tensions or violently repress its inhabitants. The promotion of socio-economic development—for example, in regard to social security, health, and housing—may also help, offering decent living conditions that reduce the appeal of financial incentives from terrorist organizations and the experience of relative deprivation in the economic realm. However, the quest for significance cannot be reduced to mere materialistic conditions: It also extends to being treated humanely in the deradicalization center, developing harmonious social interactions with the host community, and building strong emotional bonds with one's family (assuming that the latter is opposed to extremism). Optimally, to ensure that former militants succeed in their reintegration into society, regular follow-ups should be implemented with an eye to detecting and addressing potential grievances that may reignite their desire to slide back into radicalism and violence.

Providing Alternative Routes to Personal Significance

If radicalization is fueled by significance quest, then joining a radical organization and its ideology is a *means* to attaining this goal. One corollary of this proposition is that deradicalization can be induced and sustained through viable alternative means to significance quest that are more prosocial and constructive than violence. Although not typically couched in such a way, many deradicalization efforts appear to represent this perspective. For instance, one purpose of offering educational vocation to former militants is arguably to provide alternative means to personal significance, including the feelings of competence and the ability to provide for one's family. Political inclusion provides nonviolent alternative means to radical movements aiming to address individuals' sense of disenfranchisement and insignificance. Similarly, family counseling may facilitate the creation of strong affective bonds that fulfill the need to belong and feel accepted (Baumeister & Leary, 1995; Koehler, 2013), within an alternative nonviolent network.

Basic social psychological research on the substitution effect (Bélanger, Schori-Eyal, Pica, Kruglanski, & Lafrenière, 2015, Schumpe, Bélanger, Giacomantonio, Nisa, & Brizi, 2018; Schumpe et al.,2018) indicates a major way in which the presence of alternative means can play a role in deradicalization. Specifically, when alternative means are introduced, the original means comes to be seen as less instrumental to goal achievement. In turn, reduced means instrumentality is associated with reduced motivation to employ it. In other words, the presence of alternative means promotes disengagement from the original means because the latter (e.g., joining a radical organization) is perceived now as less effective for attaining the goal it is purported to serve (e.g., the significance quest).

The substitution effect is general and applies well beyond political or religious radicalization. Substitution is also relevant to other forms of deviance, for instance, participation in street gangs. As is well known, the sport of boxing has helped countless teenagers and eventual world champions with criminal pasts related to gang activity—including Raul Rojas and Adonis Stevenson—to "walk the straight and narrow." Such cases have been so recurrent that boxing schools serving as rehabilitation centers for thousands of teenagers and young adults have sprung up in recent decades, including the Westside Boxing Center in Michigan and the Crushers Club in Illinois. Substitution appears to play a role in this phenomenon. From a psychological perspective, one could plausibly assume that for numerous youngsters, criminal activities served a purpose—namely, feeling powerful or belonging to a group, which end could be served equally well if not better by becoming a successful "king of the ring." In other words, becoming part of a boxing group, physically improving oneself, and gaining respect at the gymnasium fulfill the youngsters' significance quest as much as did crime. That was likely the reason that boxing kept numerous youngsters away from carrying out felonies. It stands to reason that boxing and other athletic programs (e.g., in martial arts) could provide significance affording substitutes for deradicalized militants, thus reducing the likelihood of their recidivating.

Preventing the Reattachment to a Radical Social Network

An important reason why boxing may constitute a successful substitute activity for crime is that the particular youth culture to which the crime-prone individuals belong admires sports and heaps considerable adulation on successful athletes. In other words, members of these individuals' social networks see success in an athletic activity such as boxing as an effective means to the attainment of personal significance. Decades of psychological research indicates that the shared reality of one's group (Hardin & Higgins, 1996; Higgins, 2018)—that is, the consensual worldview of one's friends and associates—impacts a broad repertoire of cognitive, emotional, and behavioral phenomena. The anchoring of attitudes, opinions, and activities in the shared reality of one's group applies equally to the issue of recidivism into violent extremism.

Indeed, a significant amount of the reoffending risk hinges on former militants' sociocultural setting. Admittedly, ensuring that individuals' social network is immune to radicalization is easier said than done, especially when macro-level factors are concerned. Indeed, many elements of radicalization are beyond the control of well-intentioned nongovernmental organizations or even governments. As noted earlier, political and economic instability may create favorable conditions to the emergence of violent extremist groups that, in turn, increase the chances of individuals' exposure to antisocial peers. The efforts to combat the appeal of violent extremism necessitate resolve, persistence, and resources on part of the community; such resources may be hard to come by in unstable political environments. Nonetheless, striving to ensure that former militants reintegrate into a stable and peaceful social environment appears vital for the prevention of recidivism and should be an integral part and parcel of the struggle against violent extremism.

Summary

The question posed at the onset of this chapter was whether deradicalization can last. Evidence reviewed in this chapter offers a cautiously optimistic outlook on the possibility of successfully reintegrating former militants into civil society. We proposed that the likelihood of recidivism is related to factors that promoted radicalization in the first place, namely, the need, the narrative, and the network factors identified in our significance quest theory of radicalization. As in any other field of inquiry, the validity of a conclusion depends on the quality of its evidence. Though the evidence thus far is consistent with our conceptual framework, further research is needed to firmly substantiate our understanding of deradicalization in particular reference to concrete ways and best practices that minimize the likelihood of recidivism.

References

Angell, A., & Gunaratna, R. (2012). *Terrorist rehabilitation: The U.S. experience in Iraq.* Boca Raton, FL: Taylor and Francis.

Arndt, M., Greene, D., & Maksimowicz, M. (2010). *De-radicalization: You can check out anytime you like, but what will make you leave.* Monterey, CA: Naval Postgraduate School.

Arnett, J. J. (1996). Sensation seeking, aggressiveness, and adolescent reckless behavior. *Personality and Individual Differences, 20,* 693–702.

Arnett, J. J. (2000). Emerging adulthood: A theory of development from the late teens through the twenties. *American Psychologist, 55,* 469–480.

Baumeister, R. F., & Leary, M. R. (1995). The need to belong: Desire for interpersonal attachments as a fundamental human motivation. *Psychological Bulletin, 117,* 497–529.

Becker, H. S. (1966). *Outsiders: Studies in the sociology of deviance.* New York, NY: Free Press.

Bélanger, J. J., Schori-Eyal, N., Pica, G., Kruglanski, A. W., & Lafrenière, M. A. (2015). The "more is less" effect in equifinal structures: Alternative means reduce the intensity and quality of motivation. *Journal of Experimental Social Psychology, 60,* 93–102.

Bjorgo, T., & Horgan, J. (2009). *Leaving terrorism behind: Individual and collective disengagement.* New York, NY: Routledge.

Blonigen, D. M. (2010). Explaining the relationship between age and crime: Contributions from the developmental literature on personality. *Clinical Psychology Review, 30,* 89–100.

Bloom, B. L., White, S. W., & Asher, S. J. (1979). Marital disruption as a stressful life event. In G. Levinger & O. C. Moles (Eds.), *Divorce and separation: Context, causes, and consequences* (pp. 184–200). New York, NY: Basic Books.

Boucek, C. (2008). *Saudi Arabia's "soft" counterterrorism strategy: Prevention, rehabilitation, and aftercare.* Washington, DC: Carnegie Endowment for International Peace.

Boucek, C. (2009). Extremist re-education and rehabilitation in Saudi Arabia. In T. Bjorjo & J. Horgan (Eds.), *Leaving terrorism behind: Individual and collective disengagement* (pp. 212–223). New York, NY: Routledge.

Boucek, C., Beg, S., & Horgan, J. (2008). Opening up the jihadi debate: Yemen's Committee for Dialogue. In T. Bjorgo & J. Horgan (Eds.). *Leaving terrorism behind: Individual and collective disengagement* (pp. 181–192). New York, NY: Routledge

Braithwaite, J. (1989). *Crime, shame and reintegration.* Cambridge, England: Cambridge University Press.

Carter, D. B. (2012). A blessing or a curse? State support for terrorist groups. *International Organization, 66,* 129–151.

Chen, D. (2003). *Economic distress and religious intensity: Evidence from Islamic resurgence during the Indonesian financial crisis.* Unpublished manuscript. Retrieved from http://citeseerx.ist.psu.edu/viewdoc/download?doi=10.1.1.197.2377&rep=rep1&type=pdf

Cohen, S., & Wills, T. A. (1985). Stress, social support, and the buffering hypothesis. *Psychological Bulletin, 98,* 310–357.

Collier, P. (2000). Rebellion as a quasi-criminal activity. *Journal of Conflict Resolution, 44,* 839–853.

Cottam, M., Huseby, J., & Lutze, F. (2008, July). *Political psychology and criminal justice. The potential impact of street gang identity and violence on political stability.* Paper presented at the Annual Meeting of the ISPP 31st Annual Scientific Meeting, Sciences Po, Paris, France.

Cragin, K., & Chalk, P. (2003). *Terrorism and development: Using social and economic development to inhibit a resurgence of terrorism.* Santa Monica, CA: Rand.

Curry, G. D., & Decker, S. H. (1998). *Confronting gangs: Crime and community.* Los Angeles, CA: Roxbury.

Dailey, B., Davis, I., & Managuelod, J. T. G. (2013). Optimizing foreign internal defense to counter dark networks. *Small Wars Journal, 7,* 55–60.

Deci, E. L., & Ryan, R. M. (2000). The "what" and "why" of goal pursuits: Human needs and the self-determination of behavior. *Psychological inquiry, 11,* 227–268.

Decker, S. H., & Van Winkel, B. (1996). *Life in the gang: Families, friends, and violence.* Cambridge, England: Cambridge University Press.

della Porta, D. (2013). *Clandestine political violence.* Cambridge, England: Cambridge University Press.

DeLongis, A., Folkman, S., & Lazarus, R. S. (1988). The impact of daily stress on health and mood: Psychological and social resources as mediators. *Journal of Personality and Social Psychology, 54,* 486–495.

Demant, F., Slootman, M., Buijs, F., & Tillie, J. N. (2008). Deradicalisering van rechtsradicalen: Islamitische radicalen. In J. van Donselaar & P. Rodrigues (Eds.) *Monitor racisme and extremism: Achste rapportage* (pp. 255–277). Amsterdam, The Netherlands: Pallas.

Donne, J. (1990). *Poems of John Donne.* Hoboken, NJ: BiblioBytes. (Original work published 1624)

Donovan, A., & Oddy, M. (1982). Psychological aspects of unemployment: an investigation into the emotional and social adjustment of school leavers. *Journal of Adolescence, 5,* 15–30.

El-Said, H. (2015). Counter-de-rad: Setting the framework. In H. El-Said (Ed.), *New Approaches to Countering Terrorism* (pp. 13–52). London, England: Palgrave Macmillan.

Feddes, A. R., Mann, L., & Doosje, B. (2015). Increasing self-esteem and empathy to prevent violent radicalization: A longitudinal quantitative evaluation of a resilience training focused on adolescents with a dual identity. *Journal of Applied Social Psychology, 45,* 400–411.

Fink, N. C., & Hearne, E. B. (2008). *Beyond terrorism: Deradicalization and disengagement from violent extremism.* New York, NY: International Peace Institute.

Flowers, S. C. (2014). *The relationship between youth unemployment and terrorism.* Unpublished manuscript. Georgetown University.

Furnham, A. (1985), Youth unemployment: A review of the literature. *Journal of Adolescence, 8,* 109–124.

Garfinkel, R. (2007). *Personal transformations: Moving from violence to peace.* Washington, DC: US Institute of Peace.

Can Rehabilitation Last? • 195

Global Counterterrorism Forum (2012, February). *Rome memorandum on good practices for rehabilitation and reintegration of violent extremist offenders.* Retrieved from https://www.thegctf.org/Portals/1/Documents/Framework%20Documents/A/GCTF-Rome-Memorandum-ENG.pdf

Gurr, T. R. (1970). *Why men rebel.* Princeton, NJ: Princeton University Press.

Harden, K. P., & Tucker-Drob, E. M. (2011). Individual differences in the development of sensation seeking and impulsivity during adolescence: Further evidence for a dual systems model. *Developmental Psychology, 47,* 739–746.

Hardin, C. D., & Higgins, E. T. (1996). Shared reality: How social verification makes the subjective objective. In E. T. Higgins & R. M. Sorrentino (Eds.), *Handbook of motivation and cognition: The interpersonal context* (Vol. 3, pp. 28–84). New York, NY: Guilford.

Hettiarachchi, M. (2014). *Sri Lanka's rehabilitation programme: The humanitarian mission two.* Colombo, Sri Lanka: Research & Monitoring Division, Department of Government Information. Retrieved from http://www.sinhalanet.net/wp-content/uploads/2014/08/Sri-Lankas-Rehabilitation-Program.pdf

Higgins, E. T. (2018). *Shared reality: What makes us strong and tears us apart.* New York, NY: Oxford University Press.

Hirschi, T., & Gottfredson, M. G. (1983). Age and the explanation of crime. *American Journal of Sociology, 89,* 552–584.

Horgan, J. (2009). *Walking away from terrorism: Accounts of disengagement from radical and extremist movements.* London, England: Routledge.

Horgan, J., & Braddock, K. (2010). Rehabilitating the terrorists? Challenges in assessing the effectiveness of de-radicalization programs. *Terrorism and Political Violence, 22,* 267–291.

Johnsen, G. (2006). Yemen's passive role in the war on terrorism. *Terrorism Monitor, 4,* 7–9.

Johnston, A. K. (2009). *Assessing the effectiveness of deradicalization programs for Islamist extremists.* Unpublished manuscript. Naval Postgraduate School, Monterey, CA.

Kiecolt-Glaser, J. K., Garner, W., Speicher, C., Penn, G. M., Holliday, J., & Glaser, R. (1984). Psychosocial modifiers of immunocompetence in medical students. *Psychosomatic Medicine, 46,* 7–14.

Koehler, D. (2013). Family counseling as prevention and intervention tool against "foreign fighters": The German "Hayat" program. *Journal Exit-Deutschland. Zeitschrift für Deradikalisierung und demokratische Kultur, 3,* 182–204.

Krueger, A. B., & Malečková, J. (2002). Education, poverty and terrorism: Is there a causal connection? *Journal of Economic Perspectives, 17,* 119–144.

Kruglanski, A. W., Bélanger, J. J., Gelfand, M., Gunaratna, R., Hettiarachchi, M., Reinares, F., . . . Sharvit, K. (2013). Terrorism—A (self) love story: Redirecting the significance quest can end violence. *American Psychologist, 68,* 559–575.

Kruglanski, A. W., Chen, X., Dechesne, M., Fishman, S., & Orehek, E. (2009). Fully committed: Suicide bombers' motivation and the quest for personal significance. *Political Psychology, 30,* 331–357.

Kruglanski, A. W., & Fishman, S. (2006). The psychology of terrorism: "Syndrome" versus "tool" perspectives. *Terrorism and Political Violence, 18*, 193–215.

Kruglanski, A. W., Gelfand, M. J., Bélanger, J. J., Gunaratna, R., & Hettiararchchi, M. (2014). Deradicalizing the Liberation Tigers of Tamil Eelam (LTTE): Some preliminary findings. In Silke, A. (Ed.), *Prisons, terrorism and extremism: Critical issues in management, radicalization and reform.* London, England: Routledge.

Kruglanski, A. W., Webber, D., & Koehler, D. (2018). To the fringe and back: The psychology of right wing extremism. *Manuscript in preparation.*

Laub, J. H., & Sampson, R. J. (2001). Understanding desistance from crime. *Crime and Justice, 28*, 1–69.

Lemert, E. M. (1951). *Social Pathology.* New York, NY: Mcgraw-Hill.

Lemert, E. M. (1967). *President's commission on law enforcement and administration of justice, task force report: Juvenile delinquency and youth crime.* Washington, DC: US Government Printing Office.

Lemert, E. M. (1972). *Human deviance, social problems, and social control.* Englewood Cliffs, NJ: Prentice Hall.

Li, Q., & Schaub, D. (2004). Economic globalization and transnational terrorism: A pooled time-series analysis. *Journal of Conflict Resolution, 48*, 230–258.

Lipsey, M. W., & Cullen, F. T. (2007). The effectiveness of correctional rehabilitation: A review of systematic reviews. *Annual Review of Law and Social Science, 3*, 297–320.

McAuley, J. W., Tonge, J., & Shirlow, P. (2009). Conflict, transformation, and former loyalist paramilitary prisoners in Northern Ireland. *Terrorism and Political Violence, 22*(1), 22–40.

Messner, J. J. (2013, July 9). The Failed States Index 2013 launch event. *Fund for Peace.* Retrieved from http://library.fundforpeace.org/fsi13-launchoverview

Mitchell, C. (2008). The limits of legitimacy: Former loyalist combatants and peace building in Northern Ireland. *Irish Political Studies, 23*, 1–19.

Nagin, D. S., & Land, K. C. (1993). Age, criminal careers, and population heterogeneity: Specification and estimation of a nonparametric, mixed Poisson model. *Criminology, 31*, 327–362.

National Institute of Justice (2014, June 17). *Recidivism.* Retrieved from http://www.nij.gov/topics/corrections/recidivism/pages/welcome.aspx

O'Connell, E., & Benard, C. (2006). *A new IO strategy: Prevention and disengagement.* Santa Monica, CA: Rand.

Parker, K. L. (2013). Saint Louis University prison program: An ancient mission, a new beginning. *Saint Louis University Pubic Literature Review, 33*, 377–384.

Porges, M. L. (2010, January 22). The Saudi deradicalization experiment. *Council on Foreign Relations.* Retrieved from http://www.cfr.org/terrorism/saudi-deradicalizationexperiment/p21292

Reinares, F. (2011). Exit from terrorism: A qualitative empirical study on disengagement and deradicalization among members of ETA. *Terrorism and Political Violence, 23*, 780–803.

Reis, H. T., Sheldon, K. M., Gable, S. L., Roscoe, J., & Ryan, R. M. (2000). Daily well-being: The role of autonomy, competence, and relatedness. *Personality and Social Psychology Bulletin, 26,* 419–435.

Rejali, D. (2009). *Torture and democracy.* Princeton, NJ: Princeton University Press.

Schmid, A.P. (2005). Prevention of terrorism: Towards a multi-pronged approach. In T. Bjorgo (Ed.), *Root causes of terrorism: Myths, reality and ways forward* (223–240). New York, NY: Routledge.

Schumpe, B. M., Bélanger, J. J., Moyano, M., & Nisa, C. F. (2018). The role of sensation seeking in political violence: An extension of the Significance Quest Theory. *Journal of personality and social psychology.*

Schumpe, B. M., Bélanger, J. J., Giacomantonio, M., Nisa, C. F., & Brizi, A. (2018). Weapons of peace: Providing alternative means for social change reduces political violence. *Journal of Applied Social Psychology, 48*(10), 549–558.

Senate Select Committee on Intelligence (2014, December 3). *Committee study of the Central Intelligence Agency's detention and interrogation program.* Washington, DC: Author. Retrieved from http://fas.org/irp/congress/2014_rpt/ssci-rdi.pdf

Sim, S. (2012). Strategies for successful risk reduction programmes for violent extremists: Lessons from Singapore, Indonesia and Afghanistan. *Trends and Developments in Contemporary Terrorism, 103,* 55.

Sozer, M. A., & Sever, M. (2011). Violent extremism in terrorist organizations: The case of Turkish Hizbullah. *NATO Science for Peace and Security Series-E: Human and Societal Dynamics, 87,* 22–31.

Speckhard, A. (2011). Prison and community based disengagement and de-radicalization programs for extremists involved in militant jihadi terrorism ideologies and activities. *Psychosocial, Organizational and Cultural Aspects of Terrorism, 1,* 1–14.

Steinberg, L., Albert, D., Cauffman, E., Banich, M., Graham, S., & Woolard, J. (2008). Age differences in sensation seeking and impulsivity as indexed by behavior and self-report: evidence for a dual systems model. *Developmental Psychology, 44,* 1764–1778.

Steinberg, L., Graham, S., O'Brien, L., Woolard, J., Cauffman, E., & Banich, M. (2009). Age differences in future orientation and delay discounting. *Child Development, 80,* 28–44.

Stern, J. (2004). *Terror in the name of God: Why religious militants kill.* New York, NY: HarperCollins.

Stolzenberg, L., & D'Alessio, S. J. (2008). Co-offending and the age-crime curve. *Journal of Research in Crime and Delinquency, 45,* 65–86.

Tannenbaum, F. (1938). *Crime and community.* New York, NY: Columbia University Press.

Tobin, K. (2008). *Gangs: An individual and group perspective.* Upper Saddle River, NJ: Prentice Hall.

Urdal, H. (2006). A clash of generations? Youth bulges and political violence. *International Studies Quarterly, 50,* 607–663.

US Department of State (2011, August 1). *Country reports on terrorism 2010*. Retrieved from http://www.state.gov/documents/organization/170479.pdf

Vallacher, R, R., & Nowak, A. (1997). The emergence of dynamical social psychology. *Psychological Inquiry, 8,* 73–99.

Veldhuis, T. (2012). Designing rehabilitation and reintegration programmes for violent extremist offenders: A realist approach. *International Centre for Counter-Terrorism.* Retrieved from https://www.icct.nl/download/file/ICCT-Veldhuis-Designing-Rehabilitation-Reintegration-Programmes-March-2012.pdf

Wakefield, H. (2006). The vilification of sex offenders: Do laws targeting sex offenders increase recidivism and sexual violence. *Journal of Sexual Offender Civil Commitment: Science and the Law, 1,* 141–149.

Webber, D., Chernikova, M., Kruglanski, A. W., Gelfand, M. J., Hettiarachchi, M., Gunaratna, R., . . . Bélanger, J. J. (2018). Deradicalizing detained terrorists, *Political Psychology, 39,* 539–556.

Younis, N. (2015, August 15). How Isis has established a bureaucracy of rape. *The Guardian.* Retrieved from http://www.theguardian.com/commentisfree/2015/aug/16/isis-systematic-rape-sharia-justification-sex-slavery

Zuckerman, M. (1979). *Sensation seeking: Beyond the optimal level of arousal.* Sydney, Australia: Halsted.

Zuckerman, M., Eysenck, S. B., & Eysenck, H. J. (1978). Sensation seeking in England and America: Cross-cultural, age, and sex comparisons. *Journal of Consulting and Clinical Psychology, 46,* 139–149.

9 ASSESSING RADICALIZATION AND DERADICALIZATION

As noted in Chapter 3, radicalization isn't an all-or-nothing phenomenon. It is a matter of degree. Some individuals are more radicalized than others. The more radicalized individuals may be ready to commit acts of violence, while the less radicalized ones may believe that violence is justified and desirable though they themselves may not be prepared to perpetrate it (cf. Webber et al., 2018). Some individuals may reject the use of violence altogether, though they may support the use of nonviolent means to advance their political cause. These various individuals thus differ in their degree of radicalization.

Often, it is important to assess how radicalized people are to determine how much risk they pose and how they should be treated (Dugas & Kruglanski, 2014). For instance, individuals who are arrested under suspicion of terrorism may need to be appropriately classified at intake as to the security risk they pose and as to how they should be treated while in prison (e.g., whom they should reside with). Release decisions, too, are critically based on a determination of the risk a given individual would pose on re-entering the community at large. Risk assessment concerning individuals' degree of radicalization is practiced in well-endowed deradicalization programs, such as those in Saudi Arabia or Singapore. Primarily, such assessments are carried out by professionals, including forensic psychologists and social workers, who interact with the detainees, clinically interview them, observe their attitudes, and infer their intentions. In addition to the quantification of risk posed by individuals, assessment efforts may also involve the evaluation of rehabilitation and deradicalization programs as to the degree of their success in getting individuals to abandon extremism.

In what follows, we discuss, in turn, individual risk assessment and program evaluation and examine the unique problems that each pose. We also describe a psychological tool of risk assessment that we developed based on our 3N model of radicalization, pertaining to individuals' needs, the narratives to which they may be exposed, and the social networks in which they may be immersed. Assessment and evaluation processes are key to helping extremists deradicalize, re-enter society, and avoid recidivism, so it is imperative that they are understood and implemented as effectively as possible.

Individual Risk Assessment

Our approach to risk assessment involves a convergence of *observational methods* carried out by individuals familiar with the assessed person and her or his background and *self-reports* concerning individuals' attitudes and beliefs that are deemed relevant to radicalization.

Assessment by Aspects

Beyond assessing the *degree* of radicalization, it is important to evaluate *what factors* in particular have contributed to a given person's radicalization and in what proportions. As discussed, an individual may be radicalized because of strong *needs* to feel accepted or significant and to matter in the eyes of others. Alternatively, people may be radicalized primarily because of the *ideology* to which they subscribe (the narrative component of our model). Yet other persons may be radicalized primarily through the social influence of radical friends and relatives, that is, through the social *network* to which they belong. These different sources of radicalization to violent extremism are assessed by tools whose combined effects are assumed to define the degree of risk the individual poses.

We assume that the greater the number of sources of radicalization and the stronger their influence, the greater the risk of radicalization. A person known to have a sense of deep frustration and grievance, contributing to a strong significance quest, who, in addition, strongly supports extreme ideological beliefs and whose friends and relatives strongly subscribe to such beliefs as well is considered at a particularly high risk of radicalization. Such a person is considered at a higher risk, for example, than one who, while experiencing the same degree of grievance, lacks the ideological or the network sources of radicalization.

Assessing Radicalization and Deradicalization • 201

The Present Tool

The present risk assessment tool contains two related components: an adapted version of the Violent Extremist Radicalization Assessment–Short Version (VERA-SV), developed by Elaine Pressman of Carleton University, and the Significance Quest Assessment Tool (SQAT), developed by a University of Maryland team headed by Arie Kruglanski. Both tools share the same 3N model of radicalization, yet they approach risk assessment through different routes: The VERA-SV uses primarily, though not exclusively, *observations* of professionals who are in frequent contact with the detainees (primarily prison personnel) to determine these individuals' degree and type of radicalization. All available sources of information and evidence concerning the detainees— including prior arrests, court records, and family history—are also considered.

By comparison, SQAT uses the detainees' own self-reports as to their attitudes and opinions on various relevant matters to determine their radicalization, or degree of violent extremism. Jointly, these two approaches afford a comprehensive look at the detainee's degree and type of radicalization. Their combination can be used to reach informed decisions on various pertinent matters, as suggested earlier. Let's first look at the VERA-SV component, followed by SQAT, and then discuss their joint utilization.

Violent Extremist Risk Assessment–Short Version (VERA-SV)

Background and Information: What Is It?

The VERA-SV, or VERA–Short Version, is an analytical protocol for the assessment of an individual's risk of radicalization to violent extremism. It is an adapted version of the Violent Extremist Risk Assessment Protocol (VERA; Pressman & Flockton, 2014), which has been demonstrated to have both content validity and satisfactory reliability (Beardsley & Beech, 2013). The VERA-SV also relies on elements of the VERA-2 protocol, which has been shown to have both construct and user validity (Pressman & Flockton, 2012). The protocol of the VERA-SV is a modified structured professional judgment protocol. This methodology has been documented as a scientifically supported approach that provides consistency and transparency (Webster, Douglas, Eaves, & Hart, 1997; Webster, Müller-Isberner, & Fransson, 2002).

Who Can Use It?

The VERA-SV was developed for use by nonclinical staff. These users may be other academic experts training or assessing individuals, staff managing

202 • THE THREE PILLARS OF RADICALIZATION

detained individuals, general supervisory personnel working in prisons or large detention centers, and other community workers, religious advisors, and trained volunteers who come in frequent contact with assessed individuals and, hence, can contribute their impressions of these individuals to the assessment effort.

The risk indicators included in the VERA-SV address questions related to the needs, narratives, and network sources of radicalization. Specifically, they include elements pertaining to individuals' motivations, that is, needs, related to the quest for significance and the expectancy to gratify them through engagement in violence (e.g., increased through capacity and training to plan and prepare an attack). These elements include items that measure individual attitudes and beliefs related to violent ideological narratives, as well as risk indicators that pertain to personal and cyber networks with which the individual is associated.

In addition to risk *promoting* indicators, a section of the VERA-SV considers the presence or the emergence of risk-*preventing*, or risk-mitigating, factors. Items in this section also pertain to the three categories of the conceptual model on which this protocol is based—that is, to needs (whether they are gratified by nonextreme means), narratives (whether moderate narratives are salient and accessible to the individuals), and networks (whether the individual has strong ties with moderate networks). The assessment of these risk-mitigating or protective indicators is highly relevant to classification, placement, intervention, and management decisions concerning the detainees.

Elements and Use

The VERA-SV protocol contains 18 risk indicators and 4 risk-mitigating, or protective, indicators. Thus, the short version comprises a total of 22 indicators that are evaluated. Groups of these indicators pertain to questions in the needs, narratives, and network categories. Each indicator is rated on the protocol for severity. For instance, an indicator concerning the presence of a need, adherence to an extremist narrative, or connection to an extremist network may suggest greater or lesser strength of that need, narrative, or network connection. Four possible rating levels are available for each of the indicators. If no information is available for a specific indicator, the assessor documents this "lack of available information" status in the column identified as "unknown." Alternatively, the assessor documents the level of severity for the specific indicator in the "low," "moderate," or "high" column provided, as suggested by information available from reports, observations, other information or intelligence and, when possible, from information obtained from direct observation of the radicalized individual being assessed. (Guidelines for the ratings are provided in the Rating the Indicators section.)

As previously noted, the risk indicators included in the VERA-SV are divided into three categories: (a) *narratives* (including attitudes, beliefs, and ideology); (b) *networks* (i.e., social context, including personal associations, family and friendship bonds, and cyber and other social associations relevant to the individual's intention to act); and (c) *needs* (personal motivations pertinent to the search for life's meaning and significance) that serve as drivers of violent extremist action. The need category subsumes the *Training and Capacity at Violence* category. Specifically, training and capacity enable individuals to satisfy the need through violent behavior.

Rating the Indicators

The individual indicator ratings are based on the assessor's judgment using the following guidelines for severity levels: When no information is available concerning a specific indicator, the indicator is marked in the "unknown" column. The "low" mark is used when the indicator does not appear to be present at the time of assessment or is considered to be present only minimally. The "moderate" level rating is used if the indicator is present but in a relatively mild form. Finally, a "high" rating is given where the risk indicator is present at a significant level and in a relatively extreme form. The unknown rating is given a score of zero. The low rating on risk is given a score of 1; the moderate rating, a score of 2; and the high rating, a score of 3. Observers are trained to carry out these ratings by means of specific examples and are tested to ensure that they understand and agree on the meaning of the different severity levels.

Protective indicators use a reverse rating system with the exception of the unknown category, which remains at a neutral value. If the protective indicator is unknown, the rating is zero. If the protective indicator is absent, the rating is –1. If the protective indicator is present in an intermediate degree, the rating is –2. If the protective indicator is robust, the rating is –3.

Overall Risk Rating Level and Scores

The VERA-SV response sheet lists each of the VERA-SV indicators ($N = 22$) for which the assessor provides ratings in the unknown, low, moderate, or high categories. The totals of the ratings are computed on the working sheet and the summary VERA-SV form. In the case that more than one individual undertakes an evaluation of the subject, ratings of these assessors will be averaged. These scores provide one element that contributes toward a professional decision concerning the individual's degree of risk of radicalization. The final decision is not determined totally by these scores, but they at least provide a basic guideline for the final risk judgment. All evidence to justify the risk rating decisions must be available on the rating response sheets. This documentation is essential for any eventual audits. Professional judgment by a party that did not participate in the calculation of the numerical risk level can occasionally override a risk judgment based on VERA-SV. This change is only acceptable with proper justification that includes evidence and arguments for the divergent judgment.

Reliability and Accuracy of Information

Space is available in the comments section of the VERA-SV form to document the assessor's judgment of the reliability and accuracy of the information on which basis the assessment was undertaken. The assessor must be aware of the potential for deception in any information provided directly from the individual being assessed, either in an interview situation or in informal contact.

Timeliness

The VERA-SV represents a time-sensitive approach, as radicalization to violent extremism is a dynamic process. An individual's views, belief system, commitment to a narrative, networks and associations, and intention to engage in violent action can change over time. Caution should, therefore, be exercised in completing the VERA-SV to ensure that the evidence used is current. It is important to recognize that available past information may not reflect the current state of the beliefs and values of the individual, so past file information must be identified as such. If historical information is used, its date should be provided.

Repeat administrations will allow the determination of trajectories of risk over time for an individual in a reliable manner. The protocol can be repeated at predetermined intervals, providing staff with evidence-based indication of change in risk indicators. The VERA-SV could provide early risk warnings or, alternatively, an indication of positive change in an individual over the course of a rehabilitation program or other initiatives to counter violent extremism.

User Training

A training program for users of the VERA-SV protocol is required for certification. This training is intended to build confidence in the underlying methodology and procedural application of the tool. The program includes practice in the rendition of risk judgments on the different indicators and the provision of an evidence base for those judgments. Some training should be repeated on an annual basis to ensure the rater's fitness to implement the VERA-SV methodology in its various aspects.

User's Guidelines for the VERA-SV and Qualifications

After having successfully completed the training program provided by the developers, accredited trainers of the International Centre for Counter-Terrorism (ICCT) and affiliated centers, users will be qualified to apply the VERA-SV tool for the risk assessment of violent extremists. The training program transmits to trainees the objectives of the tool, its operational use, and the correct manner of interpreting and transmitting the results of the assessment. Practice cases build users' confidence, especially of those who are unaccustomed to interview techniques and strategies or who may lack clinical training.

Some training and skill in conducting interpersonal assessments or interviews is recommended for consistency of use and for understanding of appropriate probing and questioning. Probe questions are provided to users to facilitate interpersonal communication that pertains to the risk indicators. Communication skills are essential in cases where only a single opportunity may exist to obtain salient information from a source or the detainee. Users will be occupants of authorized positions where assessment, intervention programs, or monitoring of suspected or detained violent extremists are a component of their job responsibilities.

Following the Protocol and Completing Required Documentation

Users must conform to the VERA-SV protocol requirements. The information page at the front of the VERA-SV form contains the relevant details of both the assessor and the individual being assessed and must be completed before the assessment begins. The form also provides information pertaining to the context of the referral as well as the location and time of the assessment. Preparation of a standardized risk formulation report is advised. The elements of this report are included at the end of the VERA-SV record form.

Conclusion

The purpose of the VERA-SV tool is to assist the professional assessors in making defensible risk judgments, categorizing individuals on their level of risk, and identifying the most important risk indicators to be addressed in an eventual intervention program or detention. The protocol can be applied to individuals motivated by a range of different political or religious ideologies.

The Significance Quest Assessment Tool (SQAT)

Introduction and Background: What Is It?

The SQAT is a self-report measure designed to assess detainees' degree of radicalization or violent extremism. The tool can be used for either one or both of two purposes: the assessment of risk posed by an individual detainee and the assessment of a deradicalization program as to its effectiveness and impact. The SQAT has been used with detained individuals suspected of membership in the Abu Sayyaf organizations in the Philippines, as well as with Muslim community samples in Spain, Morocco, and the West Bank in Palestine. Its various subscales were found to correlate with each other as predicted by the 3N model (Kruglanski et al., 2014).

Who Can Use It?

Essentially, literate individuals who have received the appropriate training may administer the SQAT. Accordingly, its users may include academic experts trained in research and assessment, prison staff managing detained individuals, general supervisory staff working in jails or detention facilities, or religious advisors and volunteers who have received the appropriate training in the use of the tool.

Elements

Like the VERA-SV, the SQAT contains questions pertaining to all elements of the 3N model. Specifically, the overall SQAT questionnaire is subdivided into three parts: a part that inquires into respondents' quest for significance that taps the need element, a part that inquires into their acceptance of the radical, violence-justifying narrative, and a part that taps their perception of their network's (close friends) subscription to that narrative. An individual's degree of radicalization is then inferred from a combined index that averages an individual's responses on all the 3N dimensions.

Rating the Indicators and Use of the Response Categories

Assessed individuals respond to questionnaire items by marking a response on a scale with appropriate labels indicating their degree of agreement with a statement, or their degree of its endorsement. For instance, the item "Feel unimportant" on the questionnaire that taps the need for significance factor can be answered on a five-level scale ranging from "rarely or never" (1) to "very often" (5). In this case, the higher the number that the respondent checks, the greater the inferred significance loss the respondent suffers. Similarly, the item

"Armed Jihad is a personal obligation of all Muslims today" can be answered on a seven-point scale, ranging from "strongly disagree" (1) to "strongly agree (7). In this case, the higher the number corresponding to the respondent's answer, the greater the degree of violent extremist radicalization that the individual is reporting. It is important that the assessor read and understood the meaning of each question so as to properly interpret the meaning of a high or low numerical response to that item.

Response Registration

The 3N aspects are measured by the appropriate scales. The needs scale measures the respondents' need for significance by recording their responses to questions about their "significance loss and gain." Respondents' readiness to embrace the radical ideological narrative is measured by appropriate scales that would vary in accordance with the radical ideology in question. In other words, different versions of the instrument would incorporate different ideological contents, such as ones related to religious extremism, ethno-nationalist extremism, or socialist-communist extremism.

In the version of SQAT described in the following text, we assess the contents of Islamic radicalization. Accordingly, this version incorporates the scales of Islamist Extremism, Islam's Support for Violence, Attitudes toward the West, and Martyrdom. Finally, the network aspect is assessed by having respondents respond to the ideological narrative scales the way they think that their friends and family would. This approach provides information concerning the degree of extremism of the respondents' friends. Calculating the differences between respondents' answers to the two scales and the way they think their friends would answer them would reveal the extent to which the respondents are immersed in an extremist network and share the beliefs and opinions of its members.

Overall Risk Rating Levels and Scores

The quantitative response indicators derived from scales measuring each of the three Ns are summed up to yield the overall factor score (i.e., the overall need score, overall narrative score, and overall network score). Adding these three scores will give an overall risk level for a given individual. The higher the score is, the greater the inference of risk posed by the given individual. Numerical estimates of risk based on SQAT and VERA-SV can be combined by simple averaging, providing an overall measure of risk.

Timeliness

As noted in connection with the VERA-SV, radicalization to violent extremism is a dynamic process because individuals' needs, commitment to ideological narratives, and friendship networks may change over time. For that reason, both the VERA-SV and the SQAT can be used for the evaluation of deradicalization programs. In evaluating the risk posed by individuals, caution should be exercised to ensure that the evidence being used is current and to recognize that available past information may not reflect the current state of the individual's needs and beliefs.

User Training

SQAT users are required to participate in a training program that provides instructions in the methodology of the survey. The program also trains potential users on how to instruct the survey takers to respond to the survey questions and to use the response scales. The training thus imparts the manner of administering the questionnaires and impresses upon users the need to prevent respondents from communicating with each other in cases where they respond to the survey in a group setting. The various questionnaires are explained to the users and the meaning of the items is clarified. The training sessions instruct users how to reply to possible questions from the respondents and, in the event that some of the respondents are illiterate, how to read the questions to respondents in a way that would not interfere with the administration of the survey to others.

User Qualifications

Users must complete a training program that is provided by the developers, official delegates, and other qualified accredited trainers of the assessment tools (i.e., of the VERA-SV and SQAT). The successful completion of this program will provide the graduates of the training with the "user qualification" certificate.

Combining Information from the VERA-SV and the SQAT

The benefit of combining information from the VERA-SV and the SQAT lies in evaluating the risk of the potential for violent extremism posed by a given respondent via different methods, each with its unique advantages and disadvantages. The VERA-SV primarily relies on external observations of individuals of interest by persons who come into interaction with them. The

SQAT is a self-report tool that the individual responds to. Both tools provide evidence for the three basic elements that contribute to radicalization into violent extremism, namely, the needs, the narratives, and the networks in which the individual is embedded. Both tools also allow a quantitative measure of assessment on each of the three Ns involved in extremism.

The observation method used by VERA-SV might introduce *observer biases*, and the self-report method used by SQAT might introduce *respondent biases*. Thus, when used jointly, each of the methods compensates for disadvantages of its counterpart. A combined examination of information provided by the two tools can yield valuable convergent information about an individual's degree of extremism. Two separate cases can be distinguished: one in which the results of the VERA-SV and the SQAT agree (e.g., both may indicate high, moderate, or low risk of violent extremism) and another in which the two tools yield discrepant results. Agreement between the tools should give the assessor confidence concerning the risk that the given individual poses. Disagreement should provide an opportunity to consider possible reasons for the discrepancy. Analysis of the discrepancy should give insight into the risk involved and the factors that might have contributed to it.

The Temporal Course of Radicalization and Deradicalization

Both radicalization and deradicalization unfold over time. They involve a change in opinions and attitudes that typically require extensive elaboration and digestion of new information, "unfreezing" of prior opinions, consideration of novel arguments, and falling under the spell of new communicators and the pull of new social networks. The temporal course of radicalization and deradicalization has an important methodological implication. It suggests that to properly assess these processes it is necessary to measure them over time, that is, to repeat the assessment procedure (using the SQAT and the VERA tools) at different temporal points so that the degree of change may be noted.

For instance, in research by Kruglanski et al. (2016), we looked at terrorism suspects—namely, inmates of a prison in the Philippines (members of the Abu Sayyaf group)—over a two-year period. We found that over that period and with no deradicalization program in place there was a considerable radicalization of the inmates, expressed in a significantly more pronounced Islamist extremism, significantly greater support for violence as a means to political ends, and significantly more pronounced anti-Western attitudes.

Evaluating Deradicalization Programs: The Role of the Control Group

The longitudinal assessment of radicalization is particularly important in the evaluation of deradicalization programs. This importance reflects the notion that deradicalization unfolds over time: It requires the individual's growing readiness to suspend prior commitments to a radical ideology and to open her or his mind (Kruglanski, 2004) to counternarratives that advocate moderation and the abandonment of extremism. However, longitudinal measurement of detainees' attitudes over time is insufficient for adequate evaluation of deradicalization programs. In addition, it is important to include in the research design *a control group* of detainees that may be compared with the *treatment group*. Let us explain.

By treatment group, we mean individuals who were actually exposed to the deradicalization program. The control group, in contrast, consists of similar detainees who *were not* exposed to the program (perhaps they were meant to undergo the program at a later time). Without such a comparison group, any change over time in detainees' attitudes and behavior could be attributed to factors that are unrelated to the deradicalization program or its efficiency. For instance, if detainees in the treatment group became less militant over time—this might not be due to the program at all, but possibly due to their separation from the fighting group and its sphere of influence; alternatively, it could be due to historical events that happened during that period or to a number of other factors.

The control group should be tested over the same time period as the treatment group to rule out those possible extraneous (e.g., time-related) sources of influence on outcomes observed in the treatment group. Specifically, if a change in attitudes and behavior was observed in the treatment group, yet not in the control group, then time-related causes of the change could be ruled out because both the treatment group and the control group were presumably exposed to the same *general* events, such as political, social, or environmental ones. If those events, rather than the deradicalization program, were the cause of attitude change in the treatment group, the same change should have taken place in the control group as well. If it didn't, then something else must have been responsible for the change in the treatment group—hopefully, the deradicalization *treatment* itself.

Note in this connection that while general historic events that the treatment group and the control group experienced in common could not be responsible for an effect observed in only one of the groups, *local* historic events that occurred in one of the groups but not in the other could provide such explanation. For instance, if the treatment group consisted of inmates in one detention facility whereas the control group consisted of inmates in another, then specific local events that transpired in the treatment group facility but not in the control group's facility could be responsible for the observed change in attitudes of treatment group inmates that did not appear in control group inmates.

Note also that the control group needs to be *as similar as possible* in all essential characteristics (e.g., in its demographics) to the treatment group. In "true" experimental research conducted in the laboratory, this situation is achieved through random assignment of participants to the treatment and control conditions. For obvious reasons, random assignment would be impractical when it comes to evaluation of deradicalization programs. In most cases where such programs exist, the control group would just be a different group of detainees who, either by design or for circumstantial reasons, were not exposed to the treatment. Ideally then, the treatment individuals and the control individuals should be matched on all the relevant characteristics. In particular, their initial attitudes toward the political conflict at stake should be considered, along with their degree of involvement or embeddedness in the organization; their age, gender, and marital status; and anything else that might drive their attitudes and opinions on the research questions of interest.

A different methodological threat in carrying out a program evaluation research is possible *differential loss* of research participants from the treatment versus the control groups. Since taking part in the research is voluntary, some detainees might refuse it. Such refusal might well be related to detainees' attitudes and beliefs relevant to the topic under investigation—for instance, to their animosity toward the West or the distrust of scientific research due to religious fundamentalism. In short, a differential loss of participants from the treatment groups versus the control groups undermines their attitudinal parity. Should differences be found between those groups—indicating, say, that the treatment group was more moderate than the control group—these could not be readily attributable to the treatment alone because they could possibly stem from differences in the composition of the two groups created by the differential participant loss.

In Absence of the Control Group

Though having a control group is highly desirable, an inability to obtain one does not mean that data collection on the treatment group alone is fated to be uninformative. For instance, if change over time was observed in the treatment group, this would be consistent with the idea that the treatment had an effect, although the responsibility for this effect by other historical factors, occurring in the time interval between the pre- and post-measurement periods, could not be definitively ruled out. To do so, possible factors that may mediate such change might be considered.

For instance, if the change in extremist attitudes was correlated with participants' positive change toward the prison personnel, or to the deradicalization program as such, this would support the notion that it was the program that produced the effect rather than extraneous factors. If the detainees' degree of *involvement* and *success* at activities comprising the deradicalization program were correlated with the extent of observed deradicalization, this would also attest that it was the program that produced the change. In summary, obtaining systematic data pertinent to the effectiveness of the program is better than having no data, even if the conditions on the ground did not allow the implementation of a full-fledged research design including both the treatment and the control conditions.

Ethical Considerations

Research of the program evaluation variety that is carried out under the auspices of an academic institution or that is funded by a governmental agency (in the United States and Europe at least) requires authorization from a special committee to perform research with human subjects. In the United States, this committee is referred to as the institutional review board (IRB). In the case of research with prisoners or detainees, obtaining such an authorization can be difficult because of the detainees' captive status and the possibility that they are *forced* to participate in the research, rather than doing it of their own free will. In negotiating IRB approval, it is incumbent on researchers to demonstrate how their procedures minimize the risk to participants in those regards. Sometimes, such demonstrations include assurances of anonymity of the participants' responses, their voluntary participation in the research, their freedom to withdraw from the research at any time, and other similar guarantees. It may be helpful in some cases to demonstrate to IRBs that similar prior research with detainee populations produced neither ill effects nor complaints on part of the detainees or their representatives.

Researcher Safety

An additional obstacle that needs to be surmounted is the concern for the safety of the researchers. If research at a given venue is judged to put the researchers—interviewers or survey administrators—in close contact with potentially dangerous respondents, the researchers' security may be at risk. At least some agencies (e.g., the US Department of Homeland Security) are highly sensitive to such risk and flatly refuse to issue travel authorizations and approval for research where it may exist.

Placing armed prison personnel in venues where the research is carried out is a possible, albeit rather unappealing, solution to this problem. The presence of armed personnel might alter the climate of the study and introduce an atmosphere of threat and compulsion into the process; among others, it could highlight to research participants their status as detainees and might bias the research results in a particular, socially desirable, direction (e.g., by their expressing inauthentic, falsely moderate views aimed at convincing the researchers and the guards of their moderation). These issues need to be considered and negotiated with the local authorities, such as the warden of the facility, to ensure the optimal ways of dealing with the security problem.

Finally, identification of the research's funding source might introduce risk for the researchers if that particular source is perceived as illegitimate by the research respondents. For instance, in a nation with occasionally strained relations with the United States (e.g., Pakistan) identifying the source of funding as the US government could put the project in jeopardy and place the researchers' safety at risk. This situation poses a dilemma in which the data to be collected could be of unique interest, yet which collection, under the official rules of the agency, requires its complete identification.

Participants' Collaboration

As already indicated, IRB considerations typically require that respondents' participation in the research project be voluntary and that they be allowed to quit at any point during the process. In those circumstances, participants' collaboration is hardly assured and often could be problematic. The challenge, therefore, is to convince detained participants that their involvement in the research is advantageous to them. This obstacle may be quite challenging, as the detainees may be suspicious of attempts to wrest information from them, lest it be abused and worsen their already precarious situation.

If their suspicions are properly allayed, however, detainees may welcome the opportunity to speak to interviewers and express their opinions, anxieties, and concerns. After all, their time in detention is typically dull, and the opportunity to speak to intelligent people from the outside provides a welcome break from the monotony of prison life.

Last, yet of inestimable importance, is securing the full cooperation and buy-in of the prison warden and the prison personnel; they have an important role to play in enabling the execution of the research at their facility. It is they who ultimately afford access to the detainees and provide the security personnel, typically busy with other routine tasks, to fend for the safety of the researchers. They are also tasked with finding the space where the research will be conducted and the time within the prison's routine schedules—including meals, prayer times, and other daily activities—when the research effort can be fitted.

Summary

In this chapter, we discussed the assessment of individuals' degree of radicalization or deradicalization. This issue is particularly pertinent to the evaluation of inmates suspected of violent extremism in detention facilities who may be exposed to a rehabilitation program of some kind. We distinguished between two separate uses of assessment, namely, concerning the security risks potentially posed by inmates and concerning the evaluation of deradicalization programs aimed to reduce such risks. We first introduced a dual component method of assessment, including an observational method (VERA-SV) and a self-report instrument (SQAT), whose convergent results may indicate a given individual's degree of radicalization. This method, if used at intake to a detention facility, may be helpful in determining the assignment of the individual to a given section of the incarceration facility (e.g., populated by other inmates with similar levels of radicalization). It may also be useful in determining whether the individual is ready for release into the community and what type of aftercare may be specifically appropriate in her or his case.

We further discussed the issue of program evaluation and, in particular, the need for a control group, as well as other methodological considerations (e.g., differential loss of participants in treatment and control groups), to allow a clear attribution of observed differences in radicalization over time to the program as such. Finally, we examined the practical issues that typically surface when attempting to carry out a large-scale program evaluation in a facility that holds individuals suspected of violent extremism. Despite the multiple challenges that risk assessment and program evaluation may entail, we consider both as critical in reversing the process of radicalization and in preventing recidivism.

References

Beardsley, N. L., & Beech, A. R. (2013). Applying the violent extremist risk assessment (VERA) to a sample of terrorist case studies. *Journal of Aggression, Conflict and Peace Research*, 5, 4–15.

Dugas, M., & Kruglanski, A. W. (2014). The quest for significance model of radicalization: Implications for the management of terrorist detainees. *Behavioral Sciences & the Law*, 32, 423–439.

Kruglanski, A. W. (2004). *The psychology of closed mindedness*. New York, NY: Psychology Press.

Kruglanski, A. W., Gelfand, M. J., Bélanger, J. J., Sheveland, A., Hetiarachchi, M., & Gunaratna, R. (2014). The psychology of radicalization and deradicalization: How significance quest impacts violent extremism. *Political Psychology*, 35, 69–93.

Kruglanski, A. W., Gelfand, M. J., Sheveland, A., Babush, M., Hetiarachchi, M., Ng Bonto, M., & Gunaratna, R. (2016). What a difference two years make: Patterns of radicalization in a Philippine jail. *Dynamics of Asymmetric Conflict*, 9, 13–36.

Pressman, D. E., & Flockton, J. (2012). Calibrating risk for violent political extremists and terrorists: The VERA 2 structured assessment. *British Journal of Forensic Practice*, 14, 237–251.

Pressman, D. E., & Flockton, J. (2014). Violent extremist risk assessment: Issues and applications of the VERA-2 in a high security correctional setting. In A. Silke (Ed.), *Prisons, Terrorism and Extremism: Critical Issues in Management, Radicalization and Reform* (pp. 122–143). New York, NY: Routledge.

Webber, D., Babush, M., Schori-Eyal, N., Moyano, M., Hettiarachchi, M., Bélanger, J. J., . . . Gelfand, M.J. (2018). The road to extremism: How significance-loss-based uncertainty fosters radicalization. *Journal of Personality and Social Psychology*, 114, 270–285.

Webster, C. D., Douglas, K. S., Eaves, D., & Hart, S. D. (1997). Assessing risk of violence to others. In C. D. Webster & M. A. Jackson (Eds.), *Impulsivity: Theory, Assessment, and Treatment* (pp. 251–277). New York, NY: Guilford.

Webster, C. D., Müller-Isberner, R., & Fransson, G. (2002). Violence risk assessment: Using structured clinical guides professionally. *International Journal of Forensic Mental Health, 1*, 185–193.

EPILOGUE

THE LONG SHADOW OF VIOLENT EXTREMISM

In the preceding chapters, we outlined a significance quest theory of radicalization and identified its three major parameters, namely, the need, narrative and network factors (the three Ns) that typically underlie individuals' involvement in violent extremism. We noted how the psychological principles that govern violent extremism are a special case of the dynamics of extremism writ large. They address a state of motivational imbalance in which one basic need dominates the others and pushes them out of mind as it were. In the case of violent extremism, we identified the quest for significance as the dominant need, which, at intense magnitudes, prompts individuals to forget all else and be willing to make immense self-sacrifices to serve a valued cause that lends them significance. Importantly, the quest for significance alone is not uniquely tied to violence and, under the appropriate circumstances, could even lead to its very opposite: feats of humanistic self-denial aimed at eliminating the suffering of others. Whether violence or humanism will result is determined by the two remaining parameters of our theory, the narrative that ties the obtainment of significance to specific actions and the network that consensually validates the narrative and dispenses significance and veneration to those who follow its dictates.

We analyzed the relations between the 3Ns of radicalization and showed how the present analysis integrates elements identified in various prior models of radicalization by showing how they function jointly in producing violent extremism. We extended this analysis to issues raised by challenges of deradicalization and examined it in connection with the ever-present possibility of reradicalization. Finally, we examined the implications of our framework for the task of risk assessment, deemed of crucial importance in addressing the danger that committed extremists may pose to society.

We believe that when appropriately translated into specific circumstances the 3N approach offers useful guidelines for policies and best practices aimed at preventing as well as countering violent extremism. This is a worthwhile and necessary enterprise given the pernicious and costly effects that the recent wave of violent extremism has had on societies worldwide. In the final pages of this volume, we thus revisit the real-world context of violent extremism (addressed in Chapter 1) and consider some of the major ways in which terrorism has changed the world we inhabit.

It has become a cliché to say that the terrorist attacks on the World Trade Center in New York City and the Pentagon on September 11, 2001, shocked the world, shattered the self-confidence of US citizens, and wrought substantial cracks in their sense of security and stability. This tragic event and the ongoing response to it ushered in an age of anxiety in the United States and elsewhere. The specter of violent extremism has insinuated itself into major aspects of people's lives around the globe and has come to define a new normal in which ferocious violence can strike at anyone, anytime, and anywhere.

The War Path

The United States' immediate reaction to 9/11 prompted its, and its allies', invasion of Afghanistan and the routing out of the Taliban, the fundamentalist faction that had harbored Al Qaeda. Though the banishment of the Taliban occurred rather swiftly, engagement of the US military in Afghanistan has dragged on, becoming the longest-running war in American history. Despite former President Barrack Obama's insistence on the drawdown of forces in 2014, over 11,000 US troops are as of this writing to assist the Afghan army in fighting the recalcitrant Taliban insurgency. To boot, in 2003, the allies' invasion of Iraq drew the American military into further commitment. Overall, in the last 15 years, nearly 2 million US troops have been deployed to Afghanistan or Iraq. Of those troops, more than 6,000 have been killed and roughly 44,000 wounded. More than 18% have been diagnosed with a posttraumatic stress disorder or depression, and nearly 20% have suffered traumatic brain injury (Green, 2016). These statistics brought the plight of American war veterans to the forefront of our society's attention and uncovered ways in which it is woefully unprepared, beyond token gestures, to care for those who sacrificed life and limb in service of their country.

Finances

The war in Afghanistan, the invasion of Iraq, and the relentless war against terror on multiple fronts has excised considerable financial toll. The discretionary budget of the US Department of Homeland Security increased from $16 billion in 2002 to over $43 billion in 2011. Budgets of the US Coast Guard, Transportation Security Administration, and Border Patrol have all risen by over 200% since 2001, and the overall Federal Bureau of Investigations' budget, by almost 300% since that time.

By the calculation of Steven Brill, an American journalist and lawyer-entrepreneur, over the past 15 years the US government has spent $100 billion to $150 billion on inefficient or failed homeland security programs and equipment. The amount of funds spent by the US government on security is staggering, with the estimates varying between $1.7 trillion and $5 trillion (Brill, 2016).

According to Brill's analysis, much of that money was spent smartly on reinforcing vulnerable spots in major US cities deemed to constitute prime targets for terrorist attacks. For instance, the train tunnels under New York's rivers were reinforced to the tune of hundreds of millions of dollars, as was the Madison Square Garden–Penn Station complex, whose (hypothetical) destruction by a small car bomb could have had horrendous consequences. Governmental spending on security also included funding a team of experts who wrote a widely used manual titled "Engineering Security," providing guidelines on determining facilities' security and resilience. The increased funding of security also financed the posting of police at sites of potential targets, some of whom did, in fact, stave off major plots, potentially saving thousands of lives.

Immigration and Deportation

The 9/11 attacks affected substantial changes in the US immigration policy. The Homeland Security Act and the Enhanced Border Security and Visa Entry Reform Act (2002) made US visas more difficult to obtain for foreign nationals (including tourists and students), and individuals who were granted entry were further vetted through means such as fingerprints and other biometric measures. The tightening of immigration policies affected all those seeking entry into, and/or citizenship in, the United States, including applicants from countries such as Mexico and Latin America—places with no apparent relation to Islamist terrorism. The contested ban imposed by the

Trump administration on travel from several predominantly Muslim countries represents the tightening of immigration policies taken to yet a new level (Laughland, 2017).

In parallel to the tightening of entry regulations, the deportations of individuals from the United States nearly doubled from 200,000 annual deportations in the 1999–2001 period to nearly 400,000 during the first two years of the Obama administration (2009–2010). The deportees were individuals convicted of criminal offenses, the majority of which were low-level, nonviolent crimes (Green, 2016).

Air Travel

Unsurprisingly, air travel has been particularly impacted by the 9/11 attacks: Cockpit doors have been reinforced to block potential assailants from commandeering the aircraft; prohibitions have been implemented against liquid, cigarette lighters, or sharp objects on board; and frequent pat downs, body scans, and the removal of shoes have been instituted in the aftermath of the attacks. These new restrictions and procedures have multiplied by manifold the hardships of air travel and significantly increased the amount of travel time for most passengers. Despite all the security measures in place today, for many people air travel still evokes anxiety, stemming from the sense that it continues to represent an appealing and, hence, likely target for terrorists. The disproportionate scrutiny at airports of travelers of Middle Eastern origin only adds another troubling dimension to transportation by air, contributing to tensions and frustrations along ethnic lines (Green, 2016).

Surveillance, Domestic Spying, and Individual Rights

The fear of potential attacks tightened up the government's oversight of US citizens and residents, instituting an unprecedented system of domestic surveillance through a secret network of phones and Internet activity. The enormous scope of the surveillance enterprise was revealed in 2013 by Edward Snowden, a former government contractor whose disclosures shocked the nation and the world. It turned out that the budget of the surveillance state amounted to $52.6 billion in 2013, supporting an extensive intelligence community incorporating 16 spy agencies with over 107,000 employees. Additional reports have revealed that the National Security Agency alone has annually inspected about 56,000 electronic communications by regular Americans with no apparent ties to terrorism, in severe violation of privacy laws.

Art and Culture

Video Games

Beyond its impact on pervasive issues of security, the continuing war on terror has had palpable impact on art and culture in the United States. Consider video games, a pervasive marker of young people's interests. Apparently, their themes dramatically changed from pre- to post-9/11 (LaLone, 2012). In the pre-9/11 era, games revolved on themes of science fiction—the scary futures it portends for environmental destruction and power-hungry leaders trying to take over the world (characteristic also of James Bond films). In contrast, games created after 9/11 focused much more on safety, protecting one's living space from attack and unfamiliar, shadowy assailants ready to strike at anytime, anywhere.

Film

Of interest also is the film industry's response to 9/11. In his volume *Firestorm: American Film in the Age of Terrorism,* Prince (2009) argues that prior to 9/11, terrorists were portrayed as prototypical "bad guys," evil to the core, whereas following 9/11 the cinematic portrayals of terrorists became more realistic and nuanced. The latter have been characterized as "liberal fence-sitting" and were blamed for increases in Islamist terrorism during the second Bush administration (Bradshaw, 2011).

This cinematic handling of terrorism went through different phases. Immediately in the aftermath of 9/11, movies shied away from mentioning the attacks in their films for fear of offending people and being perceived as capitalizing on the disaster ("List of Entertainment," n.d.; "Post-9/11," n.d.). This phase was followed by indirect hints at terrorist plots, which, in turn, was followed by an intense and pervasive preoccupation with terrorism in cinema that has produced a deluge of movies on the topic—and shows no signs of waning anytime soon (Reilly, 2010).

Yong Volz, a professor of journalism and her colleagues at the University of Missouri, sought to determine whether 9/11 had an impact on Americans' reactions of foreign cultures, based on American box office receipts of nearly 600 foreign films from 1984 to 2006 (Volz, 2010). Her discovery was striking and indicated a significant change occasioned by the 9/11 trauma: Whereas prior to 2001, Americans tended to prefer foreign films from more exotic cultures that differ substantially from the American lore, after 2001 they favored foreign films from Western countries more culturally similar to the

United States. These findings suggest that after 9/11 Americans became more xenophobic and less tolerant of foreign people and culture.

Television

The popularity of terrorism-related themes in American films is matched by TV shows that pervasively portray terrorism-related topics. Blockbuster series like *Homeland*, *24*, *The Newsroom*, and *NCIS*, to mention a few, deal with Islamist terrorism and tend to do so in a stereotypic way that often portrays Muslims as bloodthirsty terrorists (Schilling, 2016). Add to this portrayal the extensive coverage of terrorism-related events by TV's news shows and one realizes the extent to which viewers are exposed to the terrorism phenomenon, which must only fuel the existential uncertainty and anxiety that this theme evokes.

Uncertainty Politics

The xenophobic attitude and the stereotypic portrayals of Muslims are but a symptom of a more general shift in the mentality of Americans and others under the specter of violent extremism, so salient in people's cognizance today. In an interview with *Psychology Today*, Charles Strozier, a psychoanalyst from John Jay College of Criminal Justice in New York City, suggested that the awareness of our own vulnerability cast Americans into the throes of an existential crisis, imbued by fear, "malaise about life and uncertainty about the future" (Peay, 2015). It is such uncertainty, and the psychological reaction to that uncertainty, that may have significantly impacted people's world views and political preferences.

Edward Orehek, a social psychologist at the University of Pittsburgh, and his colleagues examined the impact of threat-induced uncertainty in a set of studies (Orehek et al., 2010). In the first experiment in the series, some participants—college students at a large mid-Atlantic university—were exposed to slides depicting the attacks on the World Trade Center on 9/11. At the same time, other participants, in the control condition, viewed "neutral" slides depicting the facilities at Google. Researchers then measured all participants' need for cognitive closure, the motivational cravings for certainty, and the eschewal of ambiguity. The results attested clearly that the memory of 9/11 significantly impacted individuals' need for closure; those reminded of this threatening event measured significantly higher on a scale that assesses the need for closure than the control participants.

To be sure, memories of the 9/11 trauma or other similar attacks aren't the sole factors capable of heightening the need for closure n. In their second study, Orehek et al. (2010) measured Dutch citizens' need for closure as a function of the proportion of Muslims in their neighborhood. It turned out that the proportion of Muslims had a significant effect on Dutch participants' need for closure: The higher that proportion, the higher the need for closure and also the greater individuals' bias in favor of their own group (native Dutch) and against the Muslim foreigners, attesting to the xenophobia and aversion to otherness mentioned earlier.

In their third study, Orehek et al. (2010) investigated American adults' need for closure, their tendency to feel interdependent with others in their ingroup, and their support for tough counterterrorism measures, such as use of torture and the signing of the Patriot Act. The results showed that the need for closure is significantly related both to individuals' feeling of interdependence with others as well as to their support for tough counterterrorism measures. In a related study, these investigators also found that increased support for tough counterterrorism related to individuals' need for closure and to optimism about future safety. This finding reflected the idea that when individuals' need for closure is high, tough measures appear to them to constitute a particularly effective solution to the terrorism problem.

The significant relation between need for closure and support for torture, a particularly tough counterterrorism measure, was recently obtained in an independent research by Giacomantonio, Pierro, Baldner, and Kruglanski (2017). The study also revealed that individuals with high need for closure justify their support for torture by adopting what Jonathan Haidt referred to as moral foundations that "bind" individuals to their group (Graham et al., 2011, 2013). Specifically, *authority/subversion* refers to the moral injunction to follow and respect social hierarchies, *loyalty/betrayal* underlines the importance of faithfulness to the group, and *sanctity/degradation* stresses the importance of protecting the group from social and physical contamination, as well as support for what is sacred to the group. In short, the need for cognitive closure appears to foster a group-centric attitude (Kruglanski, Pierro, Mannetti, & DeGrada, 2006) that includes an antipathy to members of outgroups, as well as moral attitudes that elevate protection of one's group to the status of a lofty moral principle.

In the ultimate study in their series, Orehek et al. (2010) investigated the type of leader that individuals with a high need for closure will tend to support. To examine this phenomenon, the investigators presented participants—college students at a university again—with descriptions of two types of leader: A *decisive* leader, portrayed as "stable and consistent, capable of quick decisions, one who holds firm beliefs," and an *open-minded* leader, characterized as "flexible and adaptive, capable of seeing multiple perspectives, and one who believes in challenging ideas." It turned out that individuals with a high need for closure strongly preferred a decisive over an open-minded leader, whereas the opposite preference was exhibited by individuals with low need for closure.

The yearning for "strong" leadership in situations of uncertainty is strikingly illustrated by contemporary world politics. Indeed, current realities carry a great deal of uncertainty for large masses of people on the planet. Economic recession, wide-ranging war in the Middle East, the refugee crisis, extremist attacks in the world's major cities, and the specter of cyberattacks with untold consequences—all magnified by pervasive TV reporting related to terrorism—usher anxiety, fear, and insecurity about the future into people's hearts. As Orehek's research work suggests, uncertainty, in turn, breeds the need for cognitive closure, which, in turn, augments the appeal of strong authoritarian leaders who speak in definite terms and promise simple solutions to complex problems.

Indeed, as Gideon Rachman (2016) of the *Financial Times* recently commented, we are witnessing an emergence of strongmen leaders in various parts of the world, with the likes of Putin in Russia, Xi Jinping in China, Erdogan in Turkey, Sisi in Egypt, Modi in India, Orban in Hungary, and Duterte in the Philippines. Donald Trump's appeal to American voters during the 2016 electoral campaign, and his subsequent election, represents the same trend. Typically, the strongmen leaders court voter support by trading on people's insecurity and fear and promising to eradicate their causes. As Rachman (2016) puts it,

> Mr. Putin and Mr. Erdogan have portrayed Russia and Turkey as surrounded by enemies. Mr. Sisi has promised to rescue Egypt from terrorism. Mr. Xi and Mr. Modi have capitalised on ordinary people's frustrations with corruption and inequality. The Trump campaign has incorporated elements of all these themes, promising to reverse national decline and get tough with criminals and foreigners.

A characteristic element of strongmen policies is the promise to use extreme means to attain their ends. In this vein, Rachman (2016) speaks of these leaders' "willingness to ignore liberal niceties. In many cases, the promise of decisive leadership is backed up by a willingness—sometimes explicit, sometimes implied—to use illegal violence against enemies of the state." The latter typically are portrayed as the epitome of evil. Indeed, authoritarian leaders emphasize distinctions between the ingroup and the outgroup— the Manichean dichotomies between "us" and "them"—all grounded in the *binding* morality that elevates the welfare of the ingroup above all else (Graham et al., 2013). Indeed, authoritarian leaders typically are bellicose as they need to invoke threatening "enemies" to justify their extremism.

Because they espouse unrealistic "truths" in black and white—authoritarian leaders are acutely sensitive to criticism that threatens their simplistic perspectives and identify alternatives to their proposed policies. The current crop of strongmen leaders is no exception to this rule. As Rachman (2016) notes,

> In both the Putin and Xi presidencies there have been crackdowns on freedom of speech. In Turkey, Mr. Erdogan has sued almost 2,000 people for defamation. Mr. Trump misses few opportunities to insult the media and has said that he would like to make it easier for politicians to sue the press.

Though those who practice terrorism (e.g., those who radicalize and join the Islamic State) and those who fight it (e.g., strongmen leaders on today's international scene) may seem as diametrically different from each other as one might imagine, in reality they often share a deep commonality: Both embrace totalistic ideologies that depict humanity in polar opposites, and both do so in response to aversive uncertainty and confusion that they try to escape.

Summary

The wave of violent extremism that is currently sweeping the world is impacting a variety of human experience around the globe. On the concrete level, this extremism forces unprecedented monetary outlays on issues of safety and security and causes untold daily hassles to millions of air travelers. On the psychological level, it undermines people's sense of order and stability, their feelings of personal significance, and the sense of a secure and safe base for one's life pursuits. The attendant feelings of disempowerment and vulnerability commonly induce the craving for strong leadership and encourage a turn to autocracy, spinning simplistic, black-and-white narratives that offer a balmy sense of certainty, even if baseless and unrealistic.

Because different strongmen offer disparate ingroup-centered ideologies, they encourage polarization and fractionation along national, ethnic, and religious fault lines, resembling what political scientist Samuel Huntington (1997) dubbed the "clash of civilizations." Moreover, the extremism that autocracies are known for is likely to promote the unleashing of violence—the use of extreme means justified by self-righteousness and the denigration of others. This portends a dangerous, conflicted world, perennially submerged in violent strife and replete with intergroup tensions ready to explode. Consistent with this view is the statistically supported democratic peace theory (e.g., Kant, 1795/1970, de Tocqueville, 1835/1969; Ray, 1998, 2003) whereby for various reasons (e.g., leaders accountability to their electorates) democracies are less likely to engage in war than are autocracies.

All of which adds up to a compelling argument why radicalization should be resisted and counteracted by all means at our disposal. Its pernicious effects are unlikely to remain local; especially in this age of global interconnectedness, they are likely to incite chain reactions that would set the world aflame. But to fight radicalization, it is incumbent first to understand its nature. The aim of the present work was to elaborate such an understanding.

References

Bradshaw, P. (2011, September 8). 9/11 films: How did Hollywood handle the tragedy? *The Guardian*. Retrieved from https://www.theguardian.com/film/filmblog/2011/sep/08/9-11-films-hollywood-handle.

Brill, S. (2016, September). Is America any safer? *The Atlantic*. Retrieved from http://www.theatlantic.com/magazine/archive/2016/09/are-we-any-safer/492761/

de Tocqueville, A. (1969). *Democracy in America*. Garden City, NY: Anchor. (Original work published 1835)

Giacomantonio, M., Pierro, A., Baldner, C., & Kruglanski, A. (2017). Need for closure, torture, and punishment motivations. *Social Psychology, 48*(6), 335–347.

Graham, J., Haidt, J., Koleva, S., Motyl, M., Iyer, R., Wojcik, S., & Ditto, P. H. (2013). Moral foundations theory: The pragmatic validity of moral pluralism. *Advances in Experimental Social Psychology, 47*, 55–130.

Graham, J., Nosek, B. A., Haidt, J., Iyer, R., Koleva, S., & Ditto, P. H. (2011). Mapping the moral domain. *Journal of Personality and Social Psychology, 101*, 366–385.

Green, M. (2016, September 6). How 9/11 changed America: Four major lasting impacts (with lesson plan). *KQED News*. Retrieved from https://ww2.kqed.org/lowdown/2016/09/06/13-years-later-four-major-lasting-impacts-of-911/

Huntington, S. P. (1997). *The clash of civilizations and the remaking of world order*. London, England: Penguin.

Kant, I. (1795/1970). Perpetual peace: A philosophical sketch. In H. Reiss (Ed.) *Kant's political writings* (2nd ed., pp. 93–143). Cambridge, MA: Cambridge University Press.

Kruglanski, A. W., Pierro, A., Mannetti, L., & De Grada, E. (2006). Groups as epistemic providers: Need for closure and the unfolding of group-centrism. *Psychological Review*, *113*, 84–100.

LaLone, N. J. (2012). *Differences in design: Video game design in pre and post 9/11 America*. Unpublished dMaster Thesis. Texas State University, San Marcos.

Laughland, O. (2017, June 27). Trump travel ban: US supreme court partially lifts block on order. *The Guardian*. Retrieved from https://www.theguardian.com/us-news/2017/jun/26/trump-travel-ban-supreme-court-block-partially-lifted

List of entertainment affected by the September 11 attacks. (n.d.). *Wikipedia*. Retrieved from https://en.wikipedia.org/wiki/List_of_entertainment_affected_by_the_September_11_attacks

Orehek, E., Fishman, S., Dechesne, M., Doosje, B., Kruglanski, A. W., Cole, A. P., . . . Jackson, T. (2010). Need for closure and the social response to terrorism. *Basic and Applied Social Psychology*, *32*, 279–290.

Peay, P. (2015, September, 10). The traumas of 9/11 and its effects on the American psyche. *Psychology Today*. Retrieved from https://www.psychologytoday.com/blog/america-the-couch/201509/the-traumas-911-and-its-effects-the-american-psyche.

Post-9/11 terrorism movie. (n.d.). *TV Tropes*. https://tvtropes.org/pmwiki/pmwiki.php/Main/PostNineElevenTerrorismMovie

Prince, S. (2009). Firestorm: American film in the age of terrorism. New York, NY: Columbia University Press.

Rachman, G. (2016, May 16). Donald Trump, Vladimir Putin and the lure of the strongman. *Financial Times*. Retrieved from https://www.ft.com/content/1c6ff2ce-1939-11e6-b197-a4af20d5575e

Ray, J. L. (1998). *Democracy and international conflict: An evaluation of the democratic peace proposition*. Columbia, SC: University of South Carolina Press.

Ray, J. L. (2003). A Lakatosian view of the democratic peace research program. In C. Elman & M. F. Elman (Eds.), *Progress in international relations theory: Appraising the field* (pp. 205–243). Cambridge, MA: MIT Press.

Reilly, A. (2010, January 27). Film professor explores 9/11's effect on Hollywood. *Collegiate Times*. Retrieved from http://www.collegiatetimes.com/lifestyle/special_section/film-professor-explores-s-effect-on-hollywood/article_24d44cc2-331c-51d8-82c6-33b4bd9a4c16.html.

Schilling, D. (2016, February, 4). Bloodthirsty terrorists and duplicitous spies: Does TV have a Muslim problem? *The Guardian*. Retrieved from https://www.theguardian.com/tv-and-radio/tvandradioblog/2016/feb/04/muslim-television-characters-us-tv-shows-terrorist-spy-24-homeland-obama.

Volz, Y., Lee, F. L., Xiao, G., & Liu, X. (2010). Critical events and reception of foreign culture: An examination of cultural discount of foreign-language films in the US before and after 9/11. *International Communication Gazette*, *72*, 131–149.

NAME INDEX

SUBJECT INDEX

References to figures are denoted by an italic *f* following the page number. References to notes are followed by an n and the note number.